Baseball at Davenport's John O'Donnell Stadium

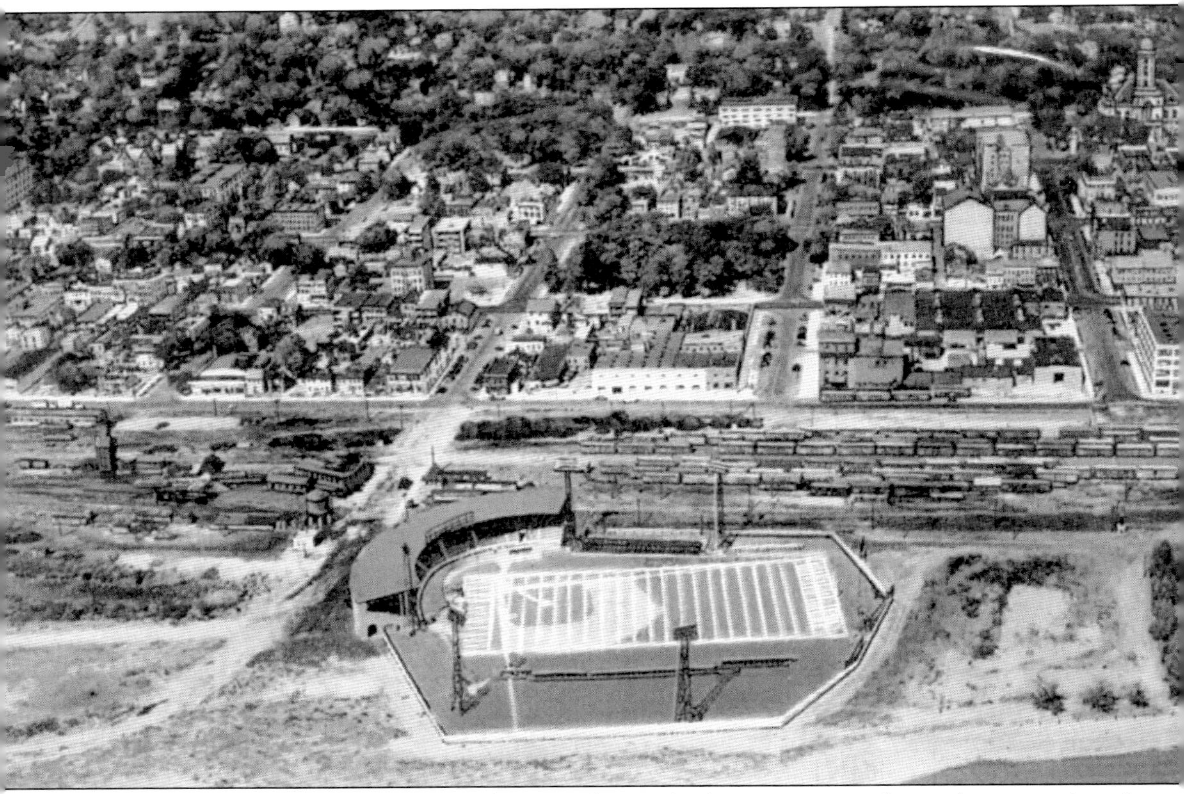

Municipal Stadium was envisioned as a multi-use facility, as seen in this early postcard, and hosted its first St. Ambrose College football game on September 25, 1931. The stadium also served as the home of Assumption High School football, but when new ownership took over the baseball club in 1986, football games at the stadium ceased.

BASEBALL AT DAVENPORT'S JOHN O'DONNELL STADIUM

Tim Rask

ARCADIA PUBLISHING

ISBN 978-0-7385-3247-9

Published by Arcadia Publishing
Charleston, South Carolina

Printed in the United States of America

Library of Congress Catalog Card Number: 2004109858

For all general information contact Arcadia Publishing at:
Telephone 843-853-2070
Fax 843-853-0044
E-mail sales@arcadiapublishing.com
For customer service and orders:
Toll-Free 1-888-313-2665

Visit us on the Internet at www.arcadiapublishing.com

Contents

ACKNOWLEDGMENTS

This book would not have been possible without the cooperation of Dorothy Wulf and her husband, Frank Wulf. By sharing the treasure trove of photographs and scrapbooks she has collected over the years, Dorothy provided an almost overwhelming record of the history of minor league baseball at John O'Donnell Stadium. The Quad City area is fortunate to have such a passionate fan of minor league baseball.

I would also like to thank the helpful staff of the Special Collections room at the Davenport Public Library, which provided historical background materials, access to back issues of area newspapers, and the photos contained on pages 11, 16 through 20, 46, and 48.

Special thanks also goes to the *Quad City Times*, especially Roy Booker, archivist for the *Times*, who permitted me to peruse the newpaper's photo collection, and to Managing Assistant Editor Gregory Swanson, who arranged for me to obtain the use of the photos found on pages 92, 97, 100, and 114 through 119.

Davenport resident and former veteran minor league ballplayer Bob Erps also graciously donated photos and related his memories of the old ballpark.

Thanks to my editor, Jeff Ruetsche, who made my first foray into publishing a smooth experience.

Any time I do baseball research, I am indebted to countless members of the Society for American Baseball Research, in this case, most notably, Bob McConnell, Lloyd Johnson, Joel Dinda, Gary Jarvis, Jerry Jackson, Bob Bluthardt, and many others who I surely am forgetting.

I had the great pleasure of living the dream of any baseball historian by spending several days pouring over the Three-I League organizational records contained in the library at the National Baseball Hall of Fame in Cooperstown, New York. For that wonderful experience, I am indebted to the Hall's Director of Research, Timothy Wiles, and his phenominally helpful staff at the A. Bartlett Giamatti Research Center.

Many friends helped support me during this project, including Eric and Susan Jones (along with their children, Johnson, Julia, and Jackson), who provided me with their hospitality during my trip to the Hall of Fame. Moral support came from Jay Yoder, Jeff and Sal Allen, Chris and Kim Baker, Dave and Cindy Gross, Craig Stafford, Dave Humes, Mollie Schlue, Tom Tapp, Ross Burkhart, Glenn Richardson, Wayne Steger, Janet Brown, and many others who I don't have the space to name.

Finally, I would like to thank my parents, Clifford and Carol Rask, for always supporting my research endeavors.

INTRODUCTION

On May 26, 1931, a Davenport teenager attended a baseball game with her family at the city's brand new Municipal Stadium. She was there to cheer on her beloved Blue Sox, a minor league team that had represented the city for two seasons in the Mississippi Valley League. The young woman, Dorothy Kohn, went home disappointed that night, as the local club dropped their home opener to their archrivals from Rock Island.

Young Dorothy was no fair-weather fan, however. She would return to the "Muny" countless times over the ensuing years to root for the home team, whether they were called the Blue Sox, the Quads, the Angels, or the River Bandits. She was active in the local booster club, worked on the Ladies Night Committee, and helped recruit new fans by assisting with season ticket drives. Eventually, Dorothy Wulf would even work for the team, starting as secretary to general manager Ken Blackman in 1963. Over the years, the Wulfs befriended many of the baseball figures who have passed through Davenport, such as a young manager named Chuck Tanner, who made his professional managerial debut the same year that Dorothy began working as the Quad City Angels' secretary.

This book contains many of the photographs that Dorothy Wulf collected over the last 70 years. As old Municipal Stadium undergoes renovations that will keep the ballpark viable well into the 21st century, enjoy a taste of some of the history that has transpired in the old ballpark. I only hope that I have been able to do justice to this valuable collection.

PROLOGUE

Pre-History: The Early Years of Baseball in Davenport

Davenport, Iowa is a city that traces its professional baseball roots to the earliest days of the minor leagues. The Northwestern League of 1879—a four-team league that consisted of teams from Davenport, along with Dubuque (IA), Rockford (IL), and Omaha (NE)—is generally acknowledged to be the first minor league west of the Mississippi. Like many leagues of the era, the Northwestern League failed to complete its scheduled season. In the June 23 issue of the *Davenport Times-Democrat*, the paper's correspondent wrote, "The Davenport base ball nine is in bad shape. It started out well with what was considered a strong nine, composed of players of recognized skill. But, for some reason or other, they either could not or would not do good work, and met with disastrous defeats in succession. These continued defeats destroyed popular interest in the game, and disheartened the stockholders, and so the dissolution of the organization became probable." At least one member of the Davenport club would go on to greater fame—second baseman Bid McPhee, who would eventually land in the Hall of Fame after an illustrious major league career with Cincinnati.

Davenport's next foray into professional baseball came in 1888, with the Central Interstate League, an eight-team circuit of clubs in Iowa, Illinois, and Indiana. This time, Davenport fielded a strong team, and posted the league's best win-loss record, 40-18. However, as the Interstate's weaker franchises folded or changed cities, the league became unstable, and disbanded in late July. Davenport managed to continue the season by taking over the former Minneapolis franchise in the Western Association, but the "Onion Wheelers" won only 4 of 25 games during their late-season stint in that league.

Nineteenth century baseball backers were ever optimistic, however, and despite the discouraging developments of the previous year, the Central Interstate reorganized to attempt an ambitious 120-game schedule in 1889, with Davenport as one of six members. As in the previous year, Davenport fielded a strong team, and the local nine took a league-leading 59-46 record into mid-September. In one of the most bizarre developments in Davenport's baseball history, the team then quit the league rather than take a scheduled road trip to second-place Quincy and third-place Springfield. Davenport had previously raised complaints about the quality of umpiring in the league, and the club was convinced that any games they played in the Illinois cities would only be robbed from them by underhanded officials. In response to Davenport's actions, the Central Interstate League unceremoniously awarded the city's franchise to an amateur club based in Monmouth, Illinois.

Professional baseball was absent from Davenport during most of the 1890s. The city briefly fielded a club in the Illinois-Iowa (or Two-I) League in 1891, but the Davenport Pilgrims posted a feeble 23-39 record, and with the club in last place, the directors disbanded the team in mid-July of that year.

The 1890s did see the first stirrings of baseball teams representing more than one of the area's cities. In 1892, the "Twins" represented the combined cities of Rock Island and Moline; while in 1895, a "Tri-Cities" entry briefly represented Davenport, Rock Island, and Moline in the Eastern Iowa League. Unfortunately, friction among representatives from the three cities caused that club to disband after playing only 32 league games and posting a record of 14-18.

The start of the twentieth century brought a renewed case of baseball fever to the city. Just as Davenport was a part of the first minor league west of the Mississippi, so too was the city part of the formation of one of the most storied leagues in minor league history—the Illinois-Indiana-Iowa League, popularly know as the Three-I. Local real estate agent Max Ochs represented Davenport at the inaugural league meeting in Peoria on January 30, 1901, where the eight-team league was formed. Meanwhile, back in Davenport, J.T. Hayes organized and ran the new River Rats ball club, which finished in fifth place, 21 1/2 games behind the winning Terre Haute Hottentots.

Subsequent clubs were not much better. The 1903 team finished with a record of 65-53, good for third place in the Three-I, but that proved to be the high-water mark of Davenport's early years in the Three-I. After seventh place finishes in 1904 and 1905, the team hit rock bottom in 1906 with a 45-74 record, which landed Davenport in last place. Attendance was so bad that the league transferred Davenport's franchise to Clinton, leaving the city out of baseball once again.

In the early twentieth century, losing a baseball team was not a devastating loss—teams and leagues came and went on an annual basis. Not surprisingly, a city the size of Davenport was considered a likely site for a team. "That Davenport should and could be a prominent figure on the baseball map is a matter that has passed the questionable stage—it is a settled thing," wrote the *Davenport Daily Times* in September, 1908. And, sure enough, a group of Davenport baseball enthusiasts, again led by J.T. Hayes, were able to win back the Three-I franchise from Clinton for the 1909 season.

To accommadate for the returning Prodigals, local fans agreed that a new ballpark was needed. As the *Daily Times* put it, "A park that is well within the city limits is deemed a necessity. Ever since Davenport was wiped off the baseball map, there have been momentary agitations to place it back on again. At each of the meetings at which baseball was discussed, the park in the west end is not adequate and should be discarded." Local fans got their wish for a new park when the club secured a lot from P.W. McManus in the western part of the city. The new 2,500-seat park was located at the end of the Second Street trolley line, near Telegraph Road, where the Davenport Three-I entry would play the next eight seasons.

Initially, the club fared little better than its predecessors, but Davenport's fortunes improved when Daniel O'Leary took over as manager in 1911. O'Leary's clubs improved steadily until the team, renamed the Blue Sox in 1913, finally snagged the pennant in 1914, topping Peoria by 3 1/2 games. Davenport almost repeated in 1915. Due to franchise relocations, the league played a split-season, with the Moline Plowboys winning the first half and Davenport the second. In a championship playoff, Moline defeated the Blue Sox, four games to two.

Davenport slipped back into the cellar in 1916, and dropped out of Three-I after the season. Due to the United States' entry into World War I the following year, the Three-I League itself suspended operations. While the league rebounded after the war, Davenport remained on the sidelines, and was without a minor league team until 1929.

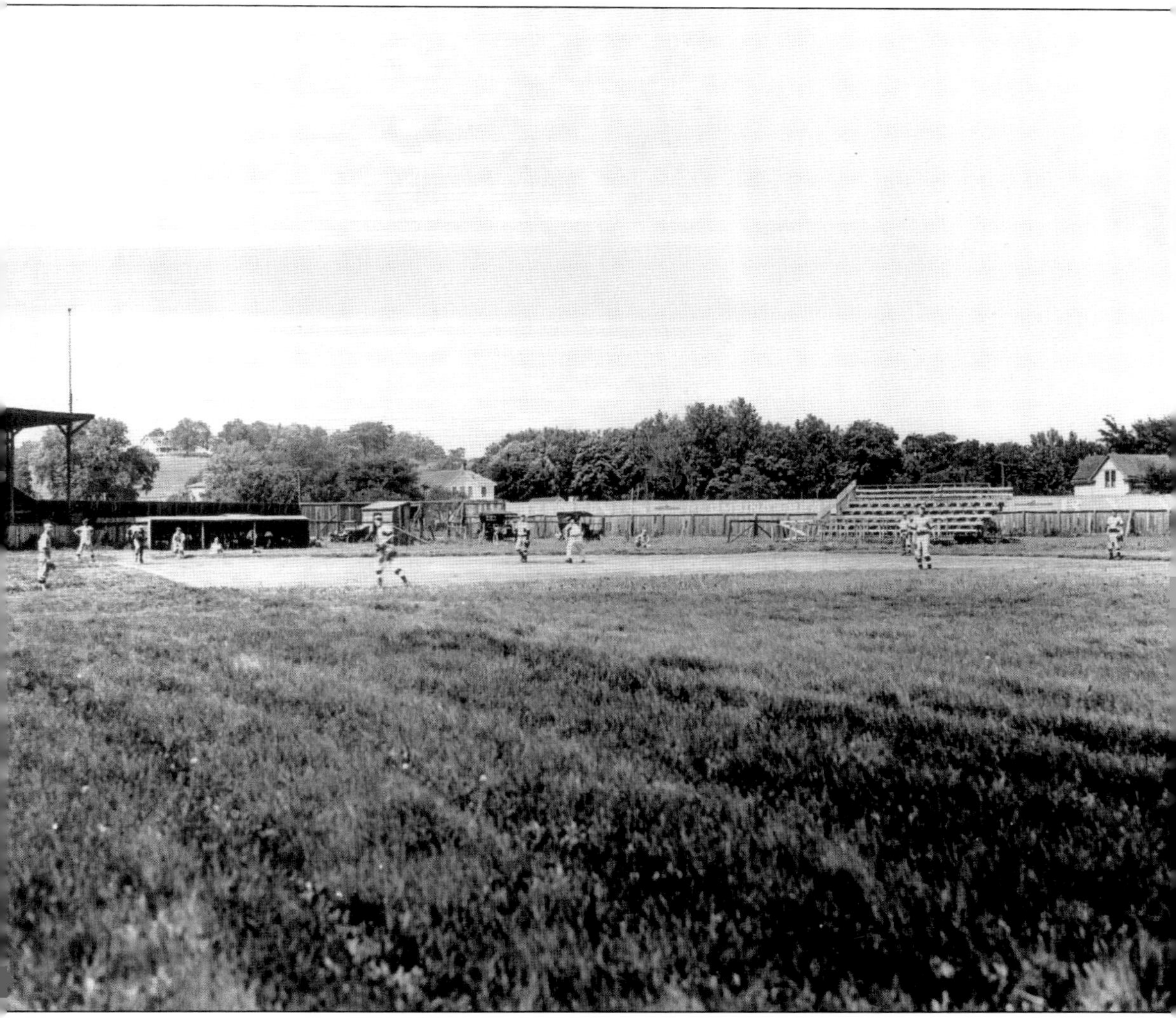

In 1909, when Davenport reclaimed the Three-I League franchise it had lost to Clinton two years earlier, local boosters built a new "base ball park" at the end of the Third Street trolley line. The "Prodigals" finished in third place in their inaugural season at the new park. Renamed the "Blue Sox" in 1913, the club would claim one Three-I League pennant, in 1914, but shut down operations after the 1916 campaign, leaving Davenport out of organized baseball until 1929.

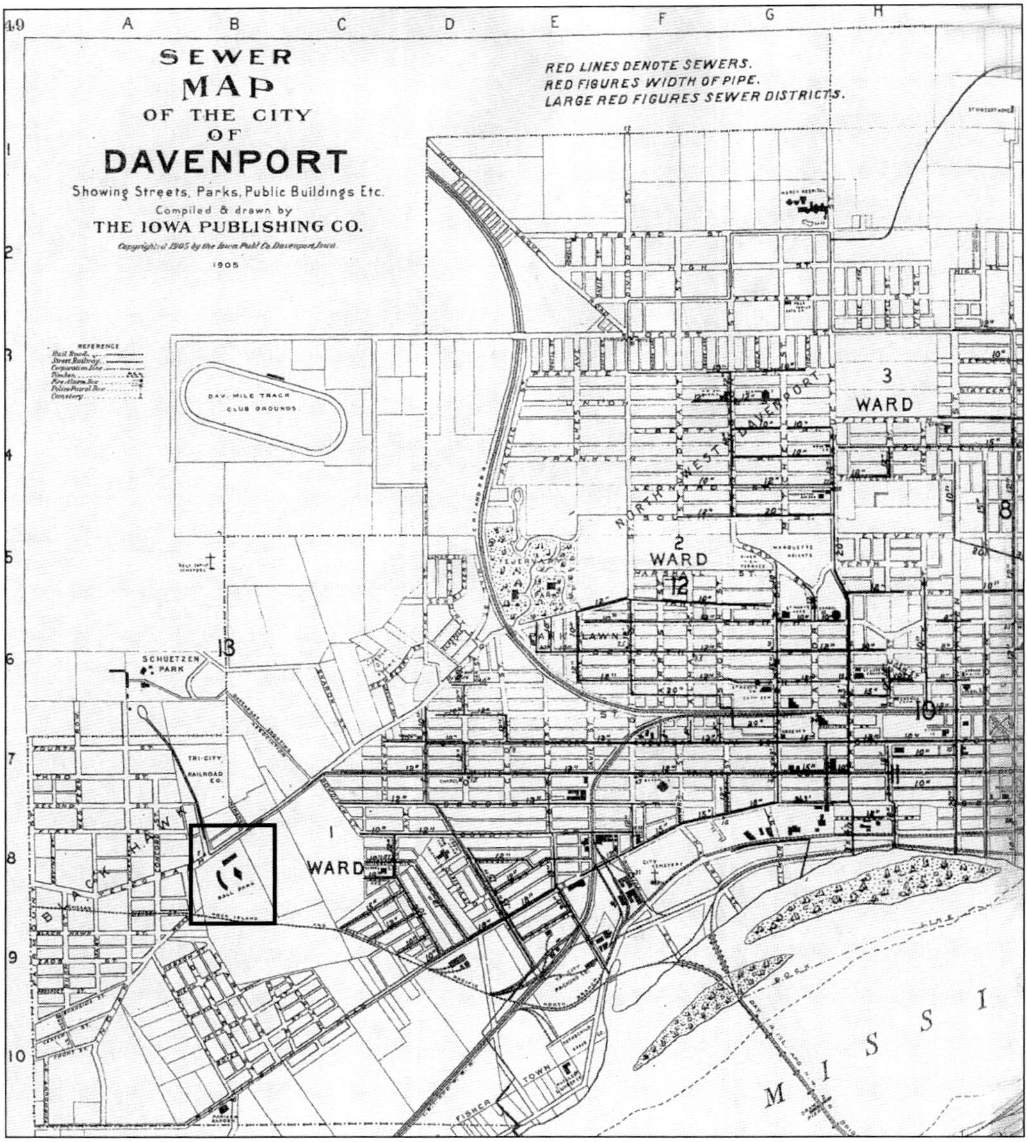

A common complaint during the early years of minor league ball in Davenport was that the park was located too far from the center of town, making it difficult to draw healthy crowds. After the Three-I League was formed in 1901, Davenport's club played in a ballpark just off Telegraph Road in the western part of the city (box in lower left).

ONE

The Municipal Stadium Era Begins

Once World War I ended, minor league baseball circuits once again sprouted up around the country, including in the Tri-Cities. Moline joined the resurrected Three-I League in 1919, and Rock Island followed suit in 1920. While the Plowboys won the 1921 Three-I League pennant under manager Earle Mack (son of the legendary Philadelphia Athletics owner, Connie Mack), both Moline and Rock Island mainly fielded second-division clubs.

In 1922, Rock Island became a charter member of the Mississippi Valley League, a circuit comprised, with the exception of the Islanders, of Iowa-based teams. After back-to-back cellar finishes in the Three-I, Moline jumped to the Valley when that league expanded to eight teams in 1924. For the rest of the 1920s, Tri-City baseball remained confined to Moline's Browing Field and Rock Island's Douglas Park, while Davenport fans looked on with envy.

After the 1928 season, the Ottumwa franchise in the Mississippi Valley League folded, giving Davenport an opportunity to reenter professional baseball. In 1929, the Davenport Blue Sox took the field at the Mississippi Valley Fairgrounds, playing their games on the infield of the racetrack. Under manager Ed Reichle, the Blue Sox fielded competitive teams (finishing third both in 1929 and 1930), but failed to draw large crowds. Attendance in 1929 was just over 40,000, while the 1930 club drew only 30,000 patrons. The low figures were blamed on the distance of the ballpark from the business district, and the lack of lights at the Fairgrounds (making Davenport one of only two clubs in the MVL unable to take advantage of the new technology of night baseball). Rumors began to circulate that Davenport would once again lose its baseball franchise.

Then, shortly after the 1930 season ended, the Davenport Levee Improvement Commission unveiled plans to construct a modern new baseball stadium on a plot of ground west of LeClaire Park at Gaines Street. As reported in the September 17, 1930 *Daily Times*, the commission's motives for building the stadium extended beyond baseball. "In order to alleviate, in part at least, the unemployment situation in this city, members of the commission have asked that the plans be drawn as soon as possible. Only Davenport labor will be used on the project, the major part of which should be completed before winter.

"The new field can be used by the citizens of Davenport for the furtherance of athletic exercises and recreation. Besides the baseball field, the plant will consist of a football gridiron, soft-ball baseball diamonds, tennis courts, large playground for children, etc. Although no definite plans have been announced by the commission, it is understood that the park will be lighted for night baseball and football."

The initial response to the proposal was overwhelmingly positive. "Provision of a modern playing field for the Blue Sox next year, which is included in the levee commission plans, guarantees Davenport organized baseball for many years," said Paul Lagomarcino, president of the baseball club. "It is impossible to continue playing at the fairgrounds and we were contemplating the surrender of our franchise in the Mississippi Valley league rather than go back to the old field another year. If lights are installed for night baseball I am positive that the Davenport club will be self-sustaining for years to come."

Davenport newspapers also approved of the plan. *Davenport Times-Democrat* sports editor, John O'Donnell called the stadium "the salvation of the national pastime in our village. Accordingly, the people who like their sport a la baseball are greeting each other with smiles and handshakes today. Their gloom has turned to sunshine and everybody is happy—or should be. Those who have burned gallons of gas taking themselves out to the fairgrounds will be able to give the car to the wife or to the kids and walk to the park because the new park will be just outside the office window."

Work on the new ballpark progressed amazingly quickly. Ground was broken at the site on November 6, 1930, even as the firm of Clausen, Kruse, & Klein, supervisors of the project, were completing the stadium plans. The following month, another local firm, Tunnicliff Construction Co., won the contract to build the $150,000, 4,000-seat stadium. Thanks to a mild winter, construction of the park proceeded smoothly, and the final cost came in at $165,000 (with $20,000 more to pay for the lighting system). By spring, the city anxiously awaited the arrival of the Mississippi Valley League season and the debut of Municipal Stadium. "It's rapidly nearing completion," wrote O'Donnell on March 8, "and soon Davenport will have one of the foremost and most modern municipal stadiums in the middle-west."

Opening day for the new park came on May 26, 1931. Three thousand fans turned out for the afternoon dedication, and were treated to a Davenport victory as the Blue Sox thumped Dubuque, 7 to 1. On June 4, night baseball came to Davenport, and 2,862 turned out to see the Rock Island Islanders defeat their cross-river rivals, 9-7. Although the Blue Sox remained a fairly lackluster team, finishing seventh, the new "Muny" stadium provided an attendance boost, as over 65,000 fans passed through the gates for league games, with another 15,000 attending exhibition contests.

Along with the new ballpark, Davenport gained another significant asset in 1931. On June 27, a 29-year-old Valley League veteran named Cletus Dixon managed his first game for of the Blue Sox. Dixon had been hired after Ed Reichle resigned after the club's slow start. Dixon was already an accomplished manager, having guided Waterloo to Mississippi Valley League pennants in 1924 and 1928. His first game with Davenport proved to be a wild affair, as the Sox spotted Moline an 11-4 lead before scoring 4 runs in the 6th inning, 4 in the 7th, and 3 in the 8th, en route to a 15-12 victory over the Plowboys. While the rest of the season lacked that dramatic flourish, Dixon's tenure with the Blue Sox would produce some of Davenport's finest baseball teams.

Cletus Dixon seemed an improbable manager for a minor league baseball team. A graduate of the prestigious University of Chicago, the chemistry major spent his off-seasons teaching at his alma mater and working on his Masters and Ph.D. degrees. But the scholar-athlete knew his baseball, too. The Sac City, Iowa native had spent his entire baseball career in the state with Mississippi Valley League clubs, starting as a first baseman with Cedar Rapids in 1922 before joining Waterloo, where he became a player-manager. Dixon wasted no time in adding to his track record of success by quickly building Davenport into a powerhouse.

In 1932, Dixon's Blue Sox dominated the Valley League down the stretch, winning the second half of a split-season with a 45-24 record. As an added attraction for area fans, the Blue Sox squared off against first-half champ Rock Island in a "Little World Series" to determine the championship. The Islanders topped the Sox, four games to two, so Municipal Stadium would have to wait a little longer for its first championship club.

That title would come to the Muny in 1933, when Dixon's Blue Sox fielded what was arguably the strongest ball club that Davenport had ever seen. Building on 1932's success, Davenport blistered the league in the first half of the season, easily winning the first half with a 40-17 record. For a second half encore, the Blue Sox posted a 42-15 record, for a phenomenal total wining percentage of .719. The outfielders powered the Blue Sox offense, led by Como Cotelle's .407 batting average and Ed Hall's 28 home runs and 151 RBIs. Young Al Piechota led the pitching with a 19-4 record, despite a mediocre earned run average of 4.55.

The Blue Sox' dominance created a problem for the Mississippi Valley League. In order to play a post-season championship series, league rules mandated that, when a team such as the Sox won both halves of the season, the team with the next best overall record would provide the opposition in the finals. Rock Island had the second-best mark, but Davenport balked at having to face their rivals from across the Mississippi in a seven-game series. The Blue Sox had won 16 of the season's 24 games against the Islanders, and argued that there should be no need to risk losing their title to a clearly inferior rival. League President Charles Logan ordered the Sox to play, however, and after a series-opening loss to the Islanders, the Davenport club asserted their dominance by winning the next four games and bringing the first championship banner home to Municipal Stadium.

The Mississippi Valley League folded after 1933, but Davenport, Rock Island, and Cedar Rapids managed to land berths in the Western League for 1934. The Western was a Class A league, a notch above the Class B Valley League, and Davenport took some time to adjust to the faster competition. After a sluggish first half in which the Blue Sox finished one game under .500, all-star pitcher Frank Lamanski (24-7, with 216 strikeouts) led Davenport to a second-half record of 41-23, good for first place and a spot in the Western League Playoffs. Circumstances forced the Western into a strange post-season playoff setup. In the first half of the season, St. Joseph, Des Moines, and Sioux City had tied for first, so all three joined Davenport in the playoffs. The Blue Sox dispatched Des Moines in the first round, three games to one, and then staged an epic seven-game series with St. Joseph. The two clubs battled neck-and-neck until the decisive game, when the Saints' Herman "Snooker" Drefs out-dueled Lamanksi by pitching a no-hitter against the Blue Sox before 5,862 fans in Municipal Stadium.

Davenport continued its string of successful seasons in 1935 and 1936. The 1935 Blue Sox won the regular season pennant by 7 games, although they were unceremoniously bounced from the playoffs by fourth-place Sioux City. The 1936 team won both halves of a split Western League season, and unlike 1933 did not have to play a championship series to claim their pennant. After 1936, however, Cletus Dixon retired from managing, having finished work on his Ph.D. Dixon left the 1937 club in the hands of Jack Fitzgerald, and while the '37 Sox were hardly a disaster, they slipped to third place in the Western with a 57-59 record.

Baseball in Davenport seemed healthy, but the Western League was in serious trouble. Rock Island had dropped out during the 1937 season, leaving the league with only five cities. Rather than try to scramble to find another city for 1938, the league voted to disband, forcing the survivors to search for slots in other leagues. Cedar Rapids and Waterloo, fellow refugees from the Western League, secured berths in the Three-I League. Davenport also tried for a slot in that circuit, but found itself battling Evansville, Indiana for major league sponsorship from the Boston Bees, which was needed to secure the eighth and final slot in the Three-I. Evansville offered Boston a free lease and won the battle for the franchise. Strangely, Davenport's detractors noted that the presence of gambling, in the form of bingo, made the city a risky proposition for minor league ball. After a successful six-year run, minor league baseball departed Municipal Stadium.

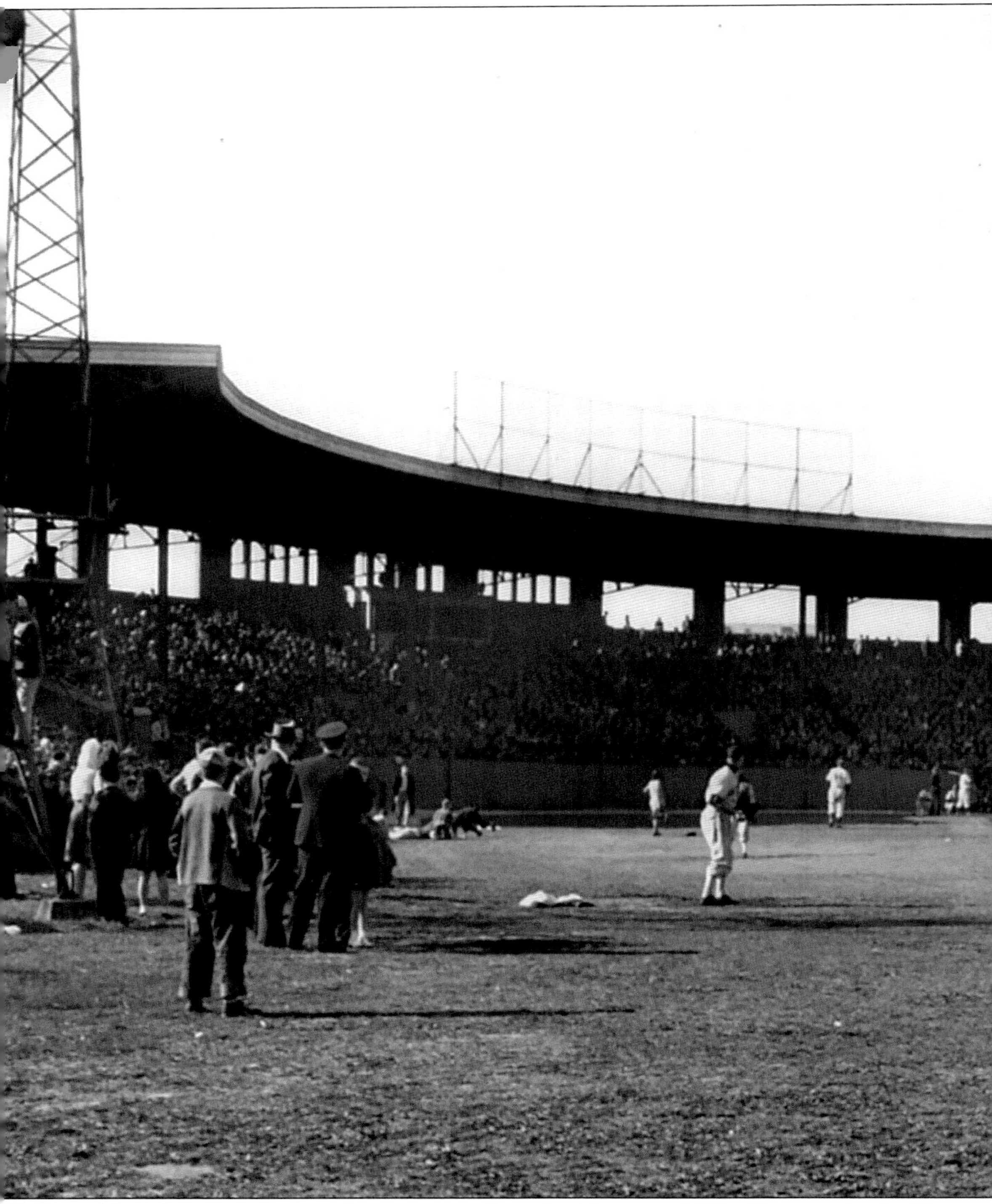

After playing two seasons for sparse crowds at the Mississippi Valley Fairgrounds, the Blue Sox moved into the new Municipal Stadium in 1931 and became accustomed to having many more fans in the stands. The club drew 80,000 for the inaugural season, a figure that included exhibition games in addition to Mississippi Valley League contests. As is the case today, the

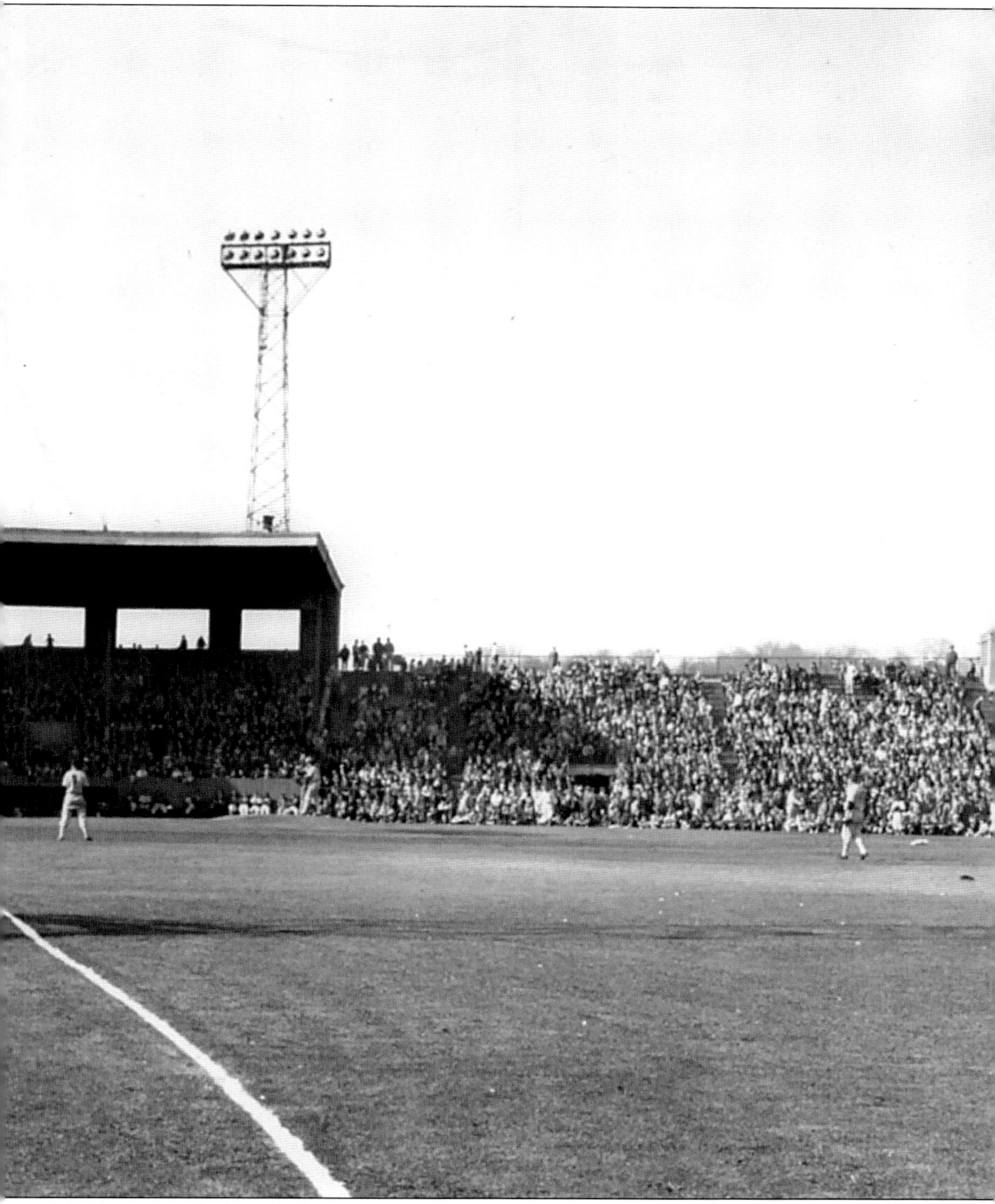

club drew particularly well when a special promotion accompanied the game. Fans often had a chance to win merchandise, including cars, or a local company or service club would provide fans with free or discounted tickets. The crowd pictured here is from a game sponsored by the Davenport Eagles Club.

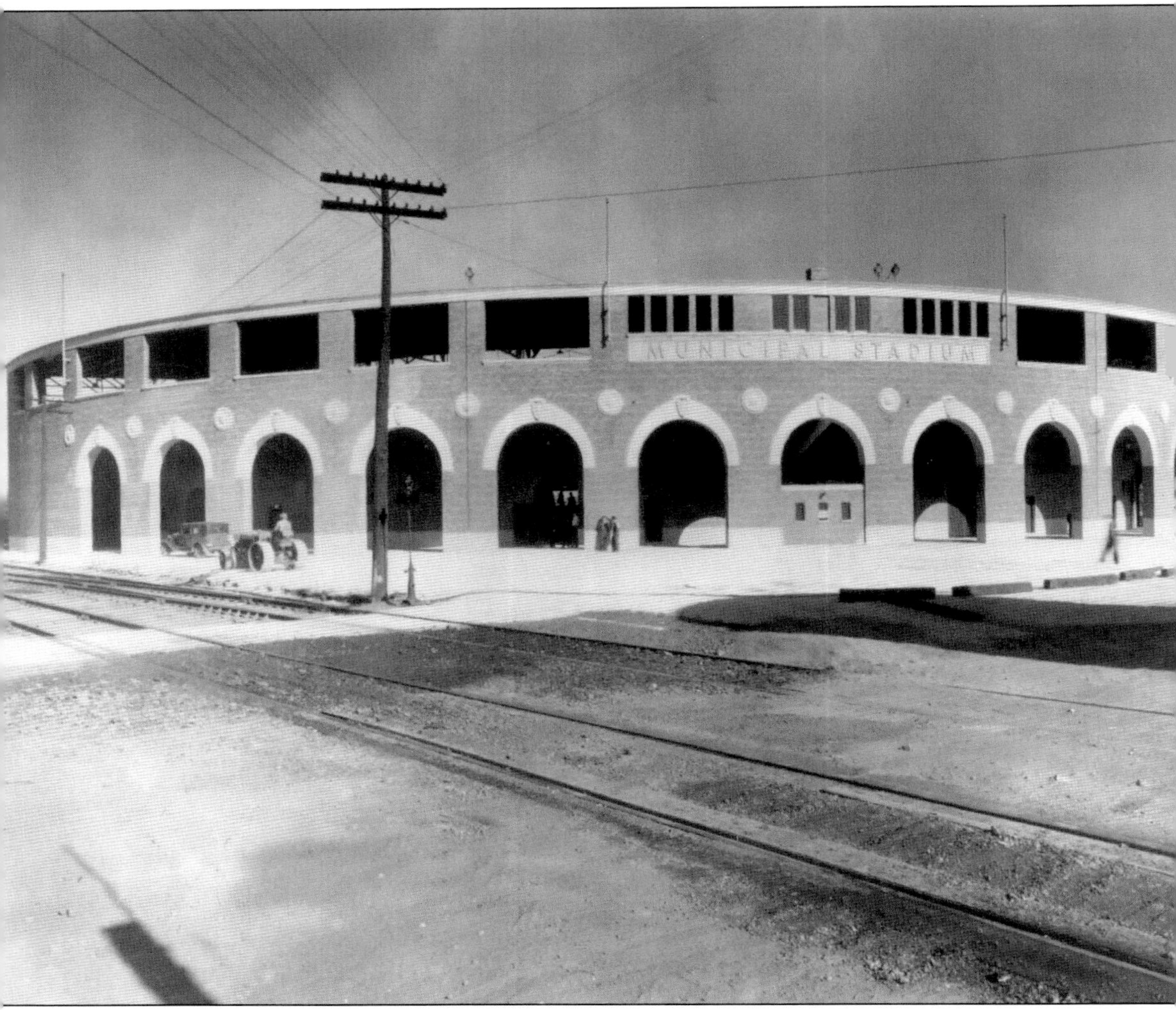

After playing two seasons before lackluster crowds at Mississippi Valley Fairgrounds, Davenport's Blue Sox moved into Municipal Stadium for the 1931 season. A crowd of 3,000 opened the new baseball palace on May 26, as the Sox trounced Dubuque, 7-1.

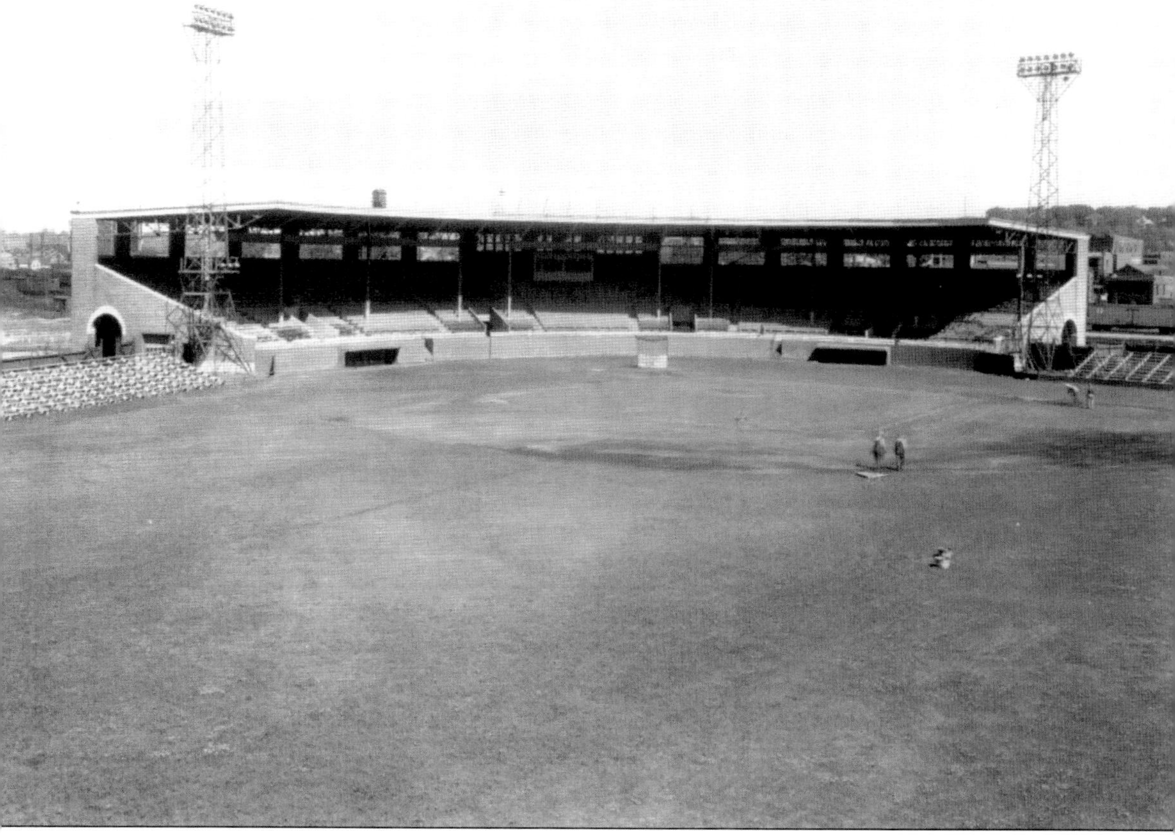

Light towers were constructed shortly after the completion of Municipal Stadium in 1931. The first night game was played June 4, 1931. Unfortunately, the archrival Rock Island Islanders spoiled the night debut by edging the Sox, 9 to 7.

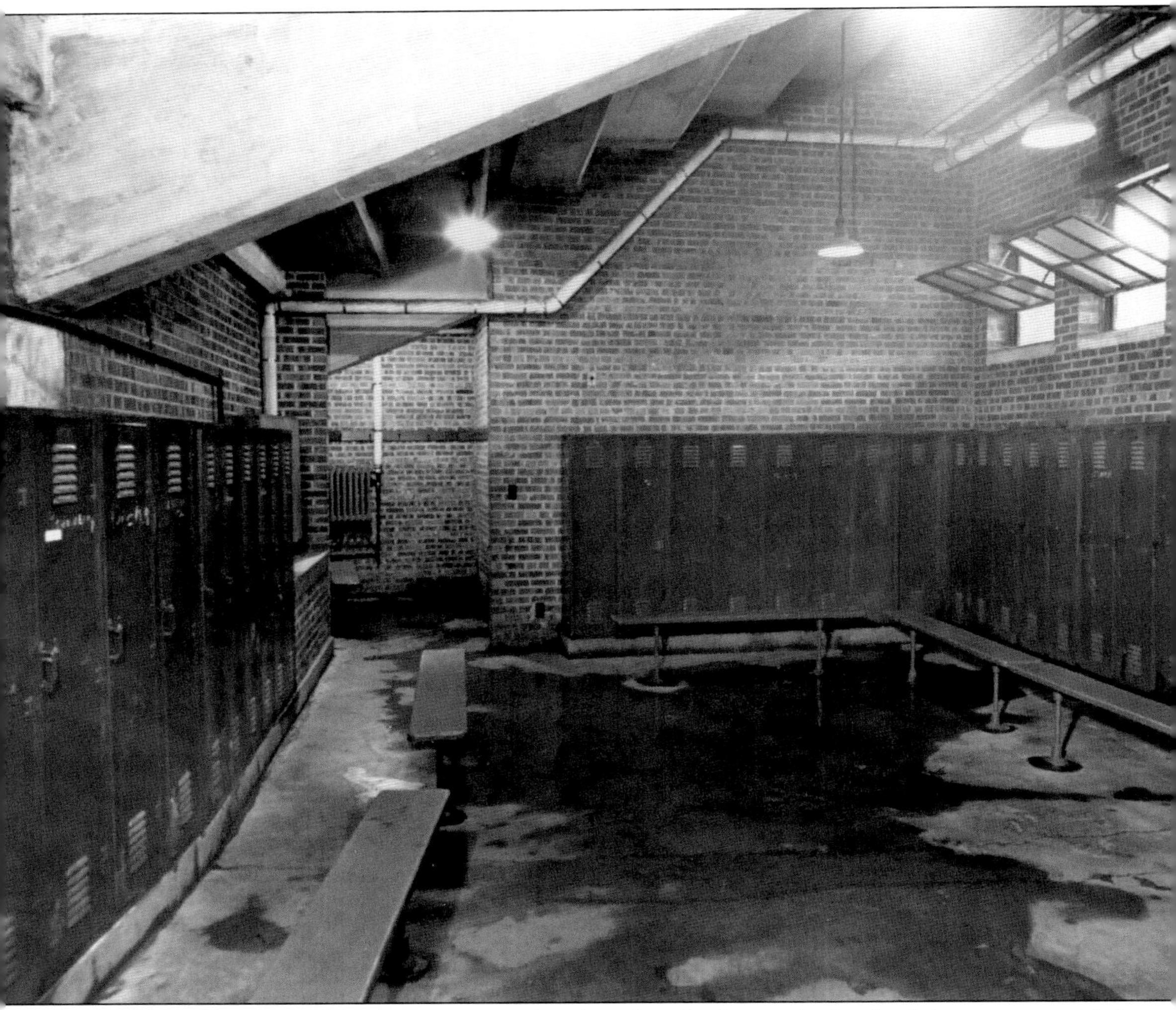

Although Municipal Stadium was considered a palace for fans, its locker facilities never provided any great luxuries for the players, as this photo from the 1930s illustrates.

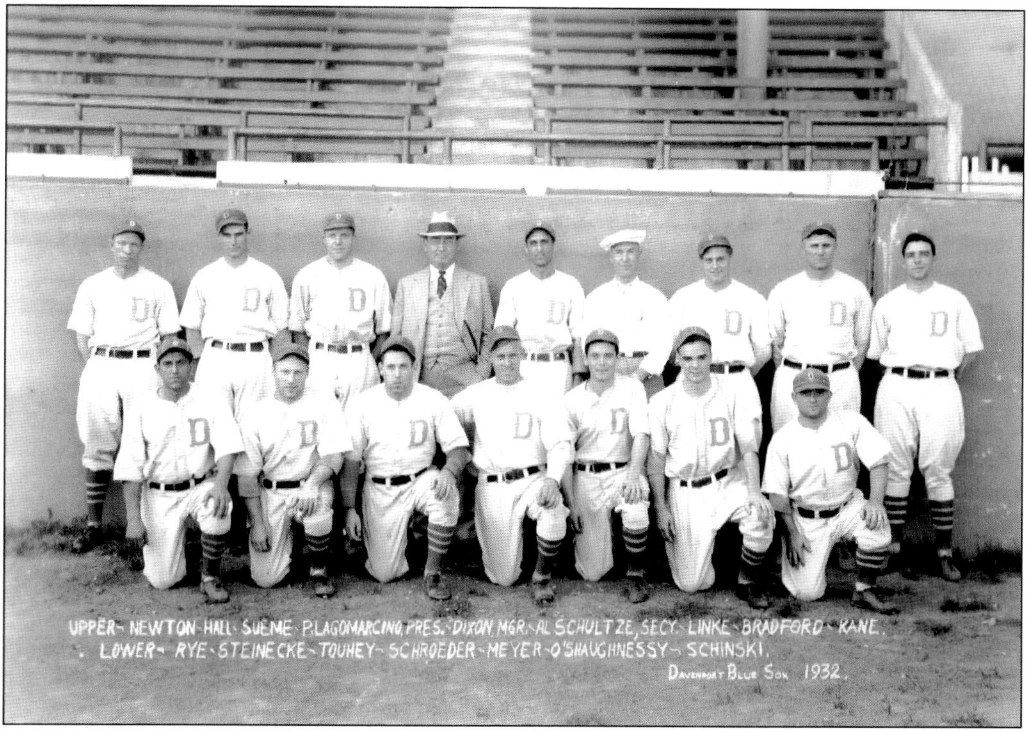

In Cletus Dixon's first full year as manager, the Blue Sox brought a second-half pennant to Municipal Stadium. Pitcher Ed Linke (back, third from right) provided the highlight of the year by throwing a no-hitter against Rock Island on September 7.

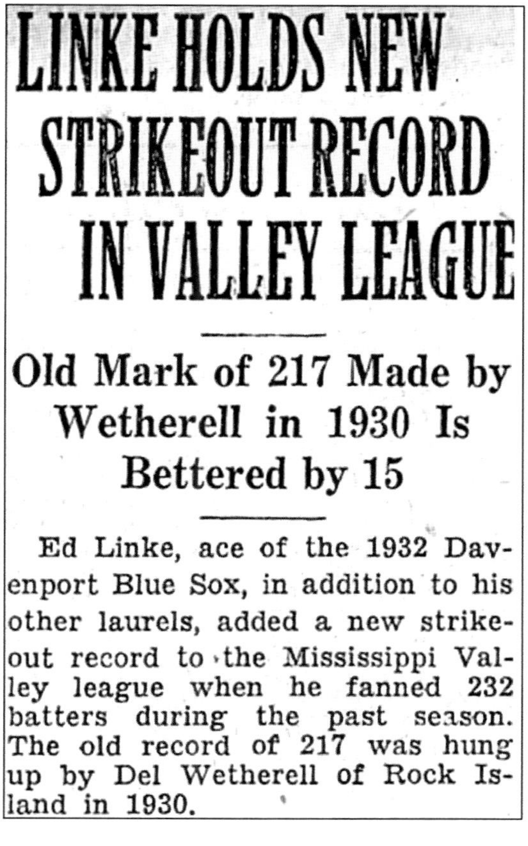

LINKE HOLDS NEW STRIKEOUT RECORD IN VALLEY LEAGUE

Old Mark of 217 Made by Wetherell in 1930 Is Bettered by 15

Ed Linke, ace of the 1932 Davenport Blue Sox, in addition to his other laurels, added a new strikeout record to the Mississippi Valley league when he fanned 232 batters during the past season. The old record of 217 was hung up by Del Wetherell of Rock Island in 1930.

Ed Linke was hardly a one-game wonder in 1932. In addition to hurling a no-hitter, he established a new league record for strikeouts. The following year, Linke would make his big league debut with the Washinton Senators. His league strikeout record still stands, as the MVL disbanded after the 1933 season and was never revived.

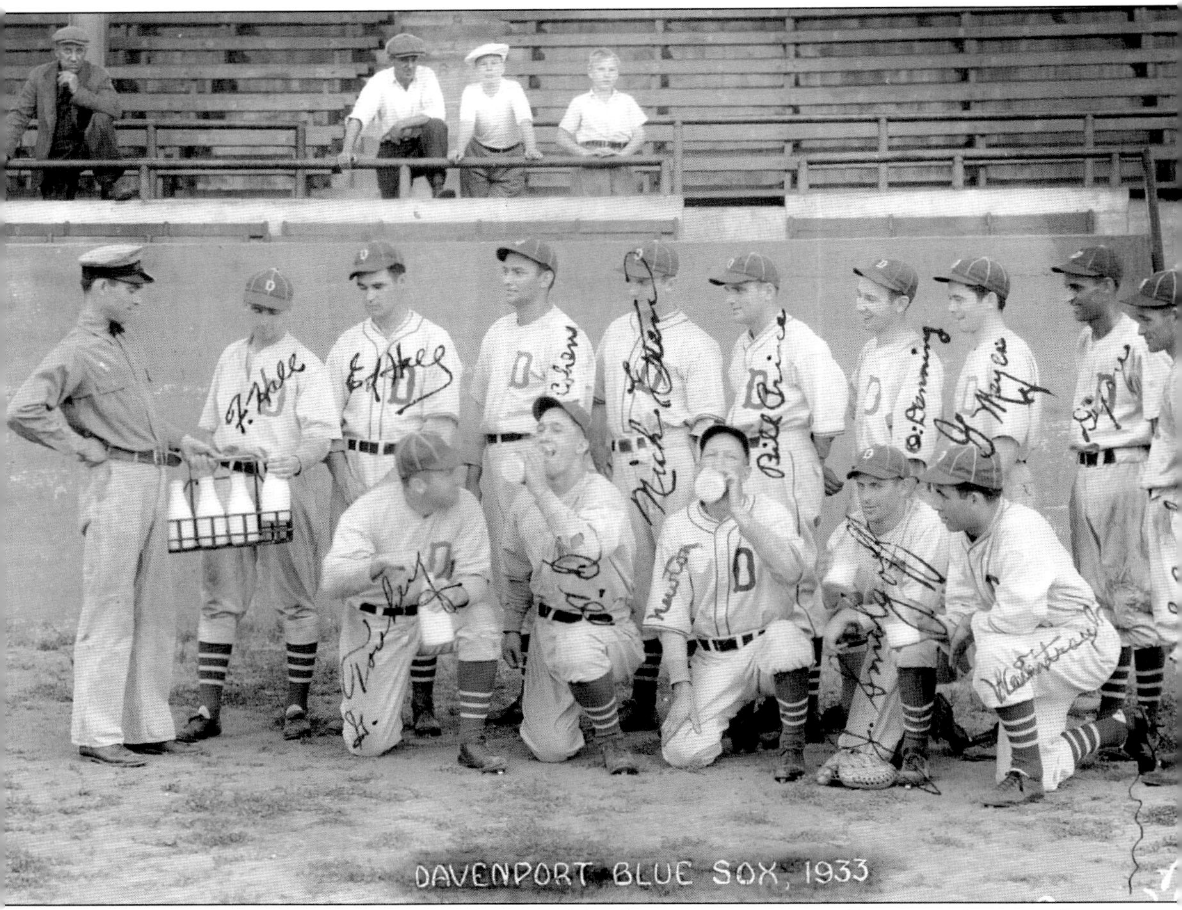

Was there something in the milk? Arguably the greatest team in Davenport's minor league history, the 1933 Blue Sox dominated the Mississippi Valley League in 1933, and easily won both halves of the split season. Still, league rules stipulated that, in the event one team claimed both halves, the team with the second best overall record would face the leaders in a championship series. Despite protests from the Blue Sox (who pointed out that they already had won 16 of 24 games against second-place Rock Island and should not have to play a seven-game series), the championship series was played, with the Blue Sox repeating their regular-season dominance of the Islanders, beating Rock Island 4 games to 1.

Unlike modern minor league franchises, Davenport's clubs of the 1930s were run locally, with no affiliations with major league teams. Davenport businessman and Team President, Paul Lagomarcino (*right*), was a prominent figure on the local baseball scene. Under his guiding hand, minor league ball thrived in Davenport.

SPORT CHATS
by
John O'Donnell
(Sports Editor)

JUST rambling around . . . . . In their first 33 games (not including Wednesday's) the Chicago Cubs batted out 177 runs while their opponents gained 157 for their records . . . . . In six games the Bruins scored 10 or more runs and were shut out only once . . . . . . that was the whitewashing handed them by Lefty Brandt when Boston played Chicago May 12 . . . . . . and have been held to one run four times . . . . . Meanwhile their playmates hammered Cub pitchers three times for 10 or more runs and took three shut-outs . . . . one by Warneke in the opening game and two dished up by Bill Lee . . . . .

At the beginning of the season the critics figured Connie Mack's supposedly haphazard aggregation would wind up in eighth place . . . Mr. Mack crossed them up and had his team well up in the first division for some time . . . . . The other day he dropped half a game behind Hornsby's Brownies in seventh place and two games ahead of the coming White Sox . . . . . . Perhaps the sports writers were right for once . . . . .

BROOKLYN has cast itself in a new role . . . . . The Dodgers are knocking down the big boys, taking two out of three from Pittsburgh and the same number from the Cubs . . . . . on their home lot . . . . . On the other hand while visiting those teams they lost all but one game . . . . Must be the Brooklyn environment . . . .

Cronin has raised his batting average 50 points . . . . But it is still only around .200 . . . . Manager Jimmy Dykes of the White Sox probably belongs to more fraternal organizations than any big leaguer . . . . . . He is a member of the Elks, Moose, Knights of Columbus and Knights of the Golden Eagle . . . . . . Animals and knights seem to be his preference . . . . . .

BOSTON Red Sox fans are a bit peeved that Joe Judge, the veteran first-baseman, was given his release . . . . The player limit forced Eddie Collins to release one man, and inasmuch as Eddie Morgan is playing bang-up ball the old-timer had to go . . . . But the fans thought he should be retained as coach, supplanting Bib Falk if necessary . . . . . Bib is an old White Sox and Cleveland player who gained more experience managing Toledo a few years ago . . . . . But Bib is rather colorless compared to Judge, and that's what the fans want . . . .

Tommy Robello, former Islander who played with Cincinnati late last season, and has been shipped to Wilmington, N. C., has remained in Cincinnati to take treatments for a sore arm. . . . . Players come and go so fast with the Columbus farm of the Cardinals' chain that bulletins on arrivals and withdrawals are issued . . . . . .

SI ROSENTHAL, the Quincy outfielder last year who did some crooning on the side, finally decided to report to Dayton . . . . . . First he had a sick sister and when she recovered he had a good job . . . . At last he decided he better get the old war club in action and signed up with Ducky Holmes . . . .

Lyn Lary and Joe McCarthy did not get along on the Yankees. . . . Joe is supposed to have suggested that Lary was minus a backbone, and Lyn put up his fists and wished to demonstrate that he was well equipped . . . . That was last year . . . . Since then the manager and his utility outfielder were far apart . . . . . And now Lary is with the Red Sox . . . . . .

THE Pacific Coast League is considering a split season . . . The reason: the Los Angeles Angels are far ahead of the rest of the league . . . . They win on the road as well as at home . . . . Dick Ward, the pitcher who won 25 games for them last year, has been returned by the Cubs . . . . Frank Demaree is batting .436 . . . . Fay Thomas has won nine consecutive games . . . . . The rest of the clubs want a new deal . . . . . .

All of the clubs apparently are in favor of the split season, even the Angels, for they find their big lead is cutting down their own attendance . . . . . L. A. won 15 straight series last year and has still to lose one this year . . . . That's some record . . . . . . Portland experienced a big shake-up . . . . . . Prince Oana, the big Hawaiian sent back by the Phillies, was shipped to Atlanta and waivers were asked on the entire club . . . . . . That's telling 'em . . . . .

GIANT fans give the following reasons for their favorites' rather poor showing . . . . (1) The Giants are in a very serious fight with able competition from the Cubs, Pirates and Cardinals . . . . (2) The new lively ball has cut down the efficiency of the Giant pitchers one run a game . . . . . . (3) The Giant batters are not profiting by the new ball, batting less as a team than they did a year ago this time . . . . . (4) Roy Parmalee, one of the Big Four last year, is still missing due to an appendicitis operation . . . . . .

Lloyd Brown, Cleveland left-hander, thinks things are getting better . . . . For three consecutive times out he pitched good ball only to lose when the Indians neglected to get any runs for him . . . . May 18 he lost after pitching a good game . . . . . . The score was 3 to

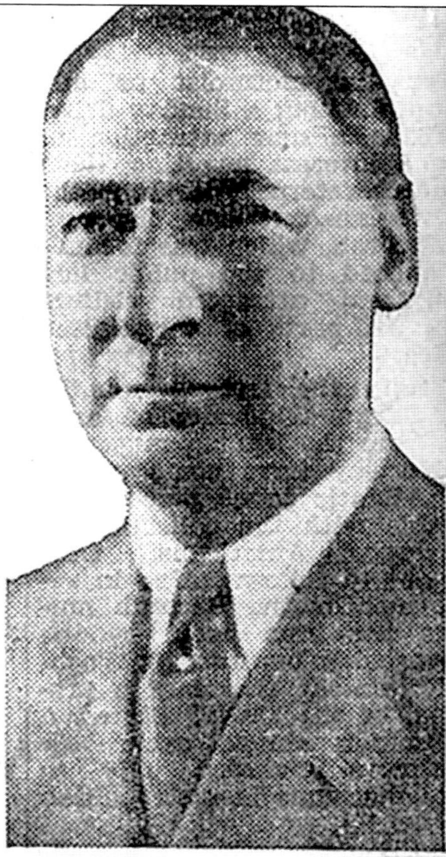

Paul Lagomarcino, president of the Davenport Baseball club since the city entered the Mississippi Valley league in 1929, is again guiding the destinies of the new Blue Sox in the Western league. Mr Lagomarcino has spent much time in an attempt to give Davenport the best to be had in baseball. It was at his suggestion that Rock Island and Davenport withdrew from the proposed Three-I league to join hands with old members of the Class A Western circuit in the organization of one of the best minor leagues in the country.

John O'Donnell's daily column, "Sport Chats" (*left*), was a fixture in the *Davenport Times-Democrat*, and later, the Times. O'Donnell used this forum to keep fans up-to-date on the local and national sports scene.

Post-Season Series Must Be Played or Forfeited, Ruling of League Chief

Paul Lagomarcino Calls Meeting of Club Directors To Decide What Action to Take on Logan's Orders—Rocks Win Argument

BY LEO KAUTZ

Davenport has been ordered, by Dr. C. R. Logan, president of the Mississippi Valley league, to play Rock Island in a post-season series or forfeit the circuit championship and pay a fine of $800, at the rate of $200 for each game forfeited.

This was the decision reached by the league president at the special meeting yesterday afternoon between representatives of the Davenport and Rock Island clubs.

Paul Lagomarcino, president of the Davenport Blue Sox, heatedly informed Dr. Logan, and Charles Beers, secretary of the Rock Island club, that his team would not participate in the series, claiming the championship games are an injustice to the Blue Sox and to Davenport fans.

At one time during the argument, Mr Lagomarcino threatened to withdraw from the Valley league but finally decided to put the matter up to a vote of the club directors who have been called together for a meeting late this afternoon.

Rocks Insist on Series

Mr Beers, representing the Rock Island club, insisted that the series be played according to the rules passed by directors of the territory and cannot play organized baseball unless Rock Island gives up its franchise.

Several directors of the Davenport club informed the writer this morning that they would not vote to play the series, no matter what the consequences, but Mr Lagomarcino claims the club cannot afford to pay an $800 fine. Legally, Dr. Logan can deduct the fine from the Davenport forfeit money.

Injustice to Club

One of the main reasons for Davenport's stand against the post-season series is that the Blue Sox have already won the championship by a clean-cut victory in both halves of the split season. However, the local club could not claim the pennant should they refuse to play the series, the Rocks being awarded the title by default.

The controversy over the 1933 post-season series to match Davenport against second-place Rock Island was big news in the Quad Cities.

YOUNG ROOKIE SOLD TO BUCS BY DAVENPORT

Sale Price Not Announced But Is Said To Be More Than $2,000

MOLESWORTH MAKES DEAL

Nick Is Batting .350 For Season—Found on Sandlots By Dixon

BY LEO KAUTZ

Nick Etten, the Mississippi Valley league's most sensational rookie outfielder this season, has been sold by the Davenport Blue Sox to the Pittsburgh club of the National league and will report to his new owners at the end of the season here.

Paul Lagomarcino, president of the Davenport club, announced the sale of Etten last night, following confirmation of negotiations with Carleton Molesworth, Pittsburgh scout who has followed the Blues for the past week. The sale price has

Sold to Pirates

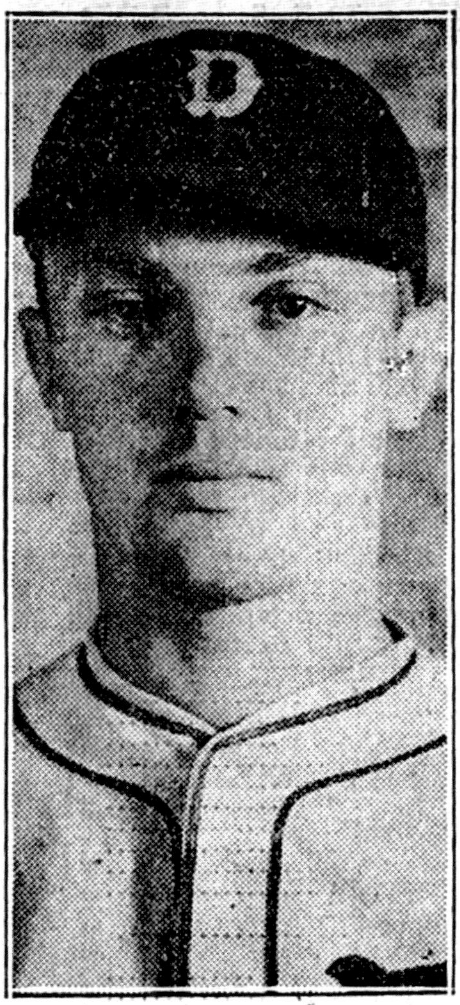

NICK ETTEN

Use Him at First Base

Molesworth, the Pittsburgh scout, states that the Pirates will give Etten a trial at first base. Every effort will be made to work the big fellow into this position. He bats and throws left handed. The Pirate scout claims Nick is

Modern fans complain about star players being moved from one minor league team to another, but player movement is no new phenomenon. For independently operated minor league clubs like the Blue Sox, the sale of a player's contract to a major league organization provided precious revenue to keep the club in the black financially.

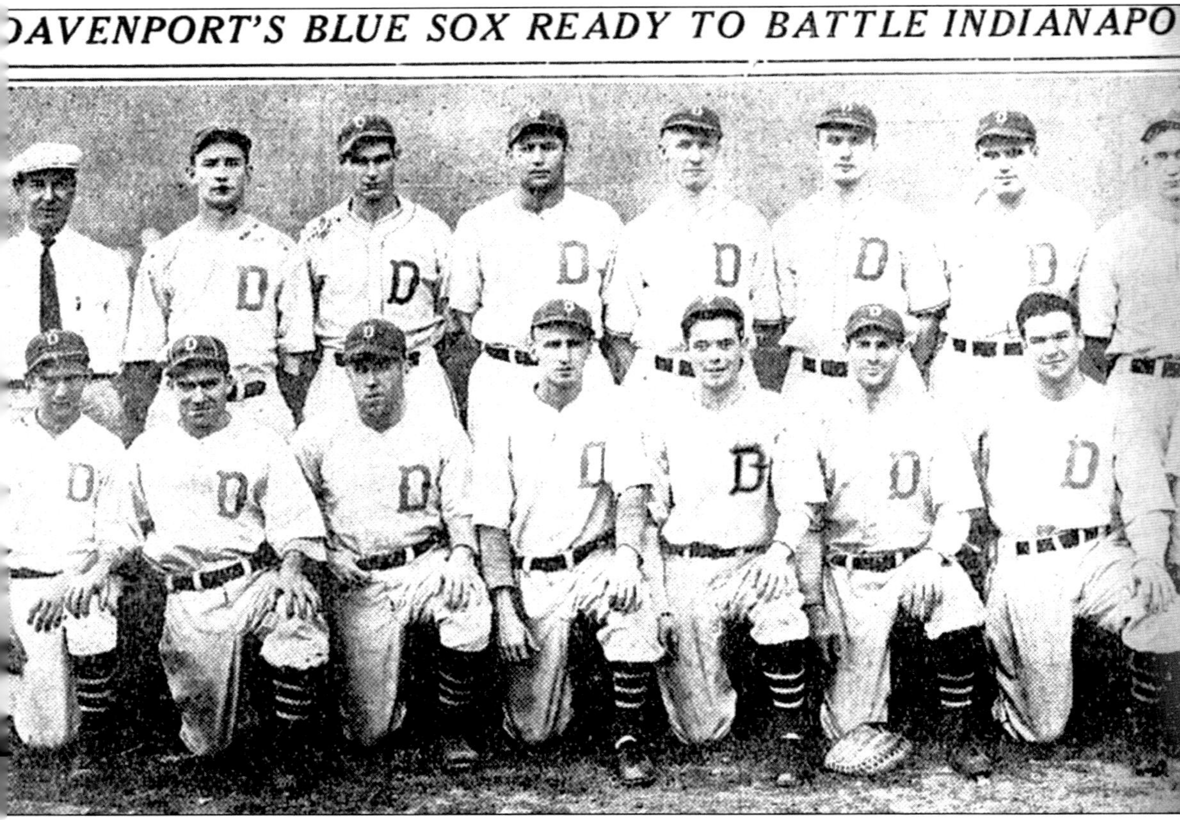

As a team in the "low minors," the Blue Sox were always eager to test their mettle against their Triple-A brethren. This headline promotes the appearance of the Indianapolis Indians of the American Association, one of the top minor leagues of the era.

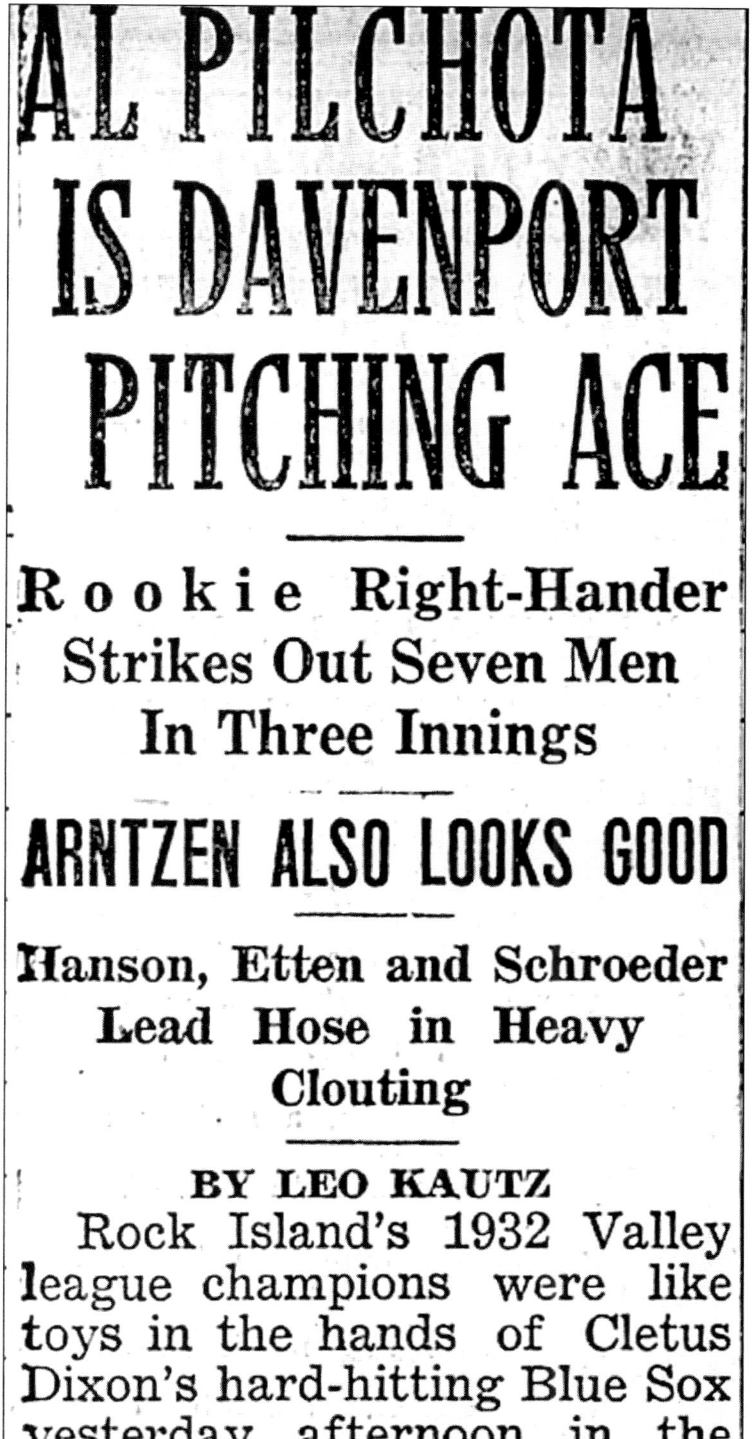

AL PILCHOTA IS DAVENPORT PITCHING ACE

Rookie Right-Hander Strikes Out Seven Men In Three Innings

ARNTZEN ALSO LOOKS GOOD

Hanson, Etten and Schroeder Lead Hose in Heavy Clouting

BY LEO KAUTZ

Rock Island's 1932 Valley league champions were like toys in the hands of Cletus Dixon's hard-hitting Blue Sox yesterday afternoon in the

A 1933 preseason headline indicates that Davenport fans (and sportswriters) were not yet familiar with young Al Piechota. They would know his name by the end of the year, as Piechota's 19-4 record led the way for the Blue Sox pitching staff.

VALLEY LEAGUE AVERAGES

(Including Tuesday Games)

TEAM BATTING

Team—	AB	R	H	Tb	Hr	Sb	Pct
Davenport	3991	867	1189	1763	82	80	.298
Rock Isl.	4025	752	1163	1653	48	141	.289
Peoria	3864	787	1094	1600	54	191	.283
Quincy	3874	703	1065	1493	44	80	.275
Springfield	3819	669	1046	1448	37	123	.274
Keokuk	4014	644	1053	1435	38	135	.262

TEAM FIELDING

Team—	Po	A	E	Dp	Pb	Pct.
Davenport	2956	1037	225	103	31	.9493
Rock Island	3042	1311	233	99	21	.9491
Peoria	2894	1293	266	88	19	.940
Keokuk	3004	1437	294	78	23	.938
Quincy	2729	1245	271	81	47	.936
Springfield	2893	1220	314	99	20	.929

INDIVIDUAL BATTING

Player—	AB	R	H	Hr	Rbi	Sb	Pct
Cotelle, D.	365	103	151	11	83	30	.410
Rosenthal, Q.	421	98	161	7	92	23	.382
Hopper, S.	341	72	121	8	87	12	.355
Etten, D	449	102	159	14	88	6	.354
Esrey, P	448	88	155	3	68	49	.346
Sueme, K	44	5	15	0	2	1	.341
Patterson, RI.	393	92	133	2	70	28	.338
Nebelung, P.	381	119	126	2	52	45	.331
Parker, RI.	415	84	136	8	90	26	.328
E. Hall, D.	461	109	150	28	149	14	.325
Mizeur, P	416	118	135	19	104	25	.325
Pickett, P-Q.	372	59	121	12	100	9	.325
Strathm'er, K	242	43	78	2	33	3	.322
Clarke, Q	448	88	144	3	75	5	.321
Sicking, K	427	81	137	1	47	22	.321
Denning, D.	352	66	112	4	70	4	.318
Thomas, S	247	53	78	4	34	7	.316
Murphy, P	181	36	57	3	27	8	.315
Anderson, RI.	465	86	144	3	68	19	.310
Heath, S	271	49	84	5	38	14	.310
Smilgoff, D.	115	26	35	4	24	2	.304
Wolf, Q	132	32	40	2	10	4	.303
Strother, D.	262	38	79	0	40	6	.302
F. Hall, D	393	79	118	4	79	6	.300
Denson, RI.	511	113	153	3	52	18	.299
Redmond, RI.	461	83	138	7	80	13	.299
Piechota, D.	87	24	26	2	23	0	.299
Lengquist, D.	64	7	19	1	16	0	.297
Meyer, D	440	128	130	11	81	9	.295
Martin, S	407	86	120	5	51	18	.295
Laskowski, P.	299	62	88	10	50	8	.294
Sanders, Q	441	109	128	3	44	21	.290
Falk, P	335	56	97	3	55	15	.290
Fitzgerald, S.	316	50	91	2	54	7	.288
Bohl, RI	118	21	34	0	17	0	.288
Shipley, P.	328	71	93	3	54	12	.284
Osborne, S	32	7	9	0	2	0	.281
Thome, P.	68	9	19	1	4	0	.279
Baker, RI	312	48	86	1	46	7	.276
Marion, Q	119	18	32	0	9	3	.269
Wagner, S	30	5	8	0	1	0	.267
Smargassi, S.	110	19	29	2	16	6	.264
Kestner, K.	448	83	118	7	48	34	.263
Munson, S-Q.	228	24	60	1	34	0	.263
Hairston, RI.	260	37	68	2	35	9	.262
Phillips, RI.	31	3	8	0	3	0	.258
Skoffic, S	39	6	10	0	4	2	.256
Bryant, Q-S.	96	15	24	3	24	0	.250
Touhey, D	84	13	21	1	12	0	.250
Tatum, K	80	15	12	0	11	2	.250
Schinski, K	64	14	16	0	5	8	.250
McIntyre, K.	28	5	7	1	6	0	.250
Seghi, P	344	54	85	5	53	4	.247
Uhas, S	168	17	41	0	11	0	.244
Beauchaine, K	373	42	90	0	44	12	.241
Strohl, Q	108	15	26	0	16	13	.241
Allison, RI	84	17	20	0	10	1	.238
Dixon, D	418	103	99	1	30	15	.237
Prince, D	76	6	18	0	9	0	.237
Hol'worth, RI	162	22	38	0	22	1	.235
Lohrman, S-K	163	29	37	4	24	6	.227
Struss, P	66	8	15	1	8	0	.227
Turner, S.	137	18	30	0	15	0	.219
Coulter, P.	47	6	10	0	11	0	.213
Jessen, RI.	29	3	6	0	2	0	.207
Lucas, K	76	10	15	1	7	0	.197
McGee, K	46	3	9	1	4	0	.196
Bradley, K.	101	12	18	1	7	0	.178
Sherer, Q	69	7	12	0	7	1	.174
Harwood, Q.	89	12	15	0	6	0	.169
Som'erfield, P	51	12	8	0	3	0	.157
Cohen, D	65	8	10	0	7	1	.154
Caldwell, K.	13	0	2	0	5	0	.154
Moore, Q	74	5	11	0	2	0	.149
Harrell, Q	75	9	11	1	7	0	.147
Gober, P	67	0	9	0	7	0	.134
Nobriga, S-Q.	48	10	6	0	3	3	.125
Kimberlin, S.	66	9	8	0	4	0	.121
Lipshin, K.	37	3	4	0	0	0	.108
Fonger, RI	13	0	1	0	0	0	.077
Sepich, P	52	6	3	0	1	0	.058
Warneke, S.	22	0	1	0	0	0	.045
Strickland, RI	65	8	2	0	3	0	.031

PITCHING RECORDS

Player—	W	L	Pct.	H	R	Bb	So
Lengquist, D.	10	1	.909	116	65	48	44
Piechota, D.	19	4	.826	192	115	141	120
Touhey, D	16	5	.762	204	102	104	170
Bryant, Q-S.	14	5	.737	163	116	96	120
Struss, P	11	4	.733	125	68	101	158
Prince, D	14	6	.700	166	100	58	125
Sepich, P	11	5	.688	187	128	92	66
Cohen, D	15	7	.682	202	100	82	88
Osborne, S.	4	2	.667	59	34	7	19
Fonger, RI.	2	1	.667	40	22	13	25
Gober, P	13	7	.650	162	96	62	104
Hol'worth, RI	14	8	.636	182	89	98	152
Nobriga, S-Q.	7	4	.636	110	51	47	40
Jessen, RI	5	3	.625	73	41	38	29
Strickland, RI	15	11	.577	230	127	87	113
Kimberlin, S.	12	10	.545	201	118	117	159
Coulter, P	8	7	.533	155	98	36	38
Bradley, P.	12	12	.500	244	118	88	106
Sherer, Q	7	7	.500	179	128	104	97
Phillips, RI.	5	5	.500	91	68	60	48
Cotelle, D	1	1	.500	14	15	15	12
Nemelin, RI.	1	1	.500	24	19	6	6

Fans followed the statistics of the Mississippi Valley League every bit as closely as fans today follow the American and National League.

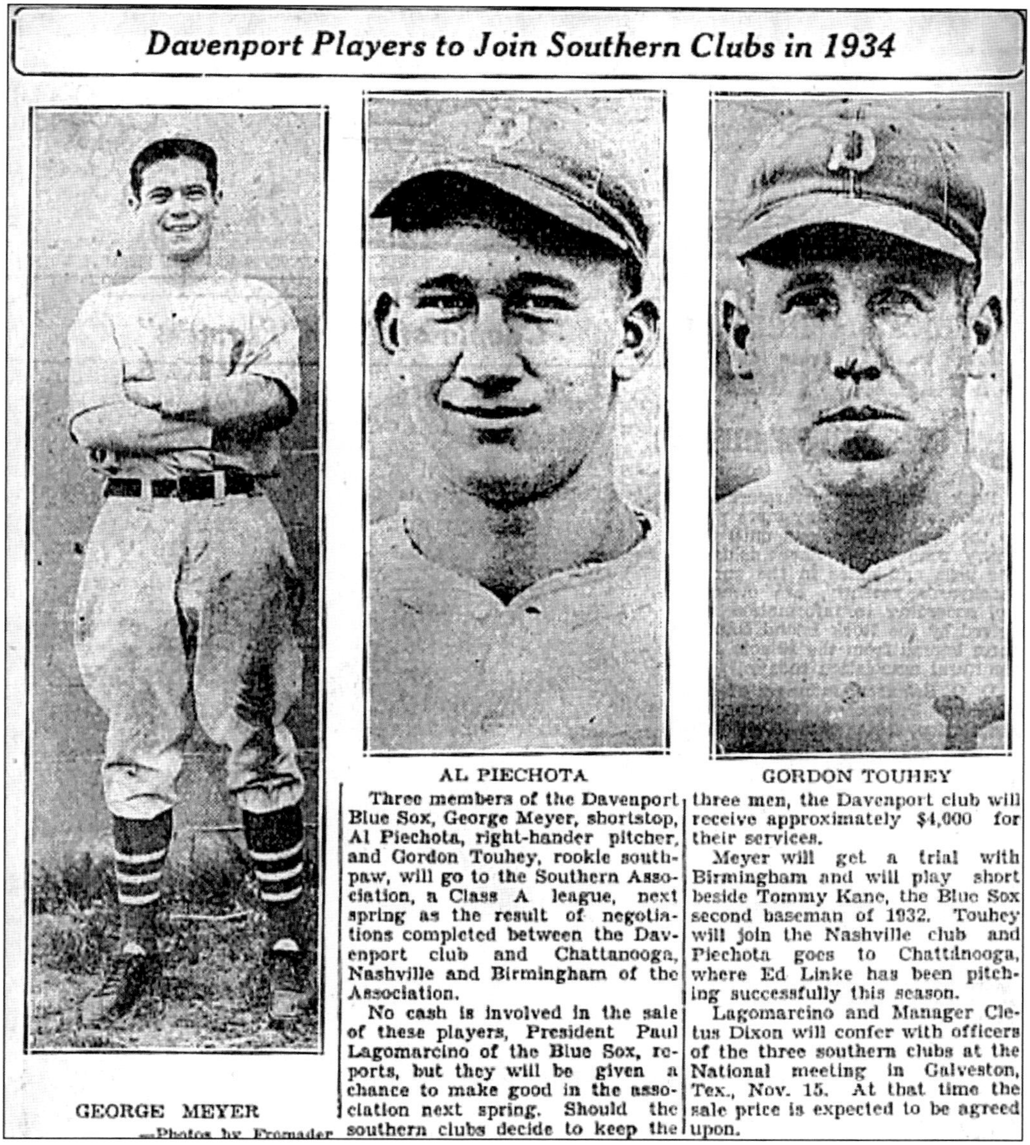

Davenport Players to Join Southern Clubs in 1934

GEORGE MEYER

—Photos by Fromader

AL PIECHOTA

GORDON TOUHEY

Three members of the Davenport Blue Sox, George Meyer, shortstop, Al Piechota, right-hander pitcher, and Gordon Touhey, rookie southpaw, will go to the Southern Association, a Class A league, next spring as the result of negotiations completed between the Davenport club and Chattanooga, Nashville and Birmingham of the Association.

No cash is involved in the sale of these players, President Paul Lagomarcino of the Blue Sox, reports, but they will be given a chance to make good in the association next spring. Should the southern clubs decide to keep the three men, the Davenport club will receive approximately $4,000 for their services.

Meyer will get a trial with Birmingham and will play short beside Tommy Kane, the Blue Sox second baseman of 1932. Touhey will join the Nashville club and Piechota goes to Chattdnooga, where Ed Linke has been pitching successfully this season.

Lagomarcino and Manager Cletus Dixon will confer with officers of the three southern clubs at the National meeting in Galveston, Tex., Nov. 15. At that time the sale price is expected to be agreed upon.

The success of the 1933 club meant that money was made from the sale of players to higher classification leagues. Here, the Davenport Times makes note of players moving up to the Southern Association.

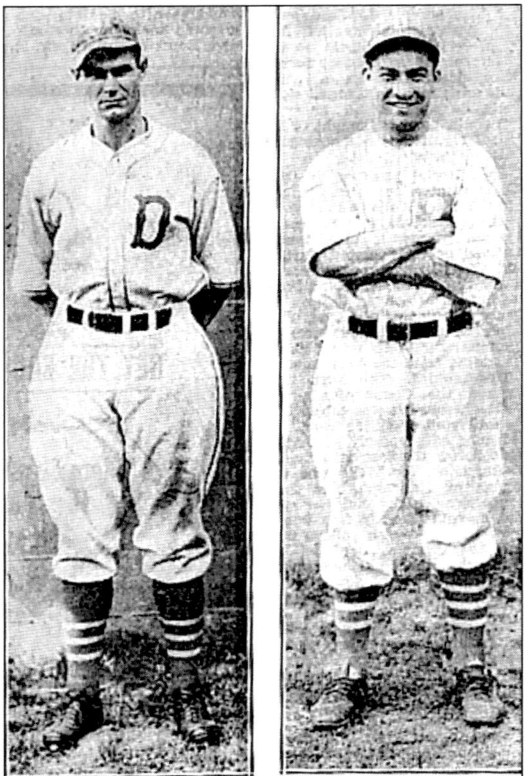

ED HALL COMO COTELLE

The 1933 Blue Sox juggernaut was led offensively by Ed Hall and Como Cotelle. Hall provided the power, with 28 homers and 151 RBI, while Cotelle batted .407 and scored 106 runs. Cotelle's on-field accomplishments were almost overshadowed by an off-field controversy. Cotelle signed a copy of a 1933 contract in the presence of Davenport's club secretary, but then neglected to have the contract notarized. Technically, that made the Sox in violation of baseball law by fielding a player who did not have a valid contract with the club. Fortunately for the Sox, the National Association absolved the club of any intentional wrongdoing, although Cotelle was declared a free agent for 1934.

Championship Series in a Nut Shell

(OFFICIAL AVERAGES)

DAVENPORT

	Ab	R	H	Tb	2b	3b	Hr	Sh	Bb	Rbi	Sb	So	Pct.	Po	A	E	Dp	Pct.
Smilgoff	1	0	1	1	0	0	0	0	0	1	0	0	1.000	0	0	0	0	.000
Touhey, p	4	1	2	2	0	0	0	0	1	2	0	1	.500	1	0	0	0	1.000
Denning, c	20	4	9	12	3	0	0	0	2	2	0	3	.450	19	3	2	0	.917
Prince, p	8	2	3	3	0	0	0	0	0	0	0	0	.375	2	5	0	0	1.000
Cotelle, cf	22	1	8	8	0	0	0	1	0	0	1	2	.364	13	0	1	0	.929
Dixon, 1b	21	3	7	7	0	0	0	2	1	0	3	2	.333	58	2	1	5	.984
Lengquist, p	3	0	1	1	0	0	0	0	0	0	0	1	.333	0	4	1	1	.800
F. Hall, 2b	19	2	5	5	0	0	0	0	2	1	2	2	.263	13	17	2	4	.938
E. Hall, lf	17	4	4	8	1	0	1	1	5	3	1	2	.235	5	1	0	1	1.000
Elten, rf	20	2	4	5	1	0	0	0	2	2	0	5	.200	6	0	0	0	1.000
Meyer, ss	21	3	4	4	0	0	0	0	3	3	2	6	.190	9	15	2	6	.923
Strother, 3b	17	3	3	4	1	0	0	0	4	3	1	1	.176	2	17	1	0	.950
Piechota, p	3	0	0	0	0	0	0	0	0	0	0	1	.000	1	3	0	0	1.000
Totals	176	25	51	60	6	0	1	4	20	18	10	26	.290	129	68	10	6	.952

Passed ball—Denning.

ROCK ISLAND

	AB	R	H	Tb	2b	3b	Hr	Sh	Bb	Rbi	Sb	So	Pct.	Po	A	E	Dp	Pct.
Hollingsworth, p.	4	2	2	2	0	0	0	0	1	0	0	1	.500	0	2	1	0	.500
Patterson, lf	19	5	8	11	1	1	0	0	4	3	0	2	.421	7	1	0	0	1.000
Sueme, c	20	3	7	13	1	1	1	0	3	3	0	2	.350	31	3	1	0	.971
Parker, rf-3b	18	1	6	8	2	0	0	0	1	3	2	2	.333	6	4	0	0	1.000
Anderson, ss	19	2	6	8	0	1	0	0	5	1	1	1	.316	10	18	3	5	.903
Baker, 2b	21	1	6	7	1	0	0	2	0	0	0	2	.286	16	17	2	4	.943
Allison, rf	11	2	3	6	0	0	1	0	0	1	0	0	.273	4	0	0	0	1.000
Hairston, 1b	21	0	5	6	1	0	0	0	2	3	0	7	.238	42	5	0	6	1.000
Jessen, p	4	1	1	2	1	0	0	0	0	0	0	0	.250	0	2	2	0	.500
Denson, cf	22	0	4	6	0	1	0	0	2	3	0	6	.182	12	0	0	0	1.000
Strickland, p	10	0	1	2	1	0	0	2	0	0	0	3	.100	2	7	1	0	.900
Bohl, 3b	12	1	1	1	0	0	0	1	1	1	0	0	.077	5	4	4	0	.692
Totals	182	21	50	72	8	4	2	5	20	19	3	26	.275	133	62	14	6	.933

Passed balls—Sueme (3).

PITCHING RECORDS

DAVENPORT

	Ip	Ab	H	R	Er	Sh	Bb	So	Wp	W	L	Pct.
Prince	19 1/3	76	22	7	6	2	10	8	0	2	0	1.000
Lengquist	9 2/3	35	6	2	0	1	2	1	0	1	0	1.000
Touhey	9	41	14	8	5	0	4	8	0	1	0	1.000
Piechota	8	30	8	4	4	2	5	9	0	0	1	.000

ROCK ISLAND

	Ip	Ab	H	R	Er	Sh	Bb	So	Wp	W	L	Pct.
Strickland	24 2/3	97	28	5	2	0	3	13	0	1	1	.500
Hollingsworth	9 2/3	47	17	16	13	3	10	7	2	0	2	.000
Jessen	9	33	6	4	0	1	2	5	0	0	1	.000

While the '33 Blue Sox were reluctant to face Rock Island in a seven-game championship series, Davenport did end up playing against the Islanders. As in the regular season, the Blue Sox dominated, and brought home their first MVL title, 4 games to 1.

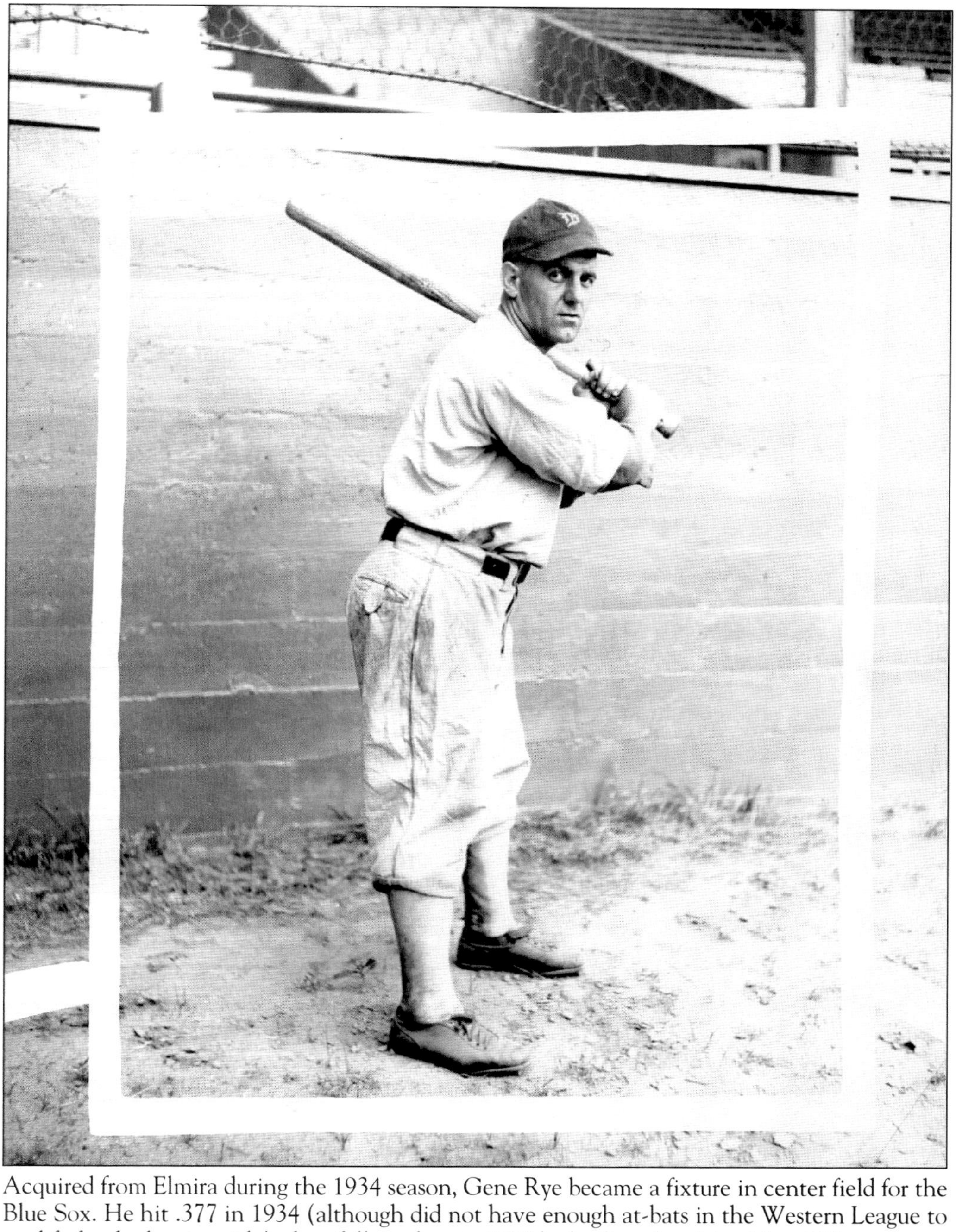

Acquired from Elmira during the 1934 season, Gene Rye became a fixture in center field for the Blue Sox. He hit .377 in 1934 (although did not have enough at-bats in the Western League to qualify for the batting title), then followed up in 1935 by leading the club with a .320 average.

No More Long Hops

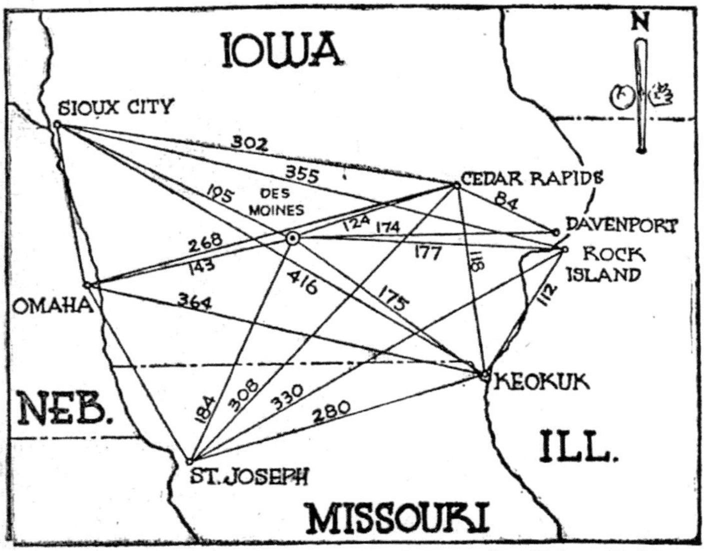

—Courtesy Des Moines Register.

With the longest hop now only 416 miles, as a result of the recent change in which Keokuk replaced Topeka in the Western League, the loop is more compact than at any other time in its history and traveling conditions are more convenient for all clubs. The above drawing shows the traveling distances between each of the league cities.

Keeping expenses low was an important part of operating a minor league club in the 1930s. When the Blue Sox joined the Class A Western League in 1934, the compact size of the league was a major selling point

Cletus Dixon Resigns as Manager of Blue Sox at Western League Meeting

BY LEO KAUTZ
Sports Editor, The Times

DES MOINES, Ia., Nov. 8.—Cletus Dixon, manager of the Davenport Blue Sox for the past three and one-half years, today presented his resignation to Paul Lagomarcino, president of the club, to take effect immediately.

Dixon's resignation came as a surprise to Lagomarcino, here today to represent Davenport at the Western league meeting. The Blue Sox manager explained that he desired to be relieved of his duties, stating that he understood a new board of directors and a new club president were to be named at the annual session in Davenport next Wednesday night.

Lagomarcino stated he would let the new board act on Dixon's resignation. Paul emphatically declared that he will not accept the presidency of the club another year. Dixon had informed Lagomarcino previously that he would not return to Davenport under a new regime and his resignation today came with the announcement that Lagomarcino would retire as president.

The eight present clubs in the Western league and a delegation from Lincoln were represented at the meeting today. Lincoln will bid for a franchise, should one of the clubs withdraw.

Charles Beers, secretary of the Rock Island club, presented a list of suggestions to the league, stating that Rock Island would not

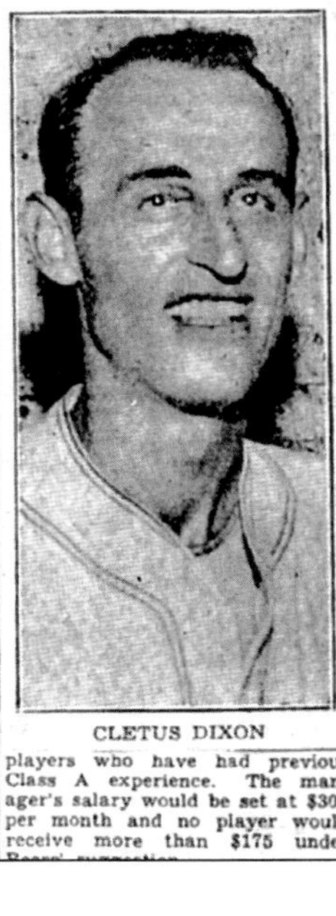

CLETUS DIXON

players who have had previous Class A experience. The manager's salary would be set at $300 per month and no player would receive more than $175 under

After three and a half years of on-field success, Blue Sox skipper Cletus Dixon resigned after the 1934 season. Fortunately for Davenport, Dixon later agreed to return for 1935, and once again led the Sox to regular-season pennant. After another championship in 1936, Dixon finally hung up his spikes for good, ending a golden era of baseball in Davenport.

Although Davenport lost an exciting seven-game final series in 1934, the attendance at the extra games helped boost overall attendance above the 100,000 mark. Pictured here is Frank "Lefty" Lemanski, one of the on-the-field reasons for the high attendance numbers. Lamanski won 24 games, more than one third of the club's total of 70. His 216 strikeouts also led the league.

Topped Everything In His Own Loop

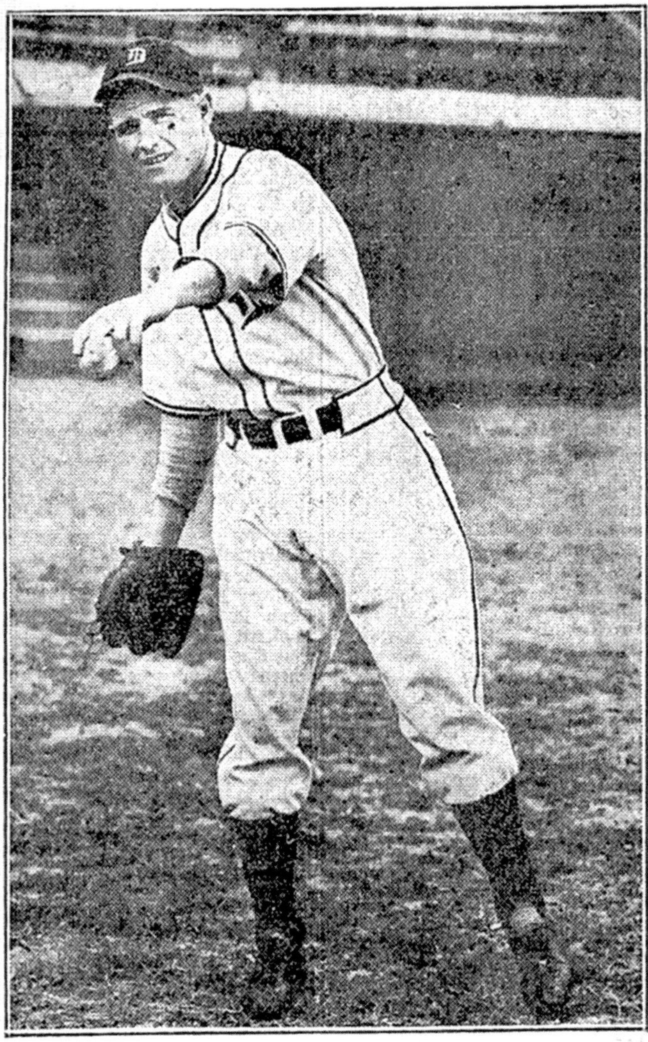

LEFTY LAMANSKI

102,438 Persons See Games At Municipal Stadium This Season; 14,700 at Playoffs

A total of 102,438 persons watched the Davenport Blue Sox in action during the 1934 season at the Municipal Stadium. The official attendance figures were released today by Secretary Al Schultze.

Of this amount 60,138 witnessed the games during the regular season; 6,000 watched the Eagles' night contest; 18,000 ladies were admitted free and 14,700 attended the six games in the two playoffs for the Western league title.

Of the 60,138 paid customers for the league games, 50,849 were adults and 9,289 were children.

Baseball Broadcasts Will Be Resumed Here July 18 If Rocks Can Raise Funds

Resuming of baseball broadcasts by Station WHBF, which was discontinued recently when President Dale Gear of Topeka, Kan., notified the Rock Island Western league club that a league rule prohibited broadcasting, appeared possible today following a long distance conversation between President Gear and C. A. Beers, secretary of the Rock Island club.

Informed by Mr Beers that the attendance has dropped off considerably since the broadcasting ban, Mr Gear said that he would take the responsibility for lifting the ban, starting July 18, in the series with Sioux City, providing, however, that in the meantime the fans of the community respond wholeheartedly to the appeal of Templar chapter, Order of DeMolay, which has charge of the sale of tickets for the opening home series of the second half.

To Affect Davenport

When the ban is lifted for Rock Island, Davenport will also be permitted to broadcast ga[illegible] though Mr Gear did not mention the Blue Sox situation. Paul Lagomarcino, president of the Davenport club, said this morning that he would get in touch with President Gear immediately with the request that Davenpor be permitted to broadcast their games as soon as Rock Island's future in the league is assured.

As soon as the Rock Island club raises enough money through their special ticket sale, the Blue Sox games will again go on the air, President Lagomarcino feels. He asks Davenport fans to do all they can to make the Rock Island campaign a success.

According to the announcement made by Mr Beers, the league president plans to make a special rule on broadcasting for the Rock [illegible]

[illegible]ance of the league rule as the other clubs are almost unanimous in their contention that the broadcasting of games shall not be permitted.

"I am making this promise in view of the tremendous load that a few individuals are carrying in Rock Island in the hope that it will be of benefit to you for the balance of the year. Any action that you take will of necessity have to be with the approval of Davenport which is so closely located to Rock Island."

In the early days of baseball on the radio, some in thought that the availability of games on the radio cut into stadium attendance. When Davenport and Rock Island joined the Western League in 1934, they had to fight for the continuation of games on the radio. "I feel that radio has built up interest in the game here and that we owe it to our fans to continue," said Davenport's Paul Lagomarcino. Rock Island's attendance suffered after the club was barred from broadcasting games on the radio. As a result, Western League President Dale Gear permitted the broadcasts to resume. Davenport followed suit in putting games on the radio.

The release of the upcoming league schedule always figured prominently in the local papers as fans geared up for the local baseball season.

WESTERN LEAGUE 1935 SCHEDULE

AT KEOKUK	AT CEDAR RAPIDS	AT DAVENPORT	AT ROCK ISLAND	AT DES MOINES	AT ST. JOSEPH	AT SIOUX CITY	AT OMAHA
READ	May 18, 19, 20 July 5, 6, 7 Aug. 27, 28, 29	May 7, 8, 9 June 24, 25, 26, 27 Sept. 2, 3	May 21, 22, 23, 24 June 22, 23 Aug. 24, 25, 26	June 7, 8, 9 July 22, 23, 24 Aug. 13, 14, 15	June 10, 11, 12 July 19, 20, 21 Aug. 16, 17, 18	June 4, 5, 6 July 13, 14, 15 Aug. 10, 11, 12	June 1, 2, 3 July 16, 17, 18 Aug. 7, 8, 9
[illegible] 10, 11, 12 [illegible] 19, 20, 21 [illegible] 6, 7, 8	THE TRIBUNE	May 16, 17 June 28,29,30,Jul.1 Aug. 30, 31, Sept. 1	May 13, 14, 15 July 2, 3, 4, 4 Sept. 4, 5	June 13, 14, 15 July 25, 26, 27, 28 Aug. 22, 23	June 16, 17, 18 July 29, 30, 31 Aug. 19, 20, 21	May 25, 26, 27 July 10, 11, 12 Aug. 4, 5, 6	May 28, 29, 30, 31 July 8, 9 Aug. 1, 2, 3
[illegible] 13, 14, 15 [illegible] 2, 3, 4, 4 [illegible] 4, 5	May 21, 22, 23, 24 June 22, 23 Aug. 24, 25, 26	FOR THE	May 10, 11, 12 June 19, 20, 21 Sept. 6, 7, 8	June 10, 11, 12 July 19, 20, 21 Aug. 16, 17, 18	June 7, 8, 9 July 22, 23, 24 Aug. 13, 14, 15	June 1, 2, 3 July 16, 17, 18 Aug. 7, 8, 9	June 4, 5, 6 July 13, 14, 15 Aug. 10, 11, 12
[illegible] 16, 17 [illegible] 28,29,30,Jul.1 [illegible] 30, 31, Sept. 1	May 7, 8, 9 June 24, 25, 26, 27 Sept. 2, 3	May 18, 19, 20 July 5, 6, 7 Aug. 27, 28, 29	BEST	June 16, 17, 18 July 29, 30, 31 Aug. 19, 20, 21	June 13, 14, 15 July 25, 26, 27, 28 Aug. 22, 23	May 28, 29, 30, 31 July 8, 9 Aug. 1, 2, 3	May 25, 26, 27 July 10, 11, 12 Aug. 4, 5, 6
[illegible] 25, 26, 27, 28 [illegible] 11, 12 [illegible] 4, 5, 6	June 1, 2, 3 July 16, 17, 18 Aug. 10, 11, 12	May 29, 30, 31 July 8, 9, 10 Aug. 1, 2, 3	June 4, 5, 6 July 13, 14, 15 Aug. 7, 8, 9	STORIES	May 7, 8, 9 July 5, 6, 7 Sept. 2, 2, 3	May 15, 16, 17 June 22, 23, 24 Aug. 28, 29, 30	May 13, 14 June 19, 20, 21 Aug. 24, 25, 26, 2[illegible]
[illegible] 29, 30, 31 [illegible] 8, 9, 10 [illegible] 1, 2, 3	June 4, 5, 6 July 13, 14, 15 Aug. 7, 8, 9	May 25, 26, 27, 28 July 11, 12 Aug. 4, 5, 6	June 1, 2, 3 July 16, 17, 18 Aug. 10, 11, 12	May 10, 11, 12 July 2, 3, 4 Sept. 6, 7, 8	OF THESE	May 13, 14 June 19, 20, 21 Aug. 24, 25, 26, 27	May 15, 16, 17 June 22, 23, 24 Aug. 28, 29, 30
[illegible] 13, 14, 15 [illegible] 25, 26, 27, 28 [illegible] 19, 20	June 7, 8, 9 July 22, 23, 24 Aug. 13, 14, 15	June 16, 17, 18 July 29, 30, 31 Aug. 21, 22, 23	June 10, 11, 12 July 19, 20, 21 Aug. 16, 17, 18	May 22, 23, 24 June 28,29,30,Jul.1 Sept. 4, 5	May 18, 19, 20, 21 June 25, 26, 27 Aug. 31, Sept. 1	BASEBALL	May 10, 11, 12 July 2, 3, 4, 4 Sept. 2, 3
[illegible] 16, 17, 18 [illegible] 29, 30, 31 [illegible]	June 10, 11, 12 July 19, 20, 21 [illegible]	June 13, 14, 15 July 25, 26, 27, 28 [illegible] 19, 20	June 7, 8, 9 July 22, 23, 24 [illegible] 13, 14, 15	May 18, 19, 20, 21 June 25, 26, 27 Aug. 31, Sept. 1	May 22, 23, 24 June 28,29,30,Jul.1 Sept. 4, 5	May 7, 8, 9 July 5, 6, 7 Sept. 6, 7, 8	GAMES

HERE'S THAT NO-HIT BATTERY

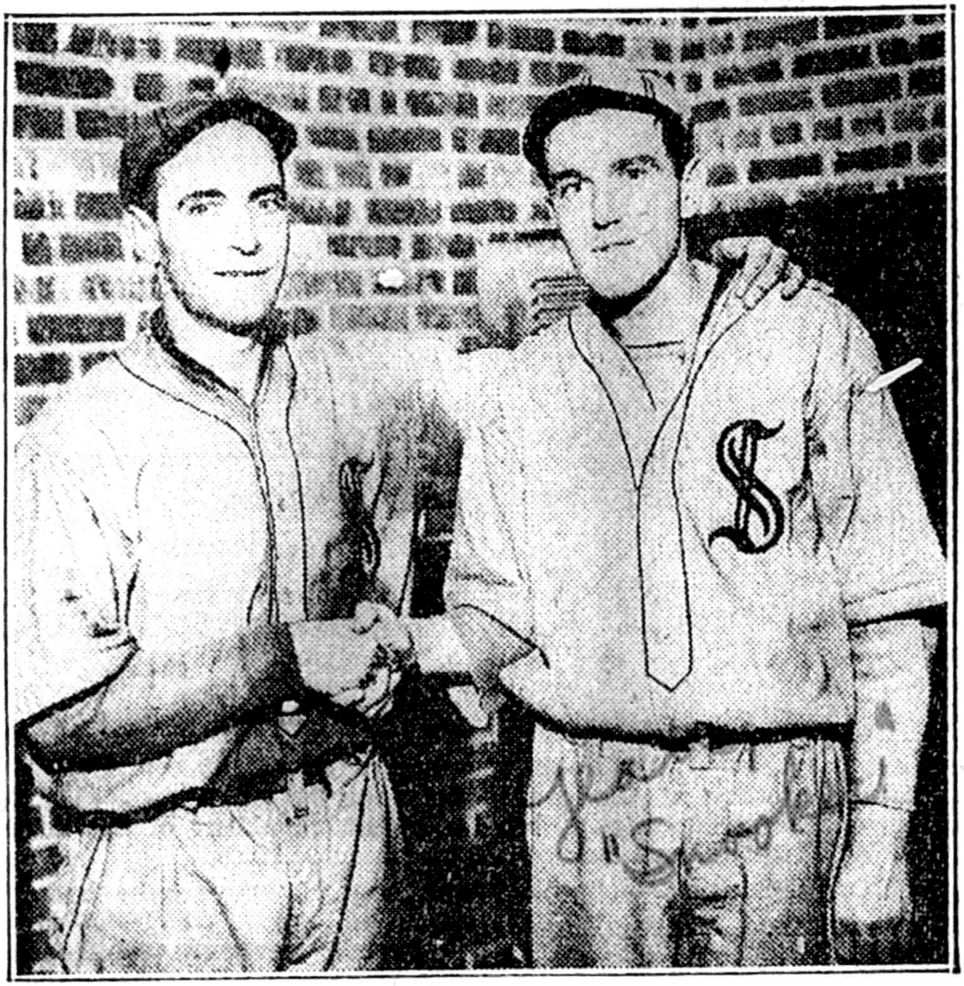

Manager Earle Brucker, (left) was heaping words of praise on Herman Drefs, (right) in the St. Joseph dressing room following last night's game, when The Times cameraman took the above picture. Brucker took charge of the St. Joe club six weeks ago and led it to the Western league title. He is sure of a job for next year as a result of that victory. Brucker, besides catching Drefs' great pitching last night, scored one run and drove in the other. He got two of the five hits off Lamanski. The Saint skipper has been the whole show in the series, driving in eight runs and leading his team at bat with an average of .310.

As in 1933, the Blue Sox ended the year by facing St. Joseph in a post-season series. This time, the stakes were the Western League Championship. The teams played a tight series that went the full seven games. In the decisive contest, Herman "Snooker" Drefs won a pitching duel with Frank Lamanski by pitching a no-hitter to give St. Joseph the title.

Davenport Receives $1,330 As Share in Title Series; Profit Shown For Season

Check For $3,350 Also Received From Brooklyn For Lamanski and Olsen—Players to Get Less Than $20 in Split But Salaries Are Paid

BY LEO KAUTZ

The morning mail brought checks totaling $4,974.40 to the Davenport Baseball club, which includes the Blue Sox' share in the post-season series and cash from the Brooklyn Dodgers for the purchase of Frank Lamanski and Russ Olsen.

Davenport's share in the three Western league series totals $1,330.15. The Blue Sox players also received $294.25 in addition to their salaries for 16 days following the schedule's close, and the Brooklyn check, after the National Association had taken its cut of three per cent, amounted to $3,350.

deducted the pool totaled $5,320.62 and was split equally among the four clubs which competed in the three series.

The Davenport club's $1,330.15 is not all profit as the player salaries for the series with Des Moines must be deducted. However, salaries for the final championship series were paid out of the league fund before the split was made. Davenport received 15 per cent of the gross receipts for all games played here, this item being for park rental and lights. An additional $50 was received after each game for policing the grounds, park help, etc.

So the Blue Sox did not fare so badly, even though they lost the championship to St. Joe. Checks received today were deposited in the Davenport bank and when the books are closed for the season President Paul Lagomarcino hopes to show club stockholders a profit for the year, something very unusual in these days of baseball.

Herman Drefs' no-hit, no-run victory over the Blue Sox here last Tuesday night cost each member of the Davenport team approximately $10. The Sox will receive less than $20 per man as the losers share of the receipts while the St. Joe players get approximately $30 each.

According to figures released today by President Dale Gear, the two series in which Davenport played Des Moines and St. Joseph played Sioux City, netted the league pool $3,382.07. The seven game series between Davenport and St. Joe brought a total of $3,974.17 into the pool after all expenses had been paid. So the league pool amounted to $7,356.24.

Of this amount, 10 per cent went to the players, the St. Joe team getting $441.37, or 60 per cent, while Davenport got 40 per cent.

When the players' shares were

The financial statement of the 1934 Davenport club seems quaint by modern standards. Although the club was a huge success on the field, making ends meet was always a struggle, especially during the hard years of the Depression.

The annual ticket drive traditionally kicked off preparation for the upcoming season. Teams of workers canvassed the city to sell season tickets and promote the local club.

Team Captains Named For Baseball Ticket Drive; 150 Workers Are Needed

Team workers, 150 of them are being rounded up by officers of the Davenport Fans association for the season ticket book campaign which will be held on Wednesday and Thursday of next week. The workers will be selected by 30 team captains who will head the drive to dispose of 1,000 books in two days.

Al Thomas, president of the Fans association, announced today the naming of the 30 captains who will meet with the campaign committee in the "barn" at Hotel Blackhawk Wednesday night.

At this meeting plans for the campaign will be outlined and each captain will select his team of five workers. The team members will then be notified of a general meeting at the

Western More Expensive

HERE ARE SOME OF THE NEW FACES IN BLUE SOX UNIFORMS

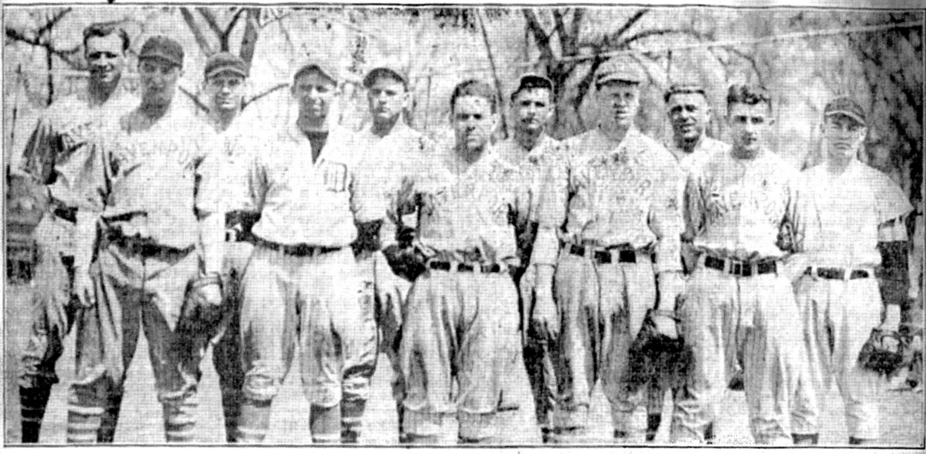

—Times Photo

Front row, left to right—Joe Dooley, Chicago outfielder; Wilbur Freck, Wisconsin outfielder; Andy Marsh, Chicago rookie outfielder; Edwin Lindstrom, Chicago rookie second baseman; Don Crowe, veteran pitcher.

Back row—John Brice, Chicago rookie pitcher; Walter Brawand, veteran third baseman, Chicago; Harry Whitehead, veteran outfielder from Southern association; Mitchell Radon, Chicago rookie pitcher; Al Hazzard, University of Illinois pitcher, and Jim Gravin, young Chicago pitcher.

Pitching of Lamanski and Grabin Features Practice Game at Blue Sox Field

Unusually effective pitching by four members of Cletus Dixon's Davenport Western league squad featured a six-inning practice game between the Regulars and Dubs at the Credit Island diamond yesterday afternoon. And when it came time to call it a day, the teams were deadlocked with two runs each.

This afternoon, at the training camp diamond, the two clubs will renew their battle but this time they'll go seven innings, and nine if necessary to break the deadlock. Manager Dixon is well satisfied with the condition of his players. They are becoming used to the tough grind and will work six hours per day from now on.

Frank Lamanski, veteran hurler from Denver, was the sensation of the mound department yesterday. He toiled three innings for the Regulars. They got one run off his delivery, due to errors, but the hits he allowed were few and far between.

Jim Gravin, rookie from Chicago, surprised even Boss Dixon with his expert pitching after relieving Lamanski. He, too, allowed one run but it wasn't all his fault.

Al Piechota and Frank Meyer pitched for the Dubs and did almost as well as Lamanski and Gravin. Hits were more frequent, due to the appearance of several veterans in the Regular lineup, but Al and Frank were tough in the pinches.

Bob Lengquist, veteran Rockford southpaw, arrived yesterday to try for his old berth on the club. He will go to work with the Sox this afternoon.

Manager Dixon is afraid his infielders will suffer serious injury on the hard Credit Island diamond. He has cut his infield practice down to less than 15 minutes for each team and will stress batting practice the rest of the week. The diamond is rough and hard, due to the absence of rain for several weeks. The condition of the lot is such that the Skipper is worried, claiming that his infielders will be a week behind others in the league for lack of practice on a smooth diamond.

The squad remained intact after the Wednesday drill but Dixon plans to issue a few pink slips tonight. He will carry the two complete teams until the season opens but several pitchers are due to start for home soon.

SPORT SHOTS

BY LEO KAUTZ

CLETUS Dixon is well pleased with the showing of his Davenport Blue Sox in Muscatine yesterday. Although the Hose didn't look like champions, they demonstrated strength in hitting and in pitching. And the spots that Dix thought might be weak gave him a pleasant surprise.

* * *

For instance, Harry Whitehouse, veteran outfielder, hasn't been hitting as expected in practice.. But yesterday he came up with a pair of solid smacks and played a nice game in the outfield. Ed Hall also clinched his job in the garden. Freck, Marsh and Dooley are fighting for the third outfield post.

* * *

Bill Prince, veteran of the Sox pitching staff last season, will be in a Davenport uniform again in a few days. Bill wired Dixon last night that he was on his way back from Albany and wanted to rejoin his old mates. So the popular right-hander will chuck 'em at the Stadium again within a few weeks.

* * *

PRINCE went to Albany of the International league but refused to sign a contract there because Albany officials wanted to farm him to the New York-Penn league. The Davenport club gave Bill a chance to make good in the Class AA circuit but refused to let him go back to a smaller league. The Western is a better league than the N. Y.-Penn, so Bill's coming home

Marvin Shelso, University of Minnesota pitcher, has been sent to Cedar Rapids. Shelso wasn't quite good enough to move any of the regular left-handers off the Blue Sox roster. York, Lamanski and Lengquist are the lefties Dixon is depending upon. Cedar Rapids needed a southpaw so Shelso moved on to the camp of the Raiders.

* * *

Russ Olson, who played with the San Francisco club in the Coast league, arrived in Davenport this morning. He will take over the shortstop berth, providing he can oust George Meyer and Frank Hall from the position. Dixon thinks a lot of the kid. He'll be in uniform this afternoon.

* * *

DIXON has 28 men on the roster today. He'll continue the practice sessions at Credit Island all week, unless Peoria can come to terms on a series of tilts in the latter city. President Paul Lagomarcino is dickering with the Tractors for a series later in the week. The Sox need competition.

* * *

The workout today started at 11 a. m. and was to continue until 3:30 without a let-up. Lunch was to be served following the drill. The same program will be followed each day. Thirteen pitchers remain on the roster. They are Lengquist, Lamanski and York, left-handers, and Hazzard, Donagan, Bradley, Crowe, Brice, Radon, Grabin, F. Meyers, Piechota and Prince, right-handers.

Denning and Smilgoff, veterans from last year, are the only catchers remaining on the roster. Hackbarth is helping Dixon with the first base work and Swanson and Lindstrom are fighting it out for second. George Meyer, Frank Hall and Russ Olson will battle for the shortstop job. Brawand is the only third-sacker on the team and he looks exceptionally good.

Minor league players of the era didn't get to spend spring training in warm locales like Florida or Arizona. Instead, players traveled to Davenport to try out for a roster spot on the local team. The Blue Sox often prepared for the season by playing exhibitions against local college and semi-pro nines.

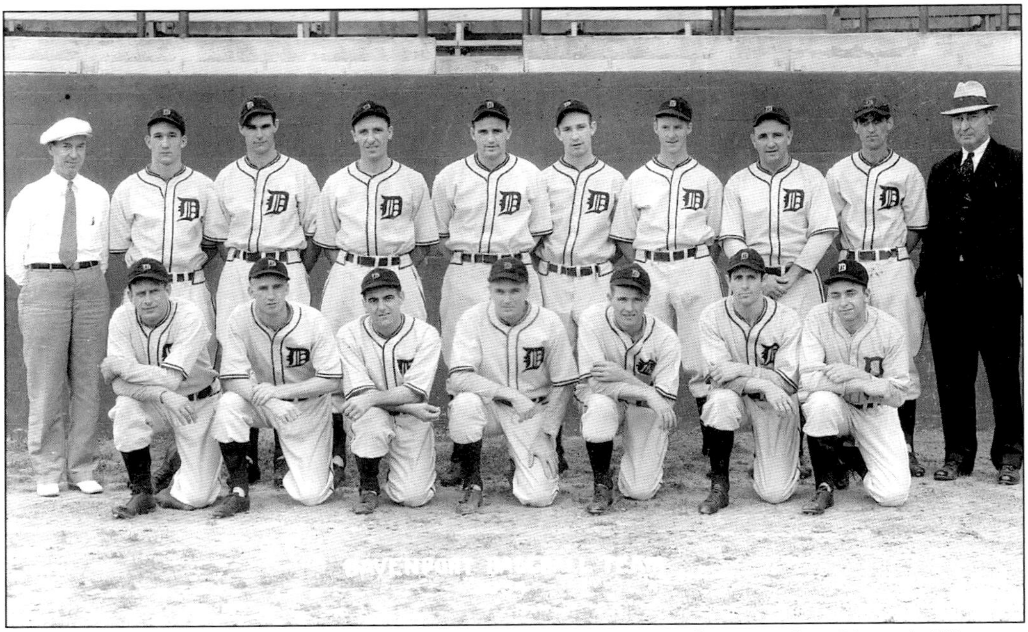

After the Mississippi Valley League folded, Davenport moved up to the Class A Western League. After a sluggish first half, the Sox rallied for a second half title and defeated Des Moines in the playoff semifinals, finally dropping a classic seven-game series to St. Joseph— the Saints' Herman "Snooker" Drefs pitched a no-hitter in the series finale.

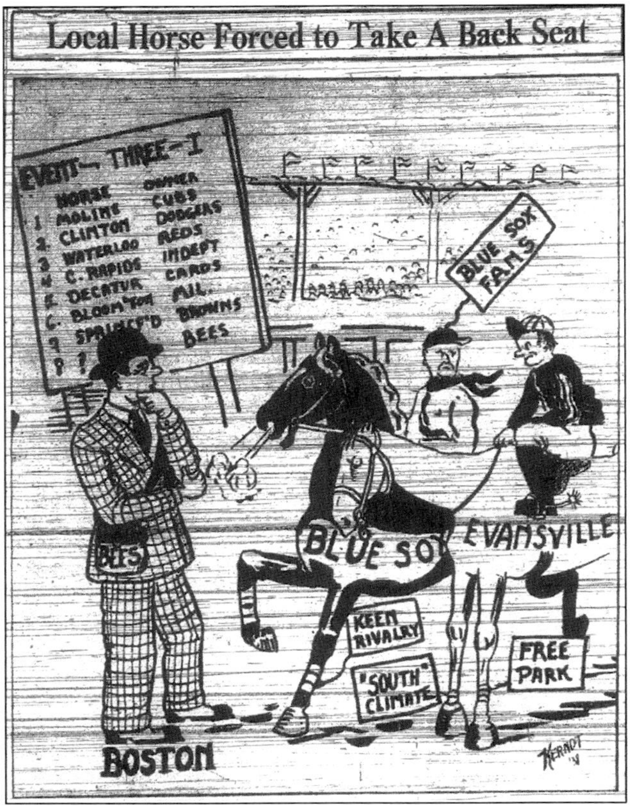

When the Western League voted to disband in January of 1938, Davenport had to fight for the eighth slot in the Three-I League with Evansville, Indiana. This cartoon, taken from the *Morning Democrat*, illustrates the big league benefactor looking over his options. In the end, the league voted 5 to 2 to admit Evansville, with only Moline and Clinton supporting Davenport's bid.

FITZ AND HIS ROOKIES TALK OVER TRAINING PLANS AT BLUE SOX CAMP

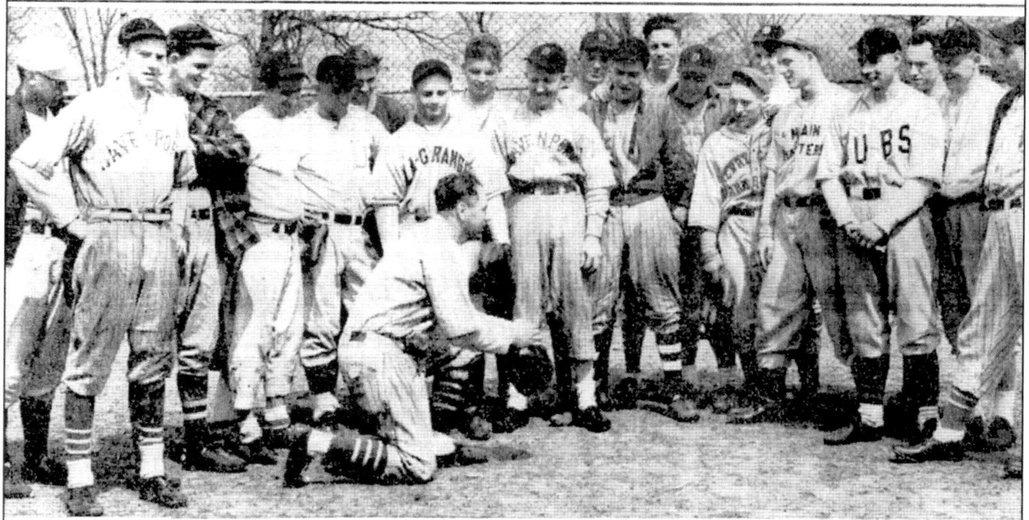

—Times Photo

Here they are, the new boss and his Davenport Blue Sox rookies who started training yesterday at the Credit Island diamond. Manager Fitzpatrick, who is giving Davenport a new deal in baseball this year, is shown kneeling in the center of his group of newcomers, several of whom are expected to land permanent berths with the Blue Sox this year. The kids came from all points in Iowa and Illinois and several from as far west as Oklahoma. Fitz will keep the youngsters hustling until Monday, when he expects to cut at least half of them loose to make room for the squad of veterans who'll start training at that time at the Municipal Stadium.

Jack Fitzpatrick took the reins of the Blue Sox in 1937, succeeding the immensely successful Cletus Dixon.

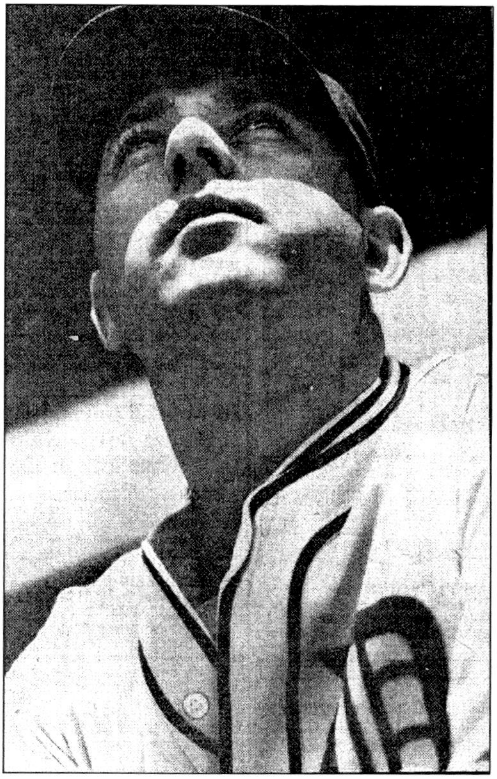

Jack Fitzpatrick had the unenviable task of succeeding Cletus Dixon as manager of the Blue Sox. Fitzpatrick led the 1937 Sox to a third-place finish in the Western League, well behind runaway champion, Cedar Rapids.

The preseason often provided fans an early look at both the Davenport club and their league rivals. With the Rock Island Islanders close by, exhibition games were common.

SWIGART WILL FACE RIVALS IN EXHIBITION

Manager Burwell of Islanders Plans to Pitch Vance Cauble

NEGRO TEAM HERE SATURDAY

Fitz Will Throw His Strongest Lineup Against Invaders

TONIGHT'S LINEUPS

ROCK ISLAND	DAVENPORT
E. Williamson, 2b	Danfield, cf
F. Denson, cf	F. Hall, 2b
C. Larson, 1b	Peddicord, 3b
Hibbard, lf	Prerost, lf
Michaels, 3b	Van Camp, rf
Kennedy, rf	Clarke, 1b
Hoover, c	Floyd, ss
Schohl, ss	Morgan, c
Cauble, p	Swigart, p

Place—Municipal Stadium.
Time—8 p. m.

Davenport's Blue Sox hoped to give local fans some idea of what they'll see in the Western league campaign, when they meet Rock Island tonight and the Indianapolis club of the Colored American league Saturday night in a pair of exhibition games at the Municipal Stadium.

Tonight the Islanders, under the leadership of Bill Burwell, former American association mound star, will invade the stadium at 8 o'clock to battle the Blues. Saturday night the colored team, rated as one of the best in the negro league, will be here to put on a swell exhibition. Both games will start at 8 o'clock. The admission tonight will be 26 cents in the bleachers and 41 cents in the grandstand.

Manager Jack Fitzpatrick of the Sox plans to start Oadis Swigart an Oklahoma youth, on the mound against the Rocks tonight. If he fares well in the three innings he is assigned to pitch, he'll be back to chuck against the Rocks in the season's opener at Douglas park Tuesday. Swigart is the only member of the Blues who has shown any sort of condition. He trained with the Oklahoma City club before coming to Davenport.

Two Other Pitchers

Following Swigart, if Fitz's plans materialize, will be Jim Goff, southpaw, and Glen Hicks, another left-hander. Rock Island expects to start Vance Cauble, their only southpaw, but other moundsmen will probably see action before the end of the ninth.

Manager Fitzpatrick expects more trouble from the Indianapolis colored team than from Rock Island. He claims the negroes boast one of the finest teams in the Colored American league.

Childs, colored second baseman, formerly played with the St. Louis Stars. He's a wonderful fielder and a steady hitter.

Henry, the center fielder, is a streak of lightning in chasing flies and one of the best hitters in the league. He was with Newark last season.

Burke, the shortstop, formerly starred with the Chicago Giants. Strong, who plays third, is the clean-up hitter and packs a mighty wallop with the willow. Gill, first sacker, is an old-timer. He is a great hitter and is claimed to be one of the best guardians of the initial sack in colored baseball circles.

Segrave, outfielder, is one of the fastest big men in baseball, according to T. R. Strong, manager of the club. He's an Indianapolis boy. Brown, right-fielder, is another fleet-footed streak. He was with the Cincinnati Tigers a year ago.

Another Satchell Paige?

Walker, the young catcher, has a great throwing arm and is also a fine hitter. Royals, who is expected to pitch against the Blue Sox, is claimed by critics to be another Satchell Paige. He's a long, rangy boy and possesses a lot of speed and remarkable control.

Rock Island expects to send its best lineup against the Davenporters. This includes Larson at first; Williamson at second; Schohl at short; Michaels at third; Hibbard in left; Denson in center and Kennedy in right. Hoover and Clark will handle the catching assignment.

The Davenport lineup is just about set and will be the same as Fitz plans to use in the season's opening game. Clarke has first clinched; Frank Hall will be at his usual position at second; Les Floyd is set at short and Spec Peddicord is certain of the third base job. In the outfield will be Joe Prerost and Al Van Camp, the sluggers of the outfit, and Elmer Danfield, a diminutive gardener who may not be able to make the grade because of his size. Hauser and Morgan will be seen behind the plate and there's a possibility that the former will be given a chance in the outfield.

The umpires for the exhibition games will be Ed Hendee and Eddie Stafford.

Blue Sox Are Defeated in Tenth By Negro All-Stars; Home Run Breaks Up Game

BY BARRETT M'DONNELL

After watching Bankhead send a long homer over the lef side of the scoreboard in the tenth inning to break up wha looked like it might turn out to be a long evening and give th Ciudad Trujillo colored all-stars a 3 to 1 victory at the sta dium Sunday night, the Davenport Blue Sox will drop dow to Burlington tonight to play an exhibition there with th Burlington Bees of the Mississippi Valley traveling league

Tonight's game at Burlington will leave the Blues wit only one night to fill out of what would otherwise be a serie with Rock Island before Waterloo comes here for the first tilt of a set Wednesday night.

Bankhead's prodigious effort on one of Lefty Schroeder's slants Sunday night came with Parnell aboard, and took the wind out of a threatened Davenport revival before it was really started.

Peddicord Ties It

After finding Lefty Metlock's drops and curves just a little too rapid for hitting designs in the first eight innings, the Sox had tied the ball game in the last of the ninth. Peddicord launched a double against the scoreboard and Flood laid down a sacrifice bunt along the third base line. In his haste to catch the man at first, who was credited with a single, Third Baseman Patterson sent the ball wide of Thomas, and Peddicord skipped in from third.

Before that the Sox had negotiated only three hits, of which Clark had two, one each in the third and fifth frames, and Spadafore one in the seventh. There had been only two Davenporters as far as third and only five balls hit out of the infield.

Dutch Schesler, most recent initiate into the stadium fold got his first call for mound duty and responded ably, yielding only five hits in as many innings of toil, and striking out five.

Score in Fourth

The visitors, just finding their land-legs again after a boat trip from Santo Domingo and a bus trip to Davenport, bunched two of their blows in the fourth to score the only early run. Patterson was safe on a fielder's choice, went to second when Schesler erred on a throw calculated to catch Williams at first, and came home on Thomas' hook to the left field foul line.

Schroeder took over in the sixth and kept things far out of danger until the ninth when an error by Clark on an attempted double play, a single by Metlock and an error by Hall on a ground ball, combined to load the bases. Spearman went out, short to first, to save Schroeder from any misery in that frame.

The 2,500 fans, many of whom came to see Satchel Paige, one of the greatest pitchers in baseball, were disappointed by his failure to appear on the scene, due to driving difficulties between New Orleans and here. He will join the club before it opens defense of the championship title in the Denver Post semi-pro tournament.

The box score:

CIUDAD TRIJILLO—	Ab	R	H	Po	A
Bell, cf	4	0	1	1	0
Spearman, rf	5	0	0	1	0
Parnell, lf	4	1	2	1	0
Patterson, 3b	3	1	0	1	1
Williams, 2b	4	0	0	3	4
Bankhead, 2b	5	1	1	2	4
Thomas, 1b	5	0	2	13	0
Palm, c	4	0	0	8	1
Metlock, p	4	0	1	0	4
Totals	38	3	7	30	14

DAVENPORT—	Ab	R	H	Po	A
Floyd, ss	4	0	0	4	2
Peddicord, 3b	4	0	1	0	5
Flood, cf	4	0	1	2	0
Hall, 2b	2	0	0	1	4
Spadafore, lf	4	1	1	0	0
Clarke, 1b	4	0	0	12	0
Van Camp, rf	4	0	0	1	0
Clark, c	4	0	2	10	1
Schesler, p	1	0	0	0	3
Schroeder, p	1	0	0	0	1
*Fitzpatrick	1	0	0	0	0
Totals	33	1	5	30	16

*Batted for Schroeder in 10th.

Ciudad .... 000 100 000 2—
Davenport .... 000 000 001 0—

Runs batted in—Bankhead (2), Thomas. Two base hit—Peddicord. Home run—Bankhead. Stolen bases—Spadafore, Williams, Patterson. Sacrifices—Schesler, Patterson, Hall. Left on base—Ciudad, 9; Davenport, 5. Base on balls—Schesler, 1; Schroeder, 2; Metlock, 1. Struck out—Schesler, 5; Schroeder, 5; Metlock, 7. Hits—Schesler, 5 in 5 innings; Schroeder, 2 in 5 innings Metlock, 5 in 10 innings. Hit by pitcher—Schroeder (Patterson). Winning pitcher—Metlock. Losing pitcher—Schroeder. Umpires—White and Stafford. Time of game—2:09.

Lose at Des Moines

DES MOINES, Ia., July 26.—(Special) — The Davenport Blu Sox dropped the final game of th series here Saturday night, 2 to 1 with Bill Prince the victim of hi club's inability to hit the offering of Edwald Pyle.

Prince allowed the Demons onl five hits, but the best his mate could get off Pyle was the sam number of safe blows.

DAVENPORT—	Ab	R	H	Po	A
Peddicord, 3b	2	0	0	1	0
Floyd, ss	4	0	0	1	2
Flood, cf	4	0	0	3	0
Hall, 2b	4	0	0	2	1
Spadafore, lf	4	0	0	5	1
Clarke, 1b	4	1	1	5	0
Van Camp, rf	3	0	2	2	0
Fitzpatrick, c	2	0	0	5	0
Prince, p	3	0	2	0	2
Totals	30	1	5	24	6

DES MOINES—	Ab	R	H	Po	A
Martinez, 2b	4	0	0	2	3
Allaire, ss	3	0	0	2	4
Criscola, cf	4	0	0	4	0

To make a little extra money, the Blue Sox frequently played exhibition games against touring clubs. Games with Negro League clubs were a lucrative draw during the 1930s.

Two

Post-War Struggles

All but a handful of minor leagues suspended operations during World War II. With the war ended in 1945, the years immediately following proved to be a boom time for minor league baseball, as Americans embraced a new era of peace, prosperity, and increased leisure time. The Three-I League wasted no time in resuming operations after the war, and Davenport was eager to win back a slot in minor league ball. Paul Lagomarcino attended the league's organizational meeting in September 1945, and when Madison, Wisconsin failed to renew its prewar franchise, league directors approved Davenport's entry back into the Three-I League.

In 1946, for the first time in its minor league history, Davenport's club operated as a farm club for a major league team, the Chicago Cubs. In their first year in Municipal Stadium, the Cubs didn't disappoint area fans. Fielding a team composed almost entirely of returning war veterans, the Davenport Cubs finished the season tied for first-place with Danville. The one-game playoff to determine the regular-season pennant winner produced one of the most memorable moments in Municipal Stadium's history. With the score tied at two in the bottom of the ninth, Davenport first-baseman Paul Swoboda clouted a two-run homer to give Davenport a 4-2 win. Jerry Jurgens of the *Davenport Times* described the scene at the time, writing, "[Manager] Kelly literally rode Swoboda as he headed plateward, but even the skipper was lost in the pandemonium that raged, with the city's rabids and the players lifting the hero to their shoulders to ride him out of the park in a fashion that reminded the writer of the days when Iowa football fans swarmed the gridiron to carry away the late Nile Kinnick after the 1939 Notre Dame game."

The honeymoon with the Cubs did not last, as Chicago pulled its sponsorship after a mediocre 1947 season. The Pittsburgh Pirates came in as Davenport's major league patron in 1948, but a last-place club drew a feeble attendance total of 45,711 for the season. Davenport was quickly earning a reputation as a "tough baseball town," and it seemed as if baseball might once again leave Municipal Stadium. A revival was coming, however, led by a dynamic new general manager.

William "Perk" Purnhage already possessed an amazing track record as a minor league general manager. In 1947, Purnhage's Waterloo White Hawks shattered Three-I League attendance records by drawing 174,064 fans. Pittsburgh brought the 1947 *Sporting News* "Executive of the Year" to Davenport, hoping he could revive attendance at Municipal Stadium. With his flair for promotion Purnhage would have fit right in to a modern minor league operation. Some of his promotions were traditional, such as Ladies' Nights, lucky number drawings, and automobile giveaways, while others seem almost bizarre. During a time when potatoes were in short supply, Purnhage wooed fans to the park by offering the fans a chance to win a 5-pound bag of spuds. Another perennial favorite of Perk's was to stage a "baby giveaway," during which a small child was presented to a stunned winner and to the delight of the crowd (the actual prize was usually a piglet or a parakeet). There was no arguing with Purnhage's results—in 1949, his first year in Davenport, attendance almost tripled, rising to 133,505.

Purnhage's schemes weren't all that attracted fans in 1949. The club's fourth-place finish earned the Pirates a spot in the Three-I playoffs, where they upset Waterloo in the semifinals, then swept Evansville in the finals to take the championship. Future Pittsburgh stars Bob Purkey and Vern Law were among the team's stars.

In the fickle world of the minor leagues, Pittsburgh pulled up operations despite the year's success, leaving Purnhage to run the club as an independent operation in 1950. Without a major league sponsor, the newly dubbed Davenport Quads were forced to scrounge for players wherever they could find them, drawing the leftovers of numerous other minor league clubs. With such a makeshift roster, the Quads managed only a 49-75 record. Still, 90,584 fans came out to Municipal Stadium to cheer the team on.

For 1951, Davenport arranged an affiliation with the Detroit Tigers. Results on the field were no better, as the Tigers recorded another cellar finish. One player in particular, though, would go on to great glory. Jim Bunning, a pitcher for the '51 Tigers, became the first former Davenport player elected to the National Baseball Hall of Fame in 1996. (He would be joined in Cooperstown in 2000 by another ex-Davenport player, Bid McPhee.)

No future Hall-of-Famers graced Municipal Stadium in 1952 (although future All-Star Harvey Kuenn played for the '52 Tigers), but at least the club stayed out of last place. A sixth-place finish, combined with declining attendance and rising club debt spelled doom. Purnhage resigned after the 1952 season, and with his departure from Davenport—and with the club in the red—the Three-I League transferred Davenport's franchise for 1953 to Peoria, Illinois. Perk would rebound to lead Clinton's return to minor league baseball in 1954 and later ran the Triple-A Albuquerque Dukes for many years.

The 1950s were a difficult time to operate a minor league baseball team. With the booming economy came new competition for the entertainment dollar of the public. Staying home to watch television in air-conditioned comfort became a more attractive evening's entertainment than coming out to the old ballpark.

Throughout the 1950s, the Three-I League struggled to maintain operations. An upstart minor league called the Mississippi-Ohio Valley League (later renamed the Midwest League) began competing for cities with the more established Three-I. Given Davenport's location and convenient stadium, the city was often mentioned in league expansion plans. Three-I president Hal Totten even gave league passes to Davenport Mayor Walter Beuse and Sports Editor John O'Donnell to keep Davenport thinking about baseball.

Davenport got the chance to get back into the Three-I in 1957. Having been rebuffed in an effort to pick up the failed Terre Haute franchise in mid-1956, the Chicago White Sox moved their Three-I operations from Waterloo to Davenport. Like the Cubs and Pirates before them, the White Sox lasted only two years in Municipal Stadium. After claiming a first-half pennant in 1958, the White Sox withdrew their franchise, and left Davenport on the outside once again.

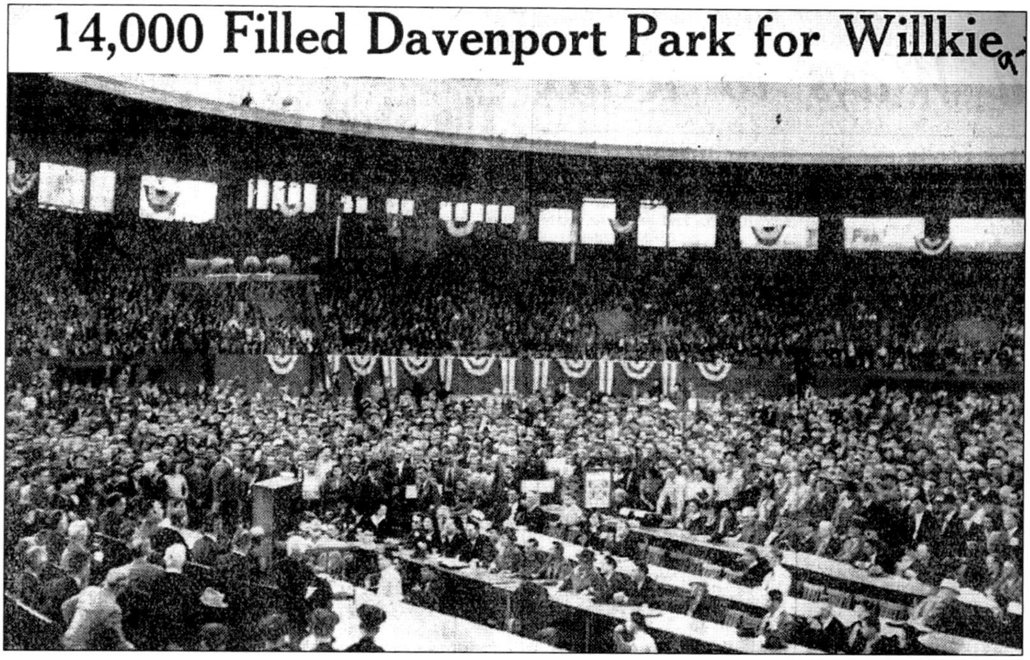

During the years Davenport did not field a minor league team, other uses were found for Municipal Stadium. Here, 1940 Republican presidential nominee Wendall Wilki makes a stump speech before a large throng at the ballpark.

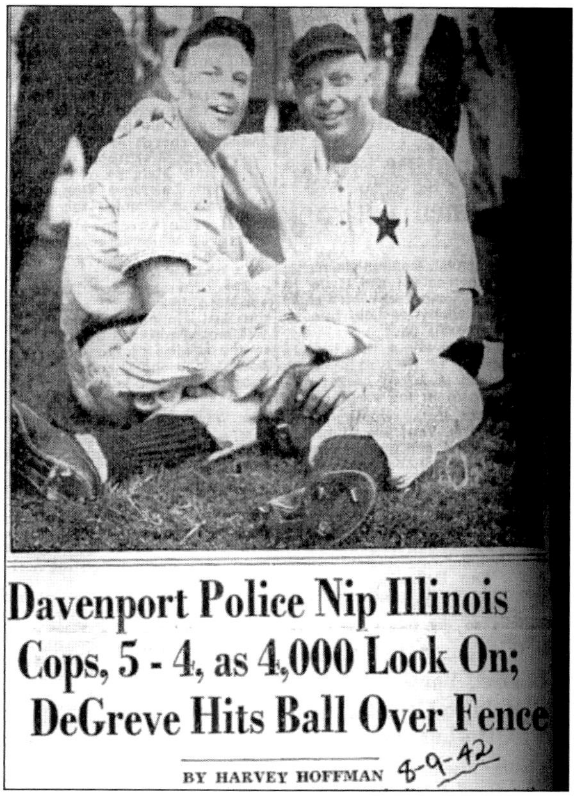

Professional baseball may have been absent from Municipal Stadium for a decade, but the diamond was not idle. Games between local clubs, such as the annual tilt pitting the Davenport Police vs. their Illinois counterparts still attracted fans to the stadium to watch the national pastime.

Hollingsworth Is Shelled by National Team

Former Islander Gives Up 12 Hits Which Account For All Runs

ONLY 4,000 ATTEND

Cold Weather Cuts Down Crowd—Leaguers Fail to Bust Fence

BY LEO KAUTZ
Daily Times Sports Editor

Johnny Lanning, veteran right-handed pitcher, didn't let a little thing like cold weather bother him last night as he hurled the Pittsburgh Pirates to a 7 to 0 victory over the St. Louis Browns before approximately 4,000 chilly fans at the Davenport Municipal stadium.

Lanning had a big edge over a former local favorite, Al "Boots" Hollingsworth, southpaw chucker for the American leaguers. Holly was around for six innings and gave up all seven of the Pittsburgh runs and 12 of their 13 hits. The National league pitcher was nicked for only four hits, one of them a questionable drive by Chet Laabs in the third which went between the legs of Alf Anderson at short without even being touched by the Pittsburgh shortstop.

The ball game did not draw as large a crowd as expected. Cold weather undoubtedly kept hundreds of potential customers away and few tickets were sold at the stadium box offices. The advance sale had reached more than 3,000 early Thursday and less than 1,000 additional tickets were disposed of before game time.

The pitching of Lanning was the bright spot of the evening's entertainment although the Pittsburgh infield did sparkle at times

Before the Battle Started

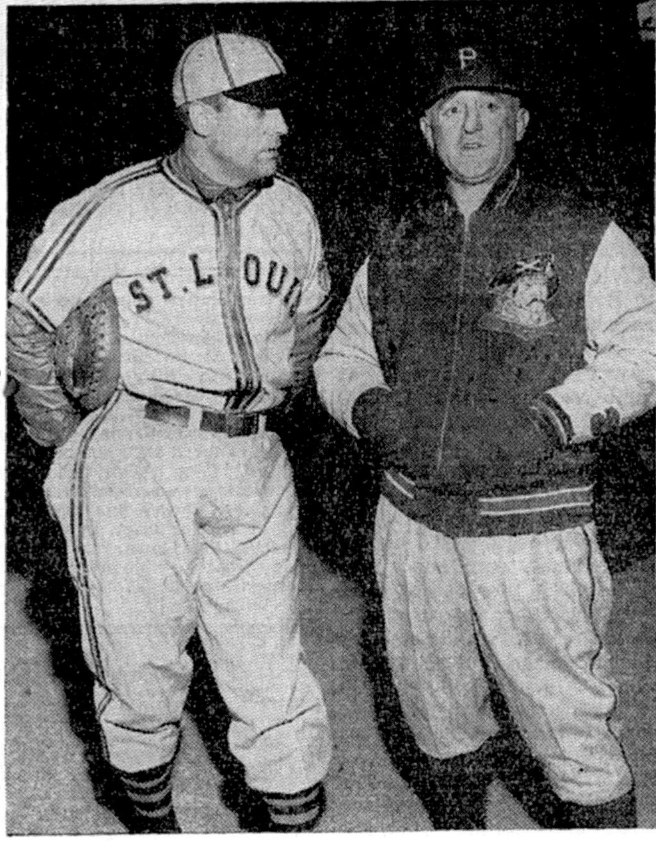

—Times Photo

Pictured here are Luke Sewell, (left) manager of the St. Louis Browns and Frankie Frisch, head man of the Pittsburgh Pirates, as they discussed ground rules just before the start of their exhibition game at the Municipal stadium last night. Frisch's sixth place National leaguers upset the third place American leaguers by a score of 7 to 0.

Very few minor leagues were able to operate during WW II. To fill the void left by the reduction in leagues, major league clubs played exhibitions in smaller cities to keep fan interest in baseball alive. A late season exhibition game in 1942 between the Pittsburgh Pirates and St. Louis Browns attracted 4,000 Quad City area fans

1946 marked not only the return of professional baseball to Davenport, but also a return to baseball for many WW II veterans. As Jerry Jurgens illustrated in his Davenport Times column, a vast majority of the 1946 Davenport Cubs spent the previous "season" in military service.

Sport-O-Scope

By Jerry Jurgens

N the eve of the departure of the Davenport Cubs—27 strong— for Quincy to open the Three-I season tomorrow, we took a sur- y of the personnel, more or less out of the sake of curiosity. W d that the average age of the squad is 22.3 years; average weight pounds, and average height, 5 feet 11 inches. By those figures l Kelly has a young ball club of normal weight and height.

Shortest man on the squad is Joe Raso, flashy second baseman who measures only five feet, seven inches, while Ned Jilton, 19-year-old hurler, is the tallest at six feet, three. The youngest is John Picchiotti, a shortstop candidate who is only 17, while Bruno Zelasko, the regular shortfielder, and Tom Calahan, right-hand pitcher are the oldest at 26. Jilton and Calahan both tip the scales at 200 pounds to top the weight department, with Tony Jacobs and Gene Davison, hurlers, the lightest at 150.

LINOIS is claimed as the home state by the most men—11, chiefl from the Chicago area; four are from Wisconsin, three from Massa usetts; two from Missouri; and one from each of Delaware, Alabama io, North Carolina, Indiana, Tennessee and Minnesota. Twenty e renewing their baseball careers after having served in the arme ces in almost every theater of operations. Six were in professiona seball last season, and one, Gene Davison of Galesburg, Ill., is i first year in organized play.

Other interesting bits of information: Joe Raso is the only switch hitter on the team; four others bat left-handed but throw right; and not one tosses from the portside and bats right. The roster contains five left-handers, three pitchers, the first baseman, and an outfielder, and all swing the willow from the unorthodox side of the dish. Joe Damato looks like Bob Hope, and judging from the amount of laughter his antics cause among his teammates, he acts like Hope.

THE ROSTER

Name and Pos.	Age	B	T	Hgt.	Wgt.	Home	Last Year
Damato, 3b	24	R	R	5'9"	175	Chicago	In Service
Raso, 2b	22	L-R	R	5'7"	170	Malden, Mass.	In Service
ul Swoboda, 1b	25	L	L	6'	175	Wilmington, Del.	In Service
uno Zelasko, ss	26	R	R	5'9"	172	Chicago	In Service
lph Davis, 3b	25	L	R	5'11"	170	Alex City, Ala.	In Service
n Picchiotti, ss	17	R	R	5'11"	163	Chicago	Leaksville, N. C
orge Pelati, ss	23	R	R	5'7"	168	Bridgewater, Mass.	In Service
lson Burbink, c	24	R	R	5'10"	180	Cincinnati, O.	In Service
be Walker, c	19	L	R	6'	185	Lenoir, N. C.	Portsmouth, Va
orge Witt, c	22	R	R	5'11"	190	Chicago	In Service
y Sowins, of	21	L	L	5'8"	170	Riverside, Ill.	In Service
rmen Mauro, of	19	L	R	6'	160	Chicago	Hagerston, Md.
y Partee, of	20	R	R	5'11"	165	Gary, Ind.	In Service
b Alford, of	23	R	R	6'	180	Kansas City	In Service
ule Zam, of	18	R	R	5'10"	170	Cicero, Ill.	Leaksville, N. C
ne Davison, p	22	R	R	5'10"	150	Galesburg, Ill.	....
rb Chmiel, p	23	L	L	6'1"	185	Chicago	In Service
d Wendt, p	24	L	L	6'	185	Marshfield, Wis.	In Service
d Jilton, p	19	L	L	6'3"	200	Johnson City, Tenn.	Nashville
Willis, p	22	R	R	6'1"	185	Stoughton, Mass.	In Service
ny Jacobs, p	20	R	R	5'9"	150	Dixmoor, Ill.	In Service
b Peterson, p	22	L	R	6'	170	Minneapolis	In Service
m Calahan, p	26	R	R	6'2"	200	Chicago	In Service
itey Prust, p	24	R	R	6'	165	Lake Mills, Wis.	In Service
l Mode, p	25	R	R	6'1"	190	Rhinelander, Wis.	In Service
rry Beiz, p	23	R	R	6'1"	172	Madison, Wis.	Leaksville, N. C
rt Taylor, p	23	R	R	5'11"	180	Troy, Mo.	In Service

Gun for Three-I Flag in Double-Header at Stadium Tonigh

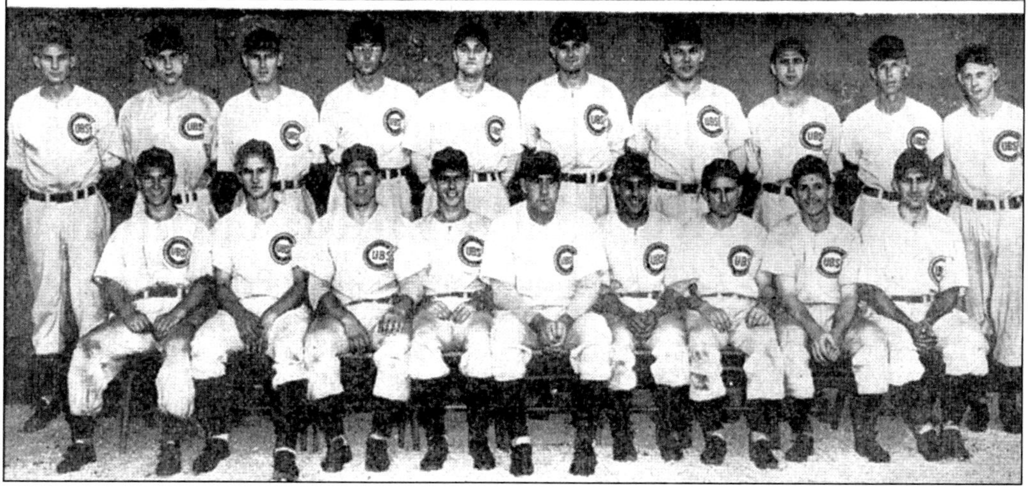

Baseball made a triumphant return to Davenport in 1946, when the Davenport Cubs battled Danville rivals to the wire in an exciting pennant race. Danville and Davenport had finished the season with identical 76-44 records, with Davenport winning the regular-season pennant in a one-game playoff. Both clubs lost in the first round of the playoffs, however, and Evansville went on to win the title.

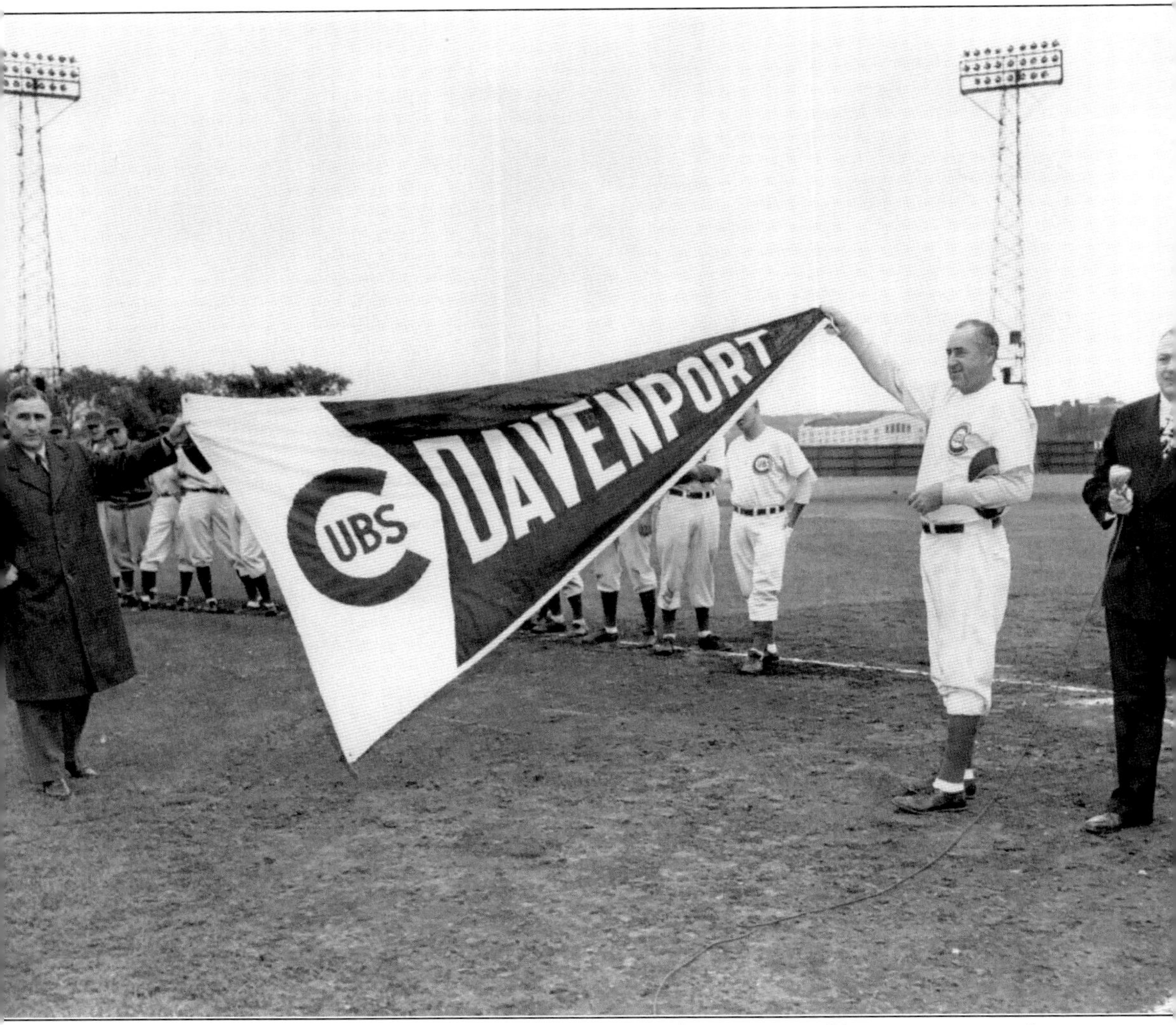

The end of WW II led to a resurgence in many minor league towns. To commemorate the return of minor league baseball to Davenport in May of 1946, longtime supporter Paul Lagomarcino (left) presented the new Davenport Cubs with a pennant to fly over the center field foul pole. Playing for the first time as the affiliate of a major league club, Davenport tied Danville for the Three-I League regular season title.

7,000 See Swoboda Win Three-I Flag With Homer

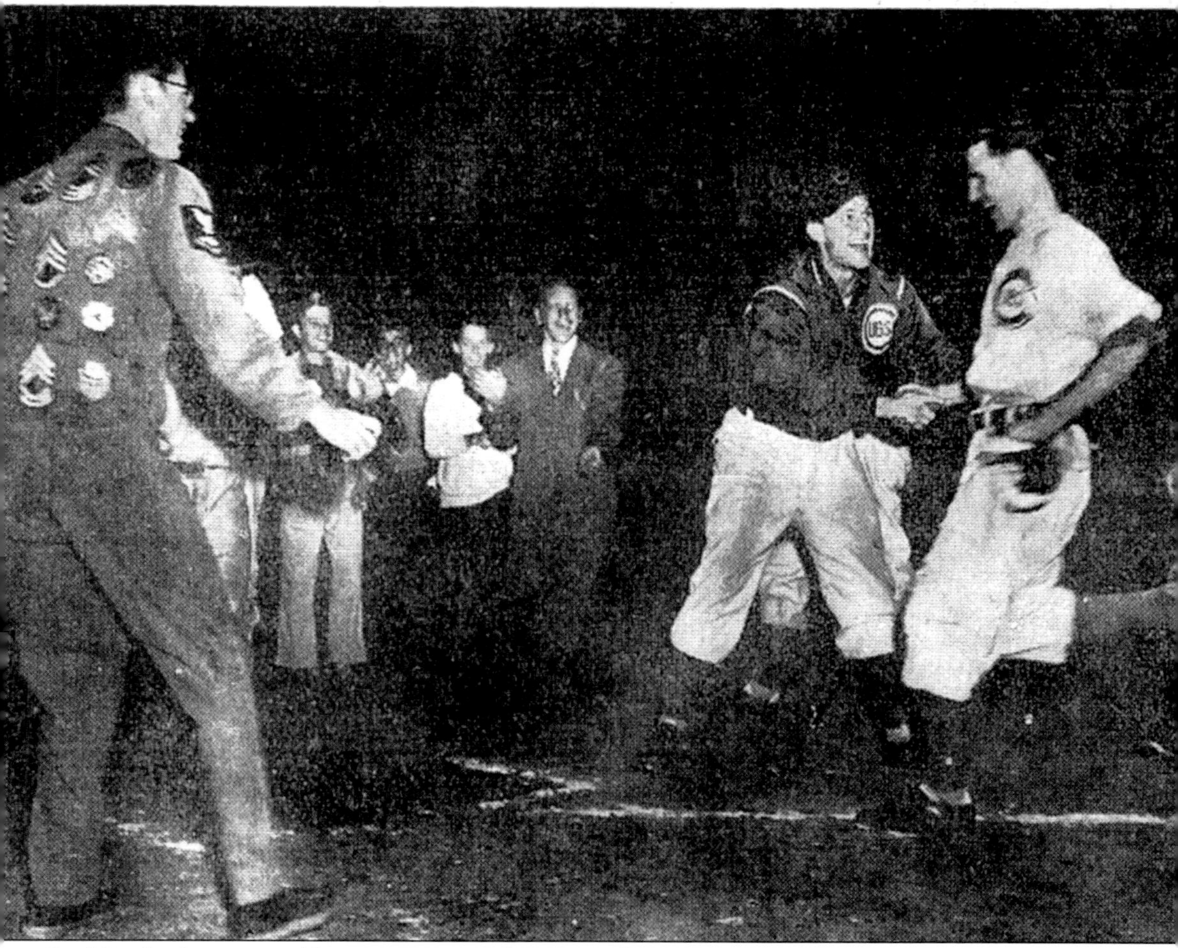

Paul Swoboda is greeted by a teammate as he crosses home plate. *Quad City Times* sportswriter Jerry Jurgens often wrote that the 1946 playoff provided one of the most memorable moments in Davenport's baseball history. First baseman Paul Swoboda knocked a two-run homer in the bottom of the ninth to defeat Danville 4-2 and give the Davenport Cubs the Three-I League regular season championship. His teammates and fans, seen in this photo crowding home plate, carried their hero off the field.

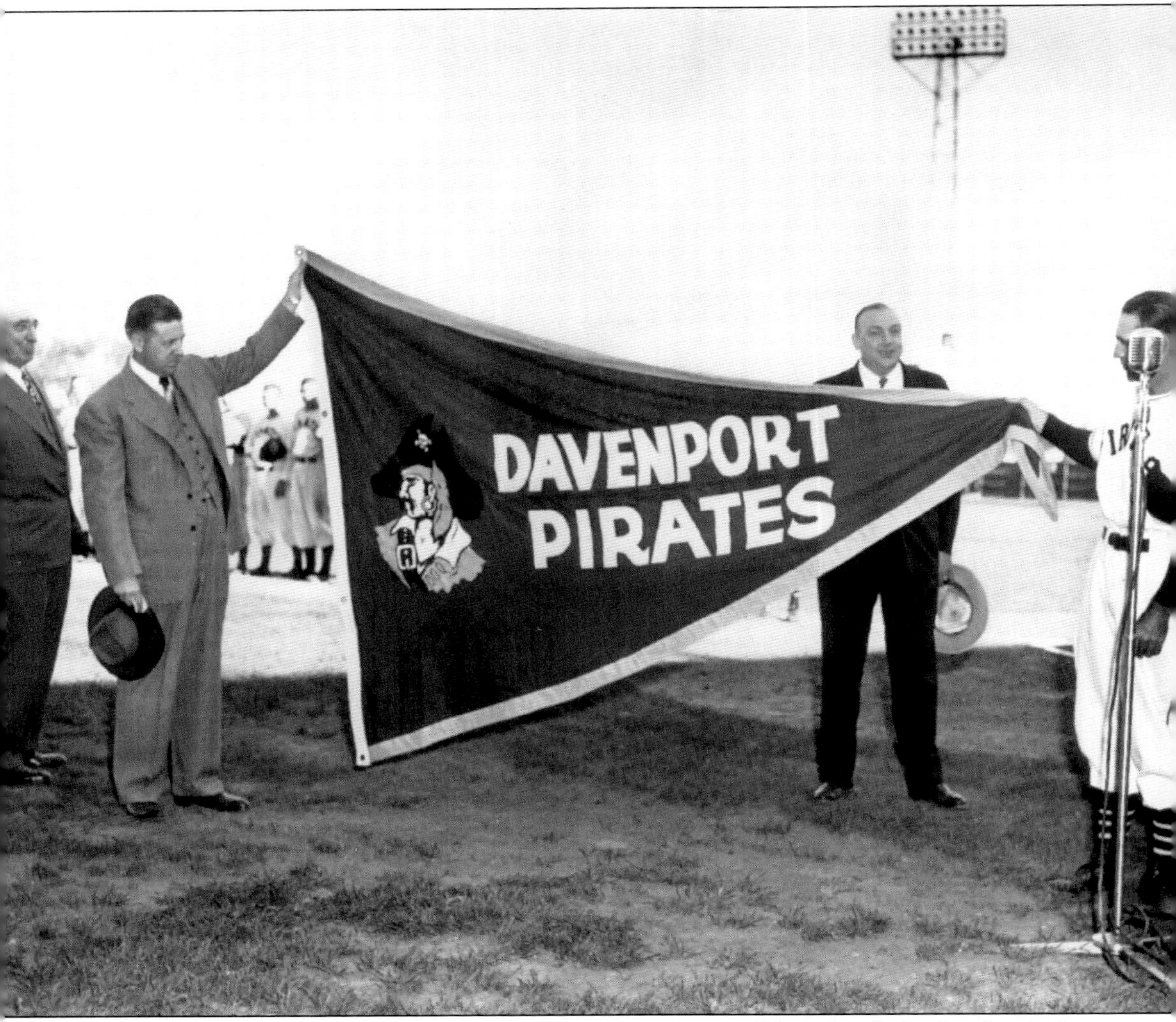

After two up-and-down seasons with the Cubs, Davenport affiliated with the Pittsburgh Pirates for the 1948 season. At the April 29 Home Opener, Ed Nicholson of the Chamber of Commerce helps manager Ival Goodman raise the new team flag, as Paul Lagomarcino and Sheriff Walter Beuse look on.

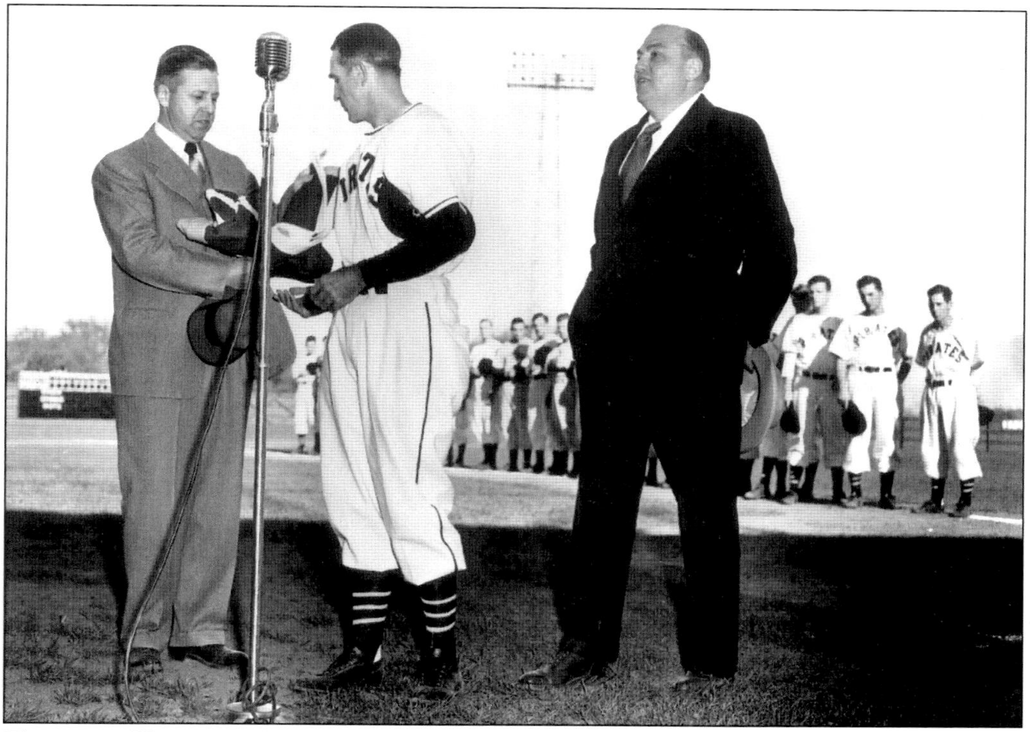

The new affiliation with the Pirates failed to improve Davenport's baseball fortunes on the field. Under Ival Goodman, Davenport finished last in the 8-team Three-I League, 40 games behind the Quincy Gems.

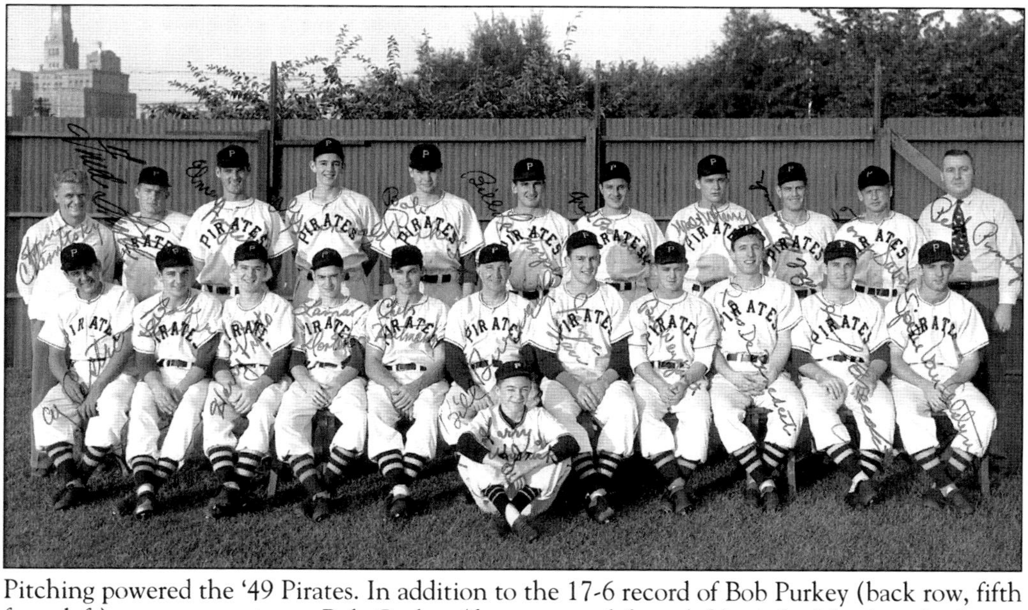

Pitching powered the '49 Pirates. In addition to the 17-6 record of Bob Purkey (back row, fifth from left), ten-game winner Bob Garber (front, second from left) pitched back-to-back one hitters in the last week of the season. The Pirates finished in fourth place at 67-59, but defeated second-place Waterloo 3 games to 2 in the semifinals before sweeping regular-season champ Evansville in the finals.

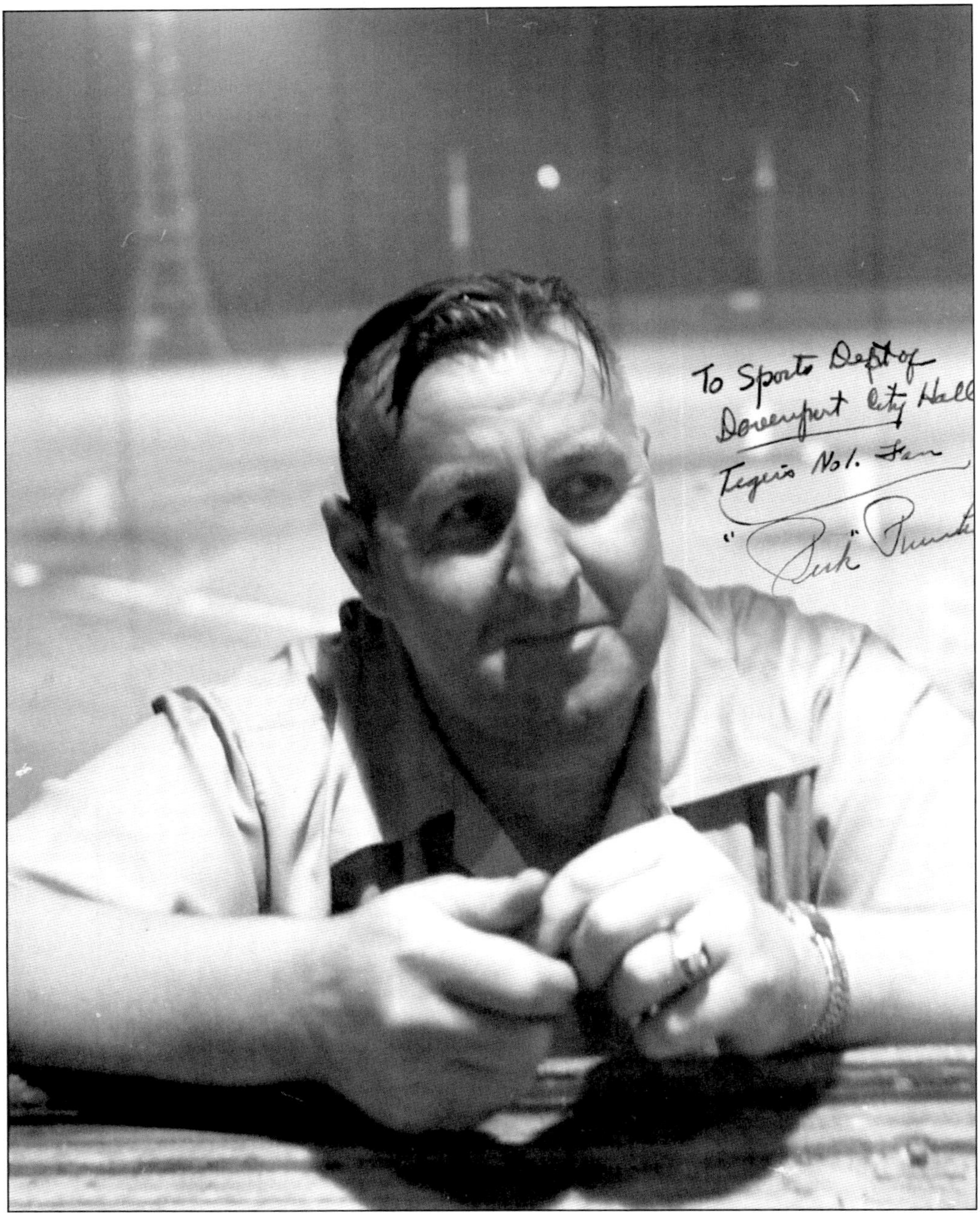

William "Perk" Purnhage achieved an amazing record of success as a minor league executive. After establishing a Three-I League attendance record at Waterloo in 1947, the Pittsburgh Pirates lured Purnhage to boost Davenport's attendance in 1949. In his first year attendance almost tripled at Municipal Stadium, thanks to a winning baseball team and Purnhage's promotional efforts. "The burden of proof for good attendance rests with the club, not the fans," according to Purnhage.

Sponsored by the Davenport Elks Lodge, Booster Night typically drew huge crowds. In 1949, 10,799 saw Bob Purkey win his 15th game of the season by beating Terre Haute, 3-0. Fans were further entertained by an argument between the Terre Haute bench and the first base umpire, which resulted in three Phillies being ejected. Here, two young fans press against the stadium fence to get a close-up glimpse of Pirate Roco Debenedetti.

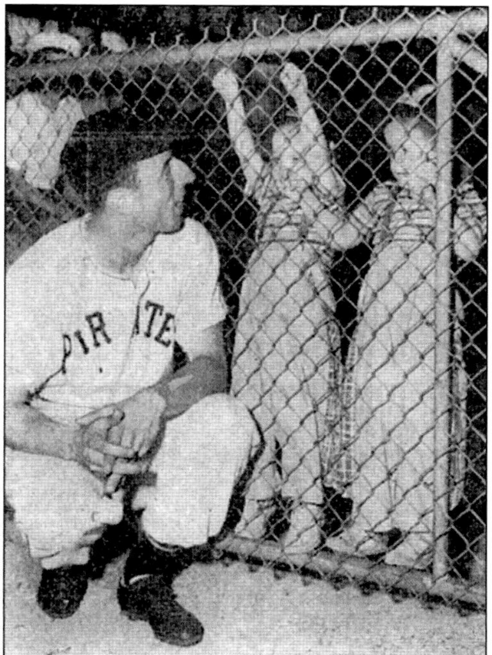

SOME of the feminine fans are really young and two little misses who attend Davenport Pirate games regularly are Larelle and Sharon Hughes, 3½-year-old twins. They are shown above talking with one of their favorite Pirates, Reno DeBenedetti, third baseman. The youngsters reside with their grandparents, Mr. and Mrs. Ivan R. Lowery, 924½ West Second street, Davenport.

This 1949 Three-I League All-Star has the distinction of being Dorothy Wulf's favorite player from the era. The flashy first-baseman, Al Grinwald, was pretty valuable with the bat, leading the club in batting average, hits, RBI, doubles, and triples. But "The Rubberman" was even more renowned for his crowd-pleasing acrobatic stretches in digging out throws to first. Grunwald never made it to the major leagues, but moved on to a career in Mexico and other Latin American leagues after his playing days in the U.S. came to an end.

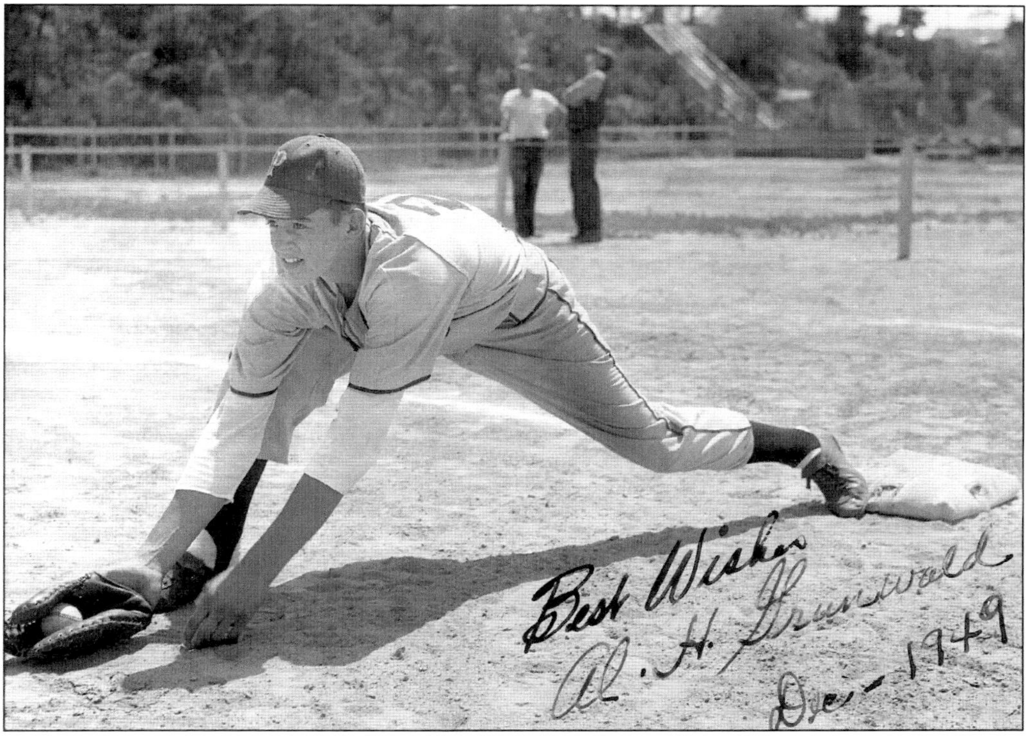

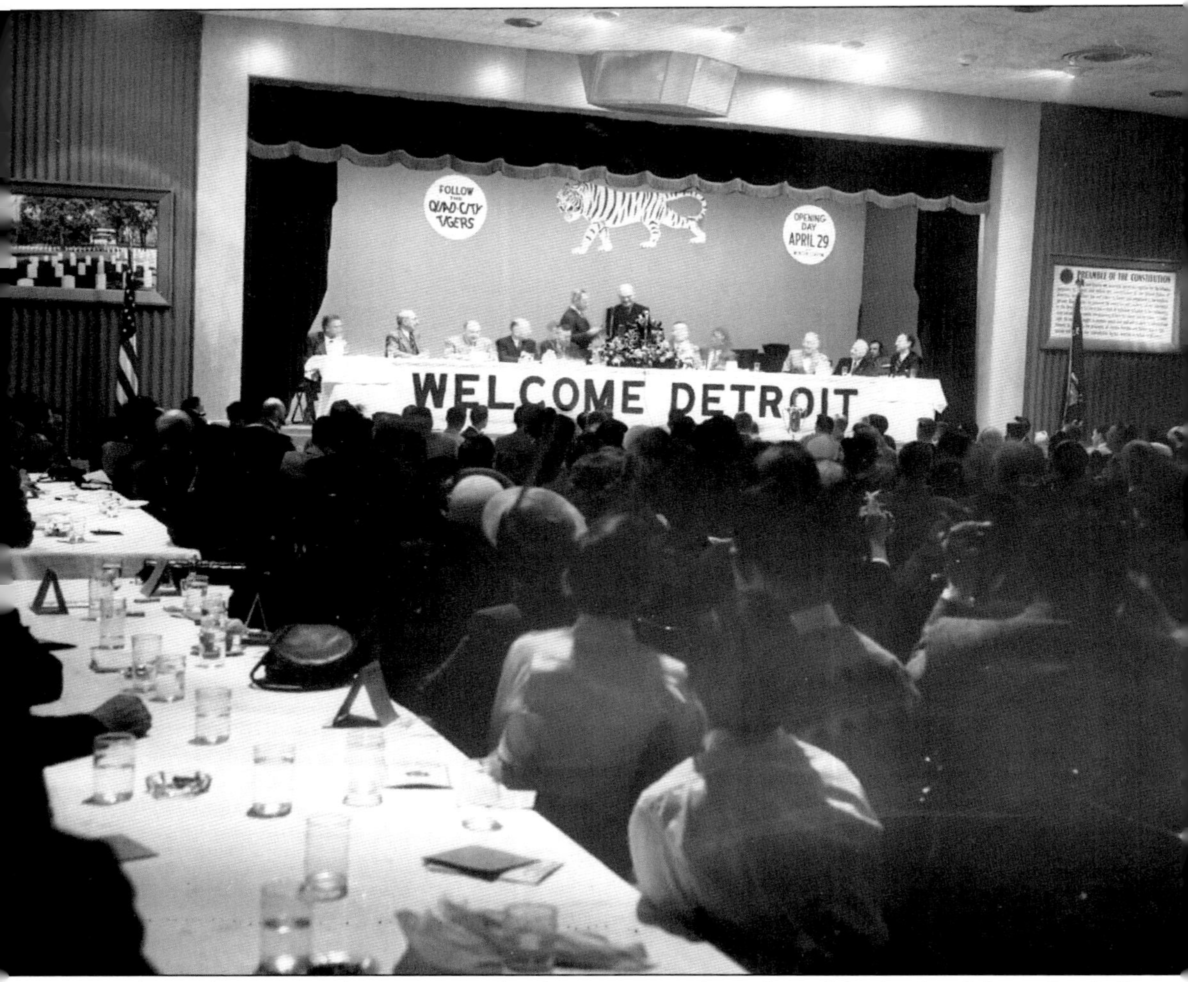

After enduring a tough season in 1950, playing as an independent club, the Quad Cities Baseball Association enthusiastically welcomed the Detroit Tigers as a major league sponsor for the 1951 season, kicking things off with a Welcome Banquet on February 8, 1951.

To encourage attendance in 1951, Perk Purnhage devised the "everyone in '51 campaign," with the stated goal of achieving a season attendance equal to the population of the Quad Cities—about 240,000. The club ended up drawing "only" 100,069, still impressive figure for a last-place team.

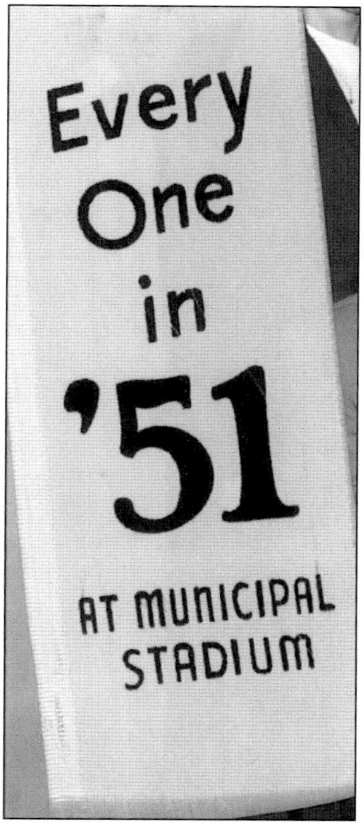

Hired by the Pittsburgh Pirates to boost attendance at Davenport, Perk Purnhage got right to work: toiling away in the Municipal Stadium office, selling tickets, and devising promotions. Attendance at Pirates games almost tripled from 1948 to 1949.

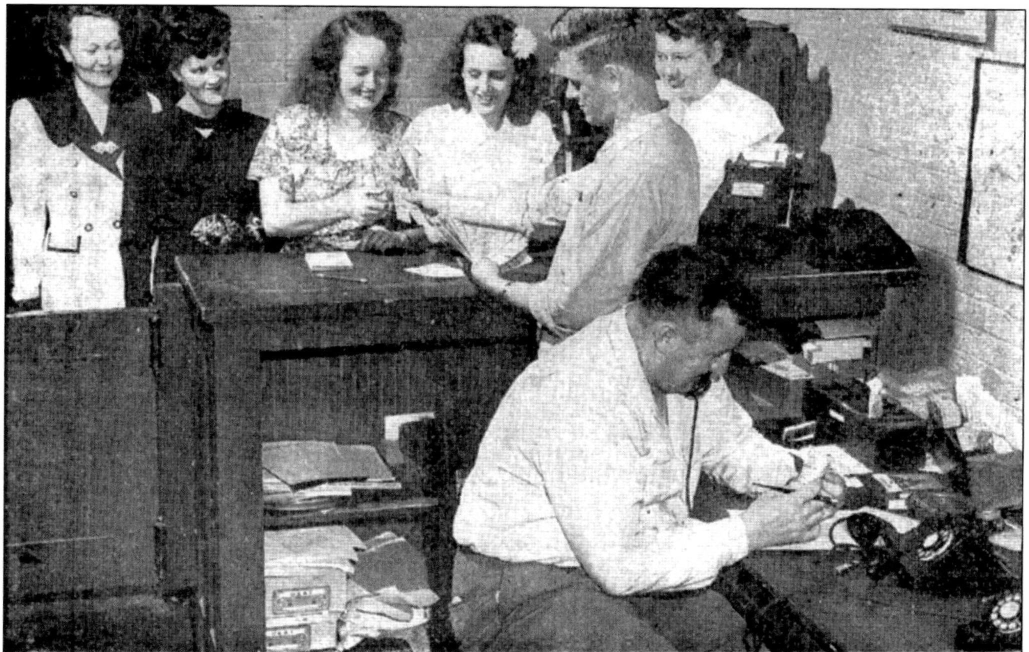

SINCE mid-January when Perk Purnhage arrived in Davenport to take over his duties as business manager of the Davenport Pirates, baseball has been foremost in the minds of local sport enthusiasts. He is shown in the foreground of the above picture busy taking reservations over the phone. Selling tickets to a group of feminine fans is Tony Chernetsky, assistant to Perk. The girls are, left to right, Gladys Behne, Carol Housley, Alice Francois, Patricia Claussen and Wanetta Buck.

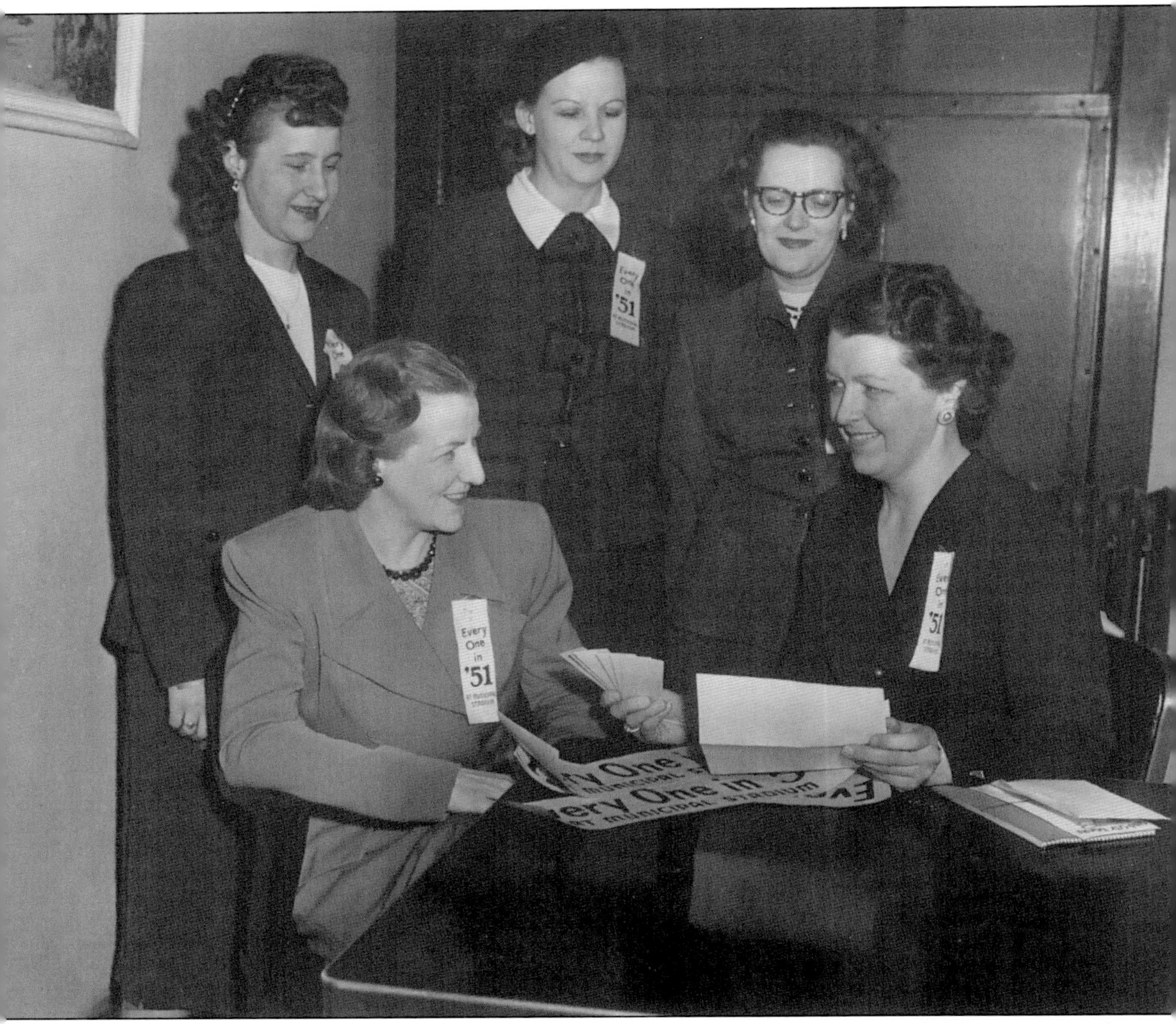

Five members of the booster club prepare promotional materials for the April 29 opener in 1951 and the accompanying ticket drive. They are, from left to right, as follows: (seated) Lucille Wolters, treasurer, and Dorothy Kohn, secretary; (standing) Jeanne Strum, Dolores Wolters, and June Link.

One of the original members of the National Association of Professional Baseball Leagues, the Three-I League celebrated its 50th Anniversary with Quad Cities as a member. Over the years, Davenport, Rock Island, and Moline each fielded clubs in the venerable circuit at one time or another.

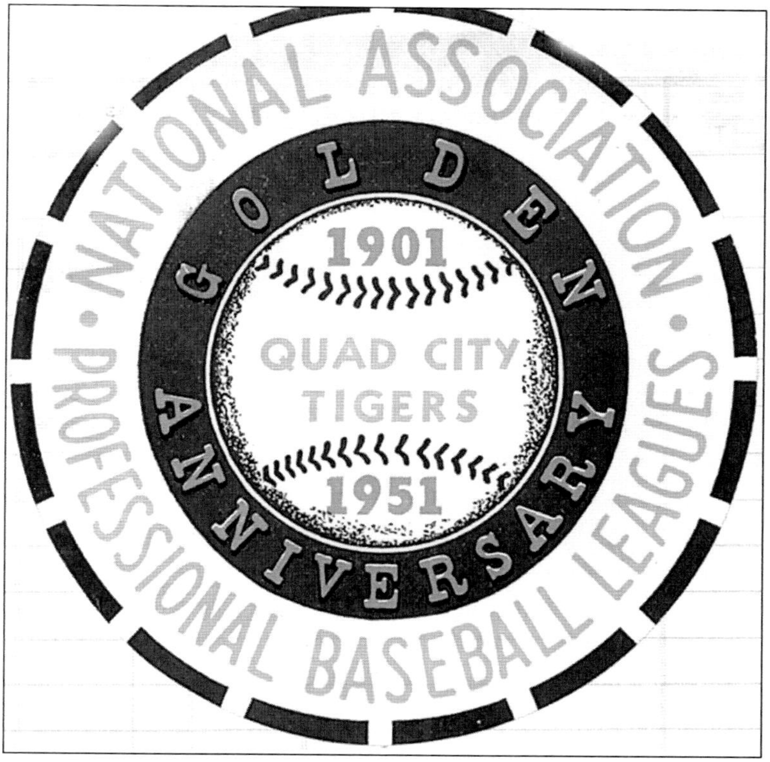

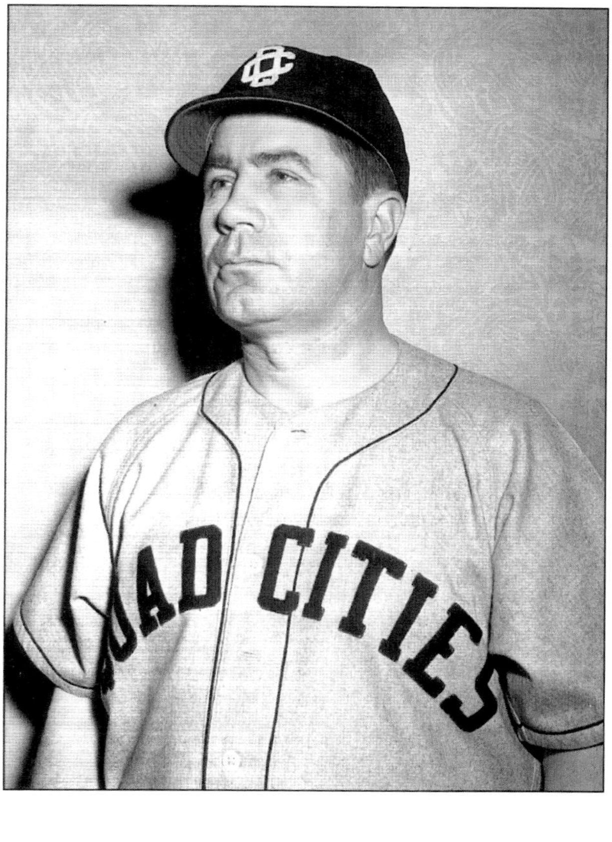

Marv Owen managed the Davenport Tigers in 1951 and 1952. The '51 Tigers brought up the rear of the six-team Three-I League with a 56-74 record. The '52 club had a slightly better percentage (54-69) but also finished 21 games behind Evansville.

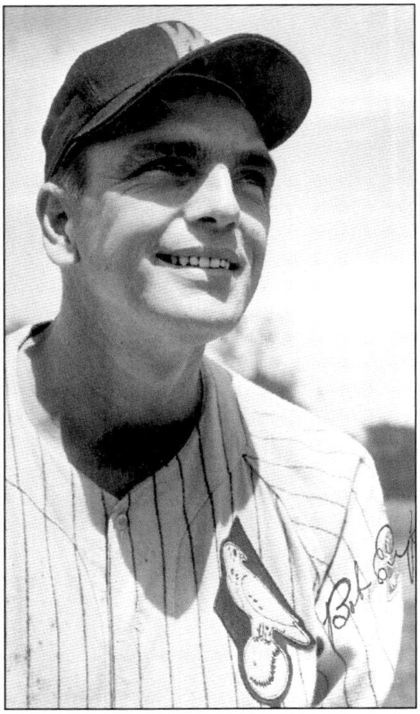

Davenport Iowa native Robert Erps, a slugging third baseman and outfielder, came home to play for the Davenport Quads in 1950 and the Quad City Tigers in 1951. Although the '51 Tigers finished in last place, Erps made the playoffs, as league rules permitted playoff-bound clubs to replace injured players by drafting replacements from the rosters of the also-rans. Cedar Rapids added league RBI leader Erps in such a postseason move, which proved to be decisive. In his only plate appearance in the semifinal series, Erps smacked a bases-loaded pinch double to complete a winning rally and send C.R. to the finals.

One of the advantages of operating as an independent club was the opportunity to sign players with local ties. The 1950 Quads featured four graduates of Davenport High (now Davenport Central). The former Blue Devils, seen below, from left to right, were: Dick Hoeksema, Bob Erps, Loras Day, and Dick Keyouth. Although the club landed in the cellar in 1950, the local connection helped boost club attendance over 90,000.

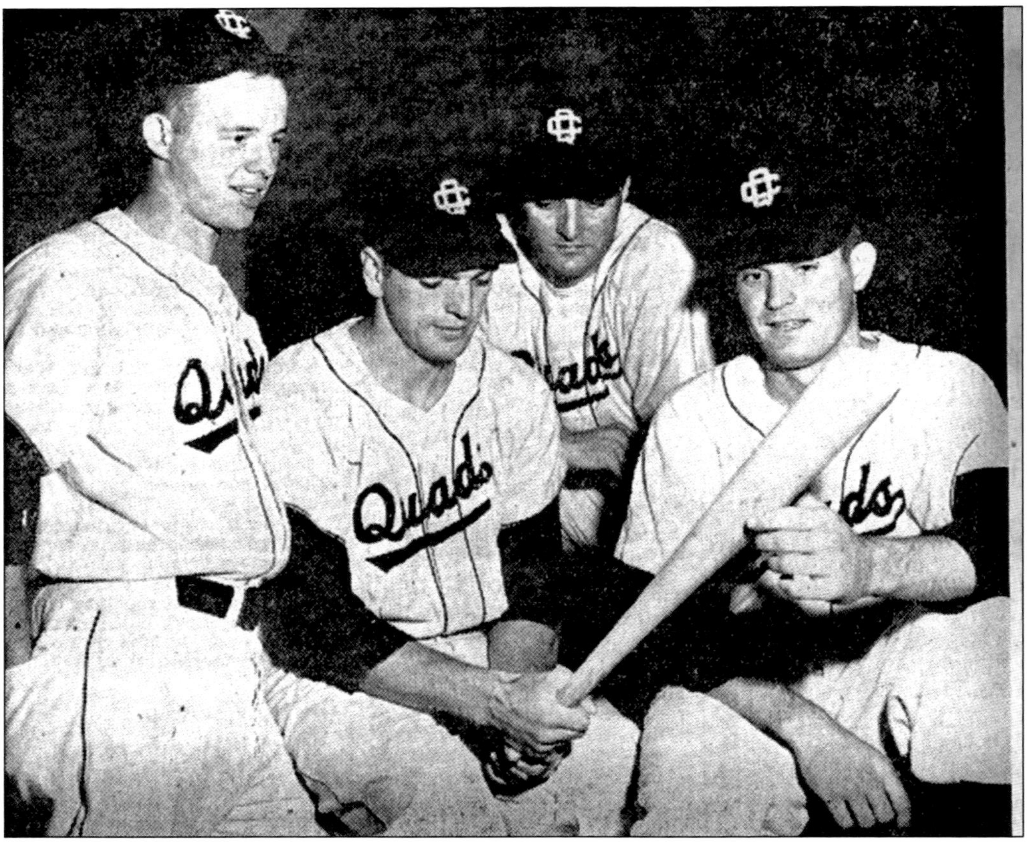

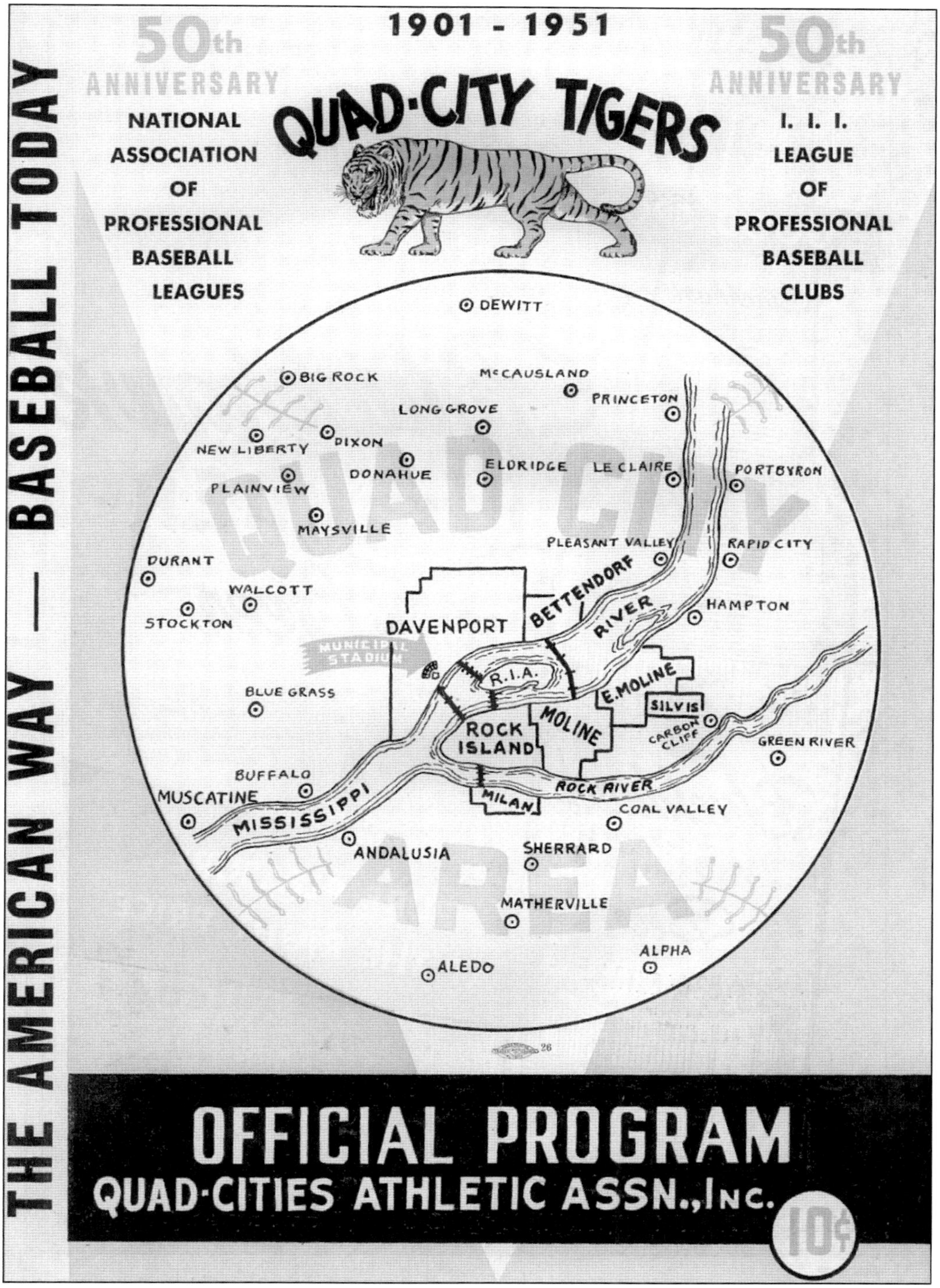

Using a regional name rather than a city was novel at the time and confused some Three-I League opponents, who were unsure whether they should refer to the "Quad Cities Tigers" or "Davenport Tigers" when posting the name on scorecards, the scoreboard, and in the media. At a league meeting in June, Perk Purnhage had to clarify for his colleagues that the club was, in fact, the "Quad Cities Tigers."

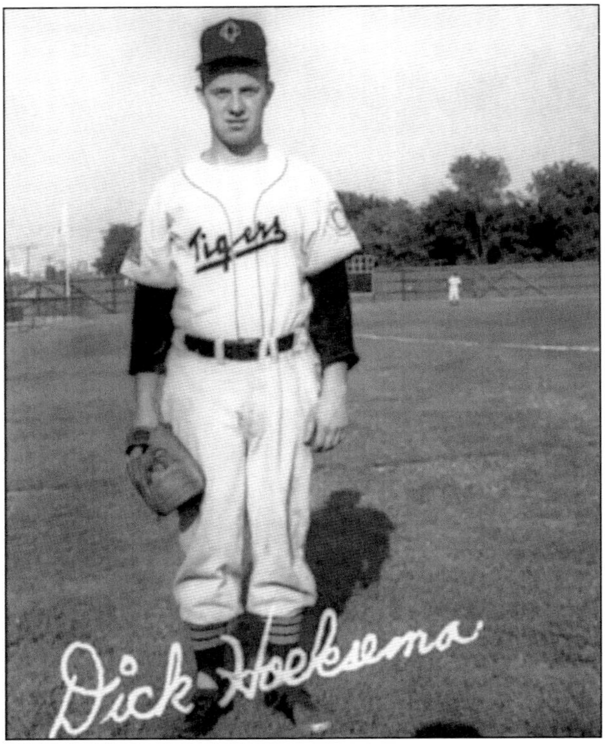

Future Hall-of-Famer Jim Bunning would become the most famous pitcher from the '51 Tigers—but Davenport native Dick Hoeksema was more renowned at the time, for his "local-boy-made-good" story. The left-handed pitcher was second in the league in strikeouts and had a hard-luck record of 11-10 (the Tigers were a dismal 54-74 overall).

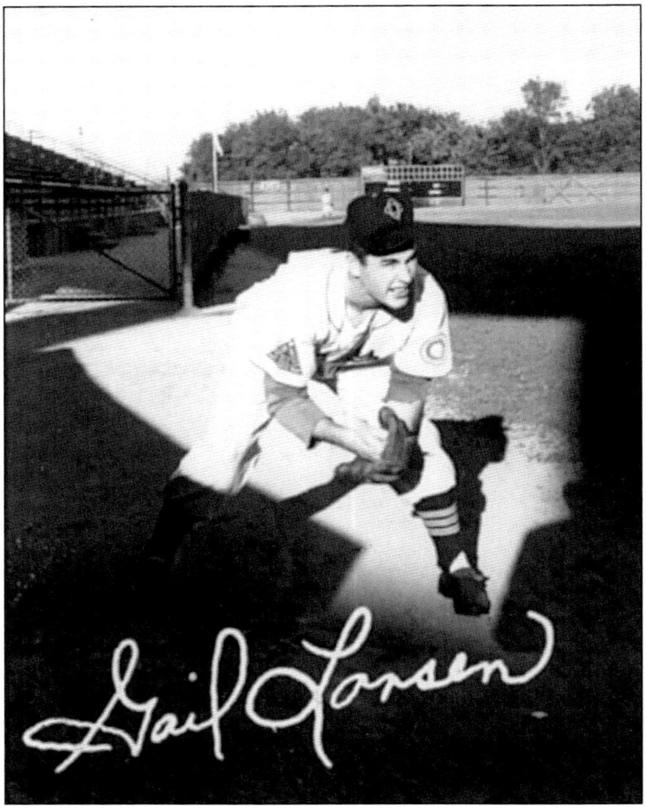

Shortstop Gail Larsen had to leave the team on August 21 when he received his induction notice from Uncle Sam, but he was still named to the Three-I League All-Star team, sharing the the honor with Evansville's Mel Cooper.

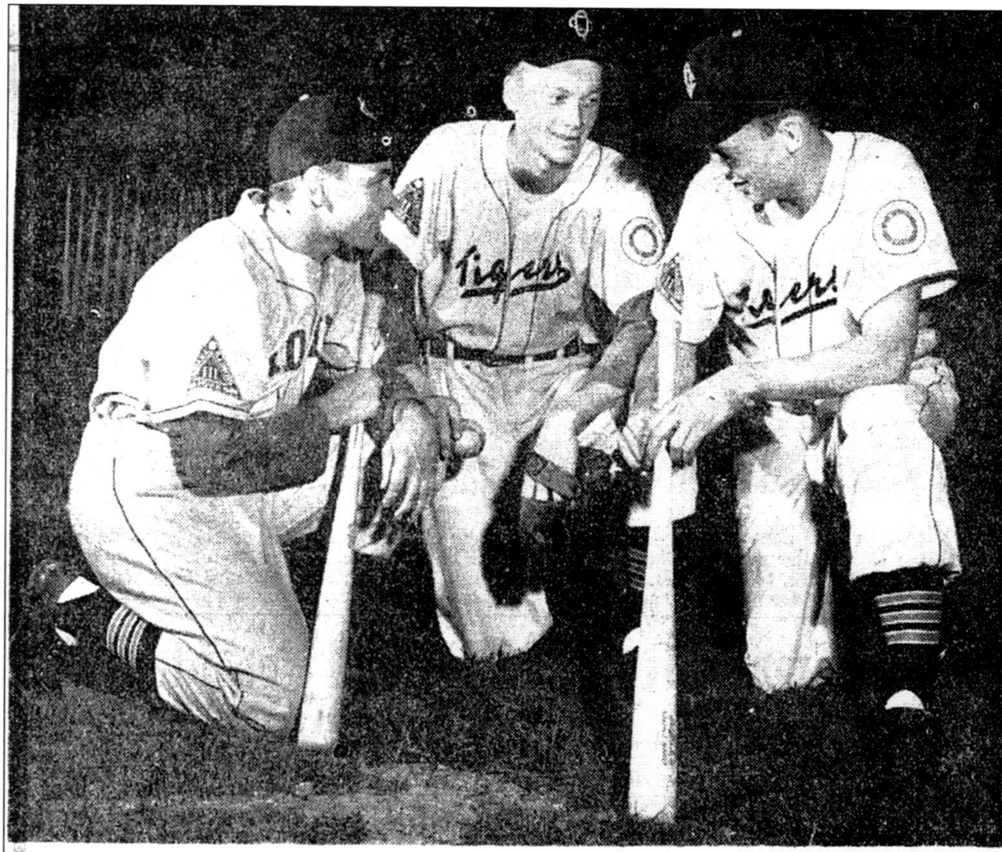

ECENT TIGER ADDITIONS — Here are the new Tigers, boys who have joined the club this week. eft to right are Bill Tuttle, Bradley bonus player; Jim Bunning, and Al Gilbert. Tuttle and Gilbert re outfielders. Bunning is a pitcher.

Future Hall-of-Famer Jim Bunning (center) joined the 1951 Davenport Tigers when he was an up-and-coming prospect in the Detroit organization. The young phenom showed flashes of brilliance during the year, such as a two-hitter against Quincy, but he finished the season with a mere 8-10 record. Bunning would go on to win over 100 games, in both the American and National Leagues. Today he represents the Commonwealth of Kentucky in the United States Senate.

Jim Bunning Blanks Gems On Two Hits

Tigers Gain 5-0 Verdict in Finale at Quincy

Evansville's Braves who don't have any trouble beating the Tigers in their home park but have yet to win a game here invade Muny stadium tonight to open a three-game series.

The Tigers returned home last night after Jim Bunning blanked Quincy, 5-0, on two hits.

Manager Marvin Olson's gang has lost all six of its games with the Braves in the Indiana city. However, earlier in the year when the Tigers were using Browning field, Moline, as their home, the Braves dropped three straight.

The job of extending that string to four this evening falls to Dick Hoeksema, the little lefty who was a 4-2 victim of the Braves in his last outing at Evansville.

his two-hitter, Lettau was doing

Nice Work, Jim

QUAD-CITY—	Ab	R	H	Po	A	E
Jones, cf	4	1	2	5	0	0
Tuttle, rf	4	1	0	2	0	0
Erps, 3b	5	0	1	0	0	0
Buranskas, 1b	4	0	1	8	0	0
Gilbert, lf	4	0	1	1	0	0
Stone, 2b	3	0	0	1	2	0
Bales, c	3	0	0	9	0	0
Larsen, ss	2	1	0	1	1	0
Bunning, p	3	2	1	0	1	0
	32	5	6	27	4	0

QUINCY—	Ab	R	H	Po	A	E
Noga, ss	3	0	0	2	6	1
Kelly, 1b	5	0	0	13	0	0
Barbarito, 3b	2	0	1	0	3	0
Smith, c	4	0	0	2	1	0
Haapala, cf	2	0	0	2	0	0
Renna, rf	4	0	1	5	0	0
Wilkinson, lf	3	0	0	1	0	0
Tretiak, 2b	2	0	0	2	2	0
Lettau, p	2	0	0	0	1	1
*Taylor	1	0	0	0	0	0
Wingo, p	0	0	0	0	0	0
†Haley	1	0	0	0	0	0
	29	0	2	27	13	2

*Struck out for Lettau in 7th.
†Grounded out for Wingo in 9th.

Quad-City .... 004 100 000—5
Quincy .... 000 000 000—0

Runs batted in—Erps 2, Gilbert, Jones. Two base hit—Jones. Sacrifice—Jones. Stolen base—Haapala. Double plays—Smith to Noga, Noga to Tretiak to Kelly. Left on base—Quad-City 7, Quincy 11. Bases on balls—Off Bunning 9, Lettau 4, Wingo 2. Struck out—By Bunning 8, Lettau 1, Wingo 1. Hits—Off Lettau 3 in 7, Wingo 3 in 2. Losing pitcher—Lettau. Umpires—Phillips and Lawson. Time—2:08.

all right on the mound but two

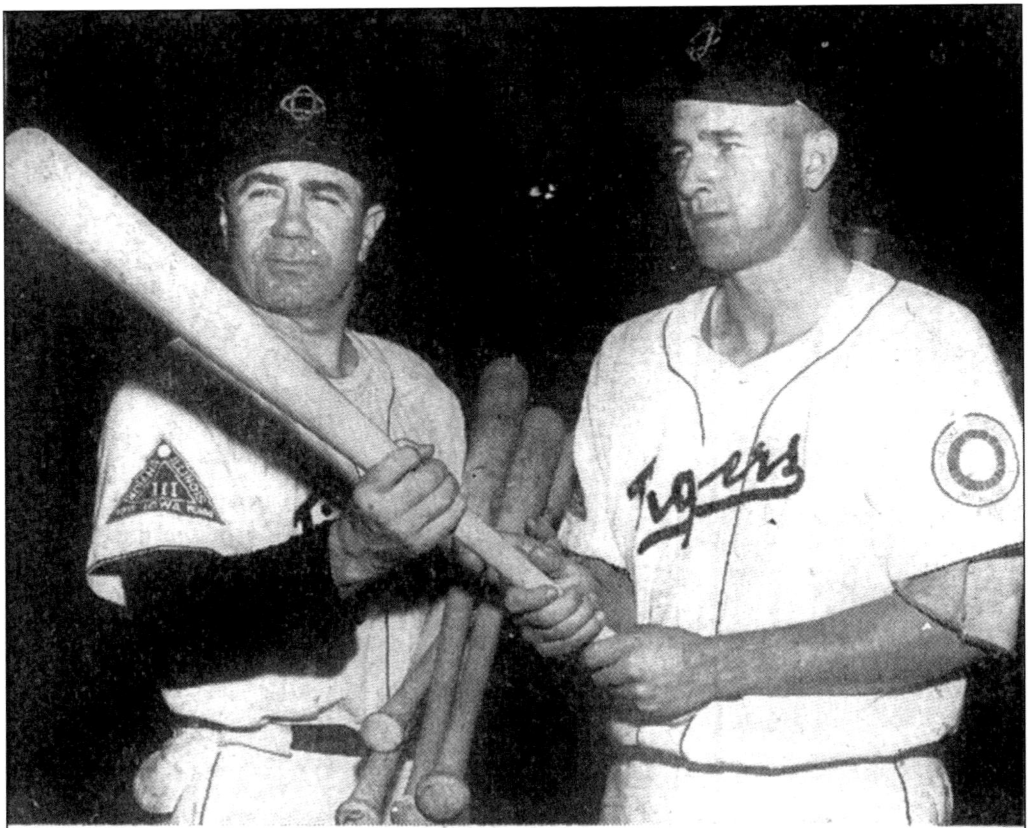

WHICH IS HOME RUN BAT?—Manager Marv Olson of the Quad-City Tigers andles an array of bats for his new outfielder, Connie Juelke, to see if any of them has wo homers in it for Saturday night's game. Juelke made his debut in a Tiger uniform riday night by clouting two over the fence. (Democrat Photo.)

Outfielder Connie Juelke made the most of his Davenport debut, swatting two home runs in his first game. Manager Marv Olson could have used such hitting more often—his two-year record at the helm of the Tigers in 1951 and 1952 was a mere 110-143.

In the early 1950s, Quad City baseball fans could follow their Quads on KSTT radio. The play-by-play man, Milo Hamilton, went on to become a recipient of the J.T. Spink award, popularly called the "broadcasters wing" of the National Baseball Hall of Fame. According to Bob Erps, Hamilton was every bit as entertaining to the players, as he provided a constant stream of jokes to ease the boredom of the long bus rides.

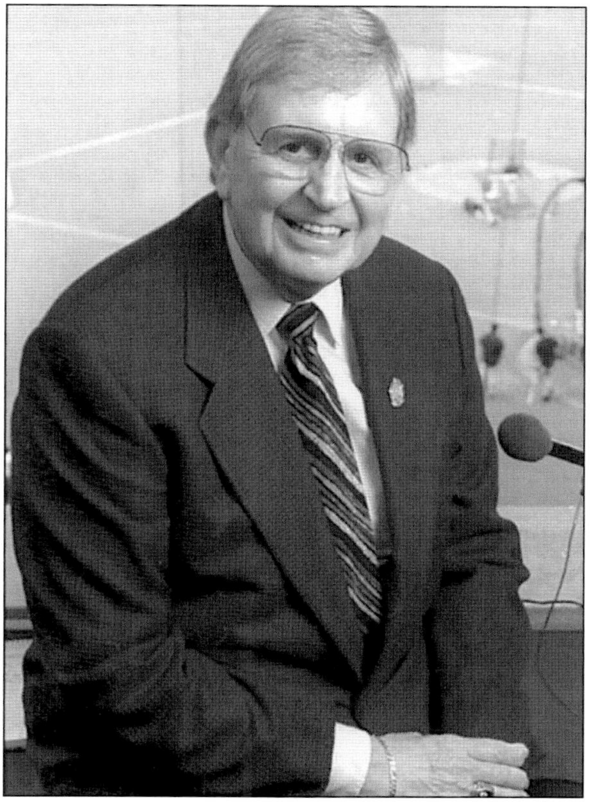

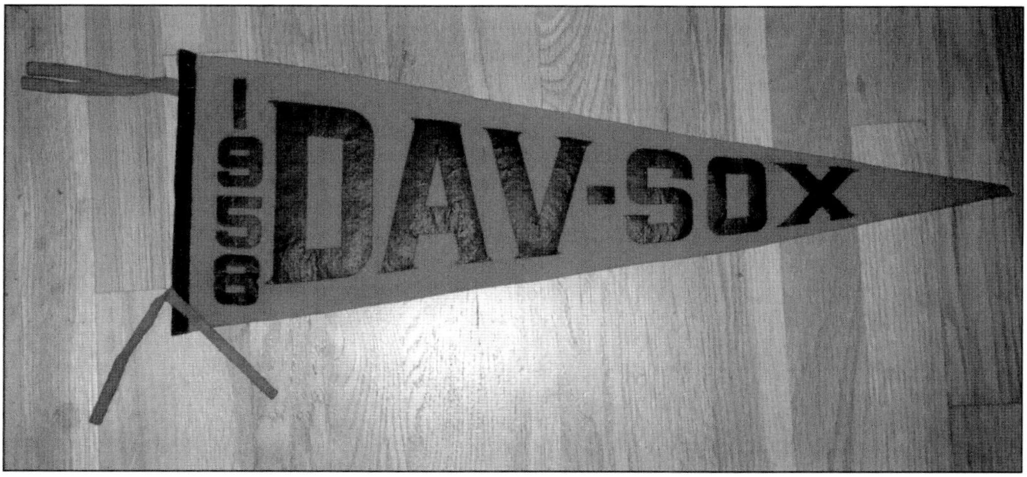

Davenport returned to professional baseball in 1957, this time with a franchise owned and operated by the Chicago White Sox. The Sox left after only two years, but did win a first-half pennant in their second year at Municipal Stadium. The Sox fell to Cedar Rapids in the league championship playoffs.

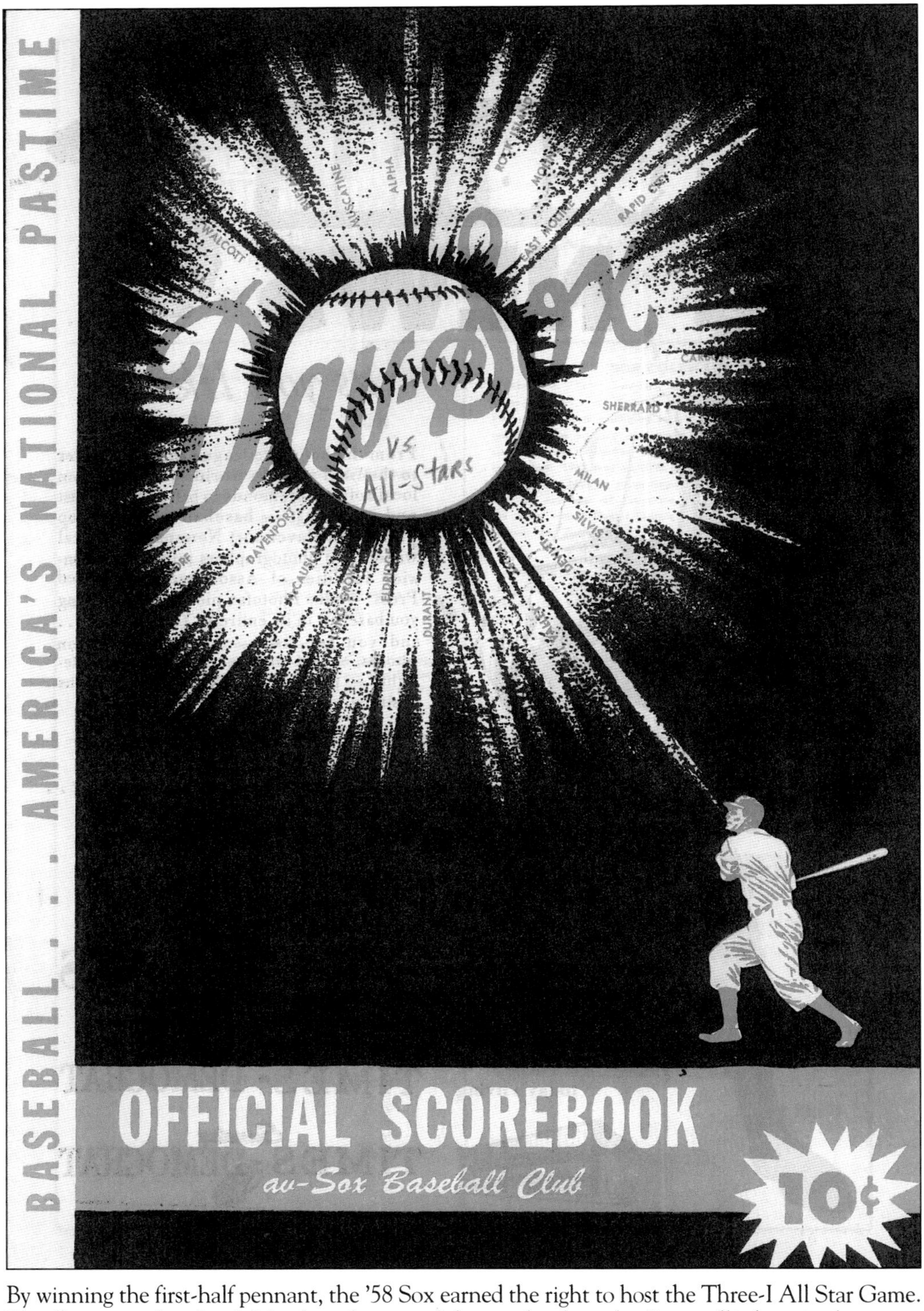

By winning the first-half pennant, the '58 Sox earned the right to host the Three-I All Star Game. The Sox squandered a 4-0 lead in the top of the ninth when the Stars rallied to tie the game. Davenport managed to tally one in the bottom of the inning, however, to take a 5-4 victory.

THREE

Stability

After the failure of the White Sox ownership of the Davenport club, Quad City area fans moved to bring local control back to the baseball club. Led by Hugo "Hooks" Kohn, the Quad City Baseball Fans Association formed to run the local baseball team. Ignoring previous failures to sustain minor league baseball at Municipal Stadium, the Association pressed forward and ushered in an era of stability that has continued to the present.

In 1960, the Association landed a franchise in the Midwest League. The Class D league (two rungs below the Class B Three-I), had been moving aggressively into the area throughout the 1950s. Originally composed of small cities in southern Illinois, the league gradually had moved north into larger markets. In 1954 new Iowa franchises in Clinton and Dubuque proved successful, and gave the league a foothold in eastern Iowa. At the same time, the Three-I League had become more spread out, increasing the travel expenses of members. Gradually the Midwest League began to take in former Three-I cities, such as Waterloo and Keokuk. In 1960, Davenport joined the Midwest League as an affiliate of the Milwaukee Braves. Despite skepticism that the Quad Cities would support the "slower" league, the Braves proved successful. Summarizing the 1960 season, John O'Donnell wrote, "The Braves have played very interesting baseball. They are a refreshing team. The customers have walked out of the park with a satisfied feeling."

Despite talk of rejoining the Three-I League, or even of moving up to the Triple-A American Association, Davenport remained in the Midwest League for the 1961 season. Any thoughts of changing leagues became moot in 1962, as the Three-I League disbanded, with three of that league's six clubs landing in the Midwest League. Since one of the refugees, Cedar Rapids, already had a working agreement with the Braves, the Quad City club dropped their affiliation with Milwaukee, and signed on with the year-old Los Angeles Angels, beginning a relationship that would continue off and on for three decades.

Although the first years of the Angels affiliation yielded no pennants, Quad City usually found itself atop the attendance figures in the Midwest League. Thanks to the support of the Quad City Fans' Association, and the leadership of general manager Ken Blackman, Quad City set a league attendance record in 1964, becoming the first Midwest League team to draw more than 100,000 fans. Success on the field gradually came the Angels way as well. The 1968 club won Quad City's first Midwest League Championship, and the 1971 club claimed a league title as well.

The 1971 season saw one major change at the stadium—a new name. Retired *Davenport Times-Democrat* sports editor, John O'Donnell, who had begun work as a sportswriter for the *Times-Democrat* two weeks after his graduation from St. Ambrose College in 1925, passed away on March 17, 1970. During the 1970 season, Bettendorf resident James Ryan circulated petitions to rename Municipal Stadium in honor of O'Donnell. "It is only fitting that Municipal Stadium be rededicated 'John O'Donnell Stadium' in honor of a man who was an integral part of the Quad City sports scene for more than four decades," wrote Jerry Jurgens of the *Times-Democrat*. On May 26, 1971, the 40th anniversary of the opening of the stadium, Davenport Mayor John Jebens officially proclaimed "John O'Donnell Stadium" the new name of the ballpark. (Unfortunately, the visiting Cedar Rapids Cardinals defeated the Angels in the rededication game, 7-3.)

Minor league baseball continued to thrive throughout the 1970s in John O'Donnell Stadium. The Angels did not win any championships after 1971, but they did field competitive teams. In 1977 and 1978, the club drew over 100,000 fans, establishing new club (and league) records both years. In fact, attendance was so good that the club flirted with moving up to the Triple-A level, one notch below the major leagues. As early as 1960, the idea had been floating around that John O'Donnell Stadium could host Triple-A baseball someday. In 1978, general manager Harry Pells openly touted the Quad Cities as a possible market for an American Association franchise. From today's perspective, it may seem strange that the Quad Cities could be considered as a market for Triple-A ball, but at the time, cities the size of Springfield, Illinois and Evansville, Indiana operated in the American Association. Still the efforts to move up came to naught, and the Quad Cities remained a fixture in the Midwest League.

Although the Quad City franchise was a fixture of the Midwest League, by the mid-1980s John O'Donnell Stadium was starting to show its age. To maintain the old ballpark, various improvements were undertaken. In 1983, some repairs were made to the bleachers and the lighting system, and major changes came later in the decade. After the Fans' Association sold the team to Chicago businessman Henry Semrow in 1986, plans were drawn for a major overhaul of the facility. Semrow sold the club after only one year to another Chicagoan, Rich Holtzman, but the stadium improvements moved forward. From 1987 to 1989, the old football bleachers along the third base line were torn down, the roof was repaired, the press box was expanded, the parking lot was paved, the box seats were expanded, and a new scoreboard was erected. In 1990, the *Quad City Times*' Steve Batterson wrote, "The city of Davenport's $2.3 million restoration of the 59-year-old stadium has turned John O'Donnell Stadium into one of minor league baseball's true gems as it sits on the banks of the Mississippi."

Fans flocked to the revamped facility. Whereas an attendance of 100,000 has once been the standard for excellence, the club consistently drew over 200,000 per season in the early 1990s. In 1992, the club attracted more attention by adopting a new nickname, discarding the nickname of their major league parent club—the Angels—and replacing it with the new moniker, Quad City River Bandits.

Disaster struck the stadium in 1993, however. As rains soaked the upper Midwest during the spring and summer that year, the Mississippi River left its banks and left much of the area under water. Floodwaters surrounded John O'Donnell Stadium, forcing the team to move its home games to various parks in the area, including North Scott High School in Eldridge and Brady Street Field in Davenport. The club weathered the disaster, and rebounded, drawing a record attendance in 1994. Still it was clear that improvements needed to be made at the ballpark to prevent any future flood damage.

Threatened with the loss of the team in 1996, the city of Davenport made $500,000 worth of improvements to the playing surface and locker rooms. More flooding occurred in 2001, however, and while the team was able to return to John O'Donnell Stadium by the Fourth of July, it was evident that further changes would be needed at the ballpark.

In 1999, the current ownership group—Seventh Inning Stretch, LLC, headed by Kevin Krause—had begun negotiating with the City of Davenport for extensive renovations to John O'Donnell Stadium. Although the talks turned acrimonious at times, a plan was finally approved in 2002. At then end of the 2003 Midwest League season, a major overhaul to the stadium began. The exterior façade of the old park was left in place, but the entire interior was gutted to make room for the $12.5 million overhaul, which included new seating areas, luxury boxes, locker room and training facilities, and an earthen berm around the outfield to protect the park against future Mississippi River floods. The ball club received a makeover as well, with a new nickname—The Swing of the Quad Cities—selected for the 2004 season.

After more than seventy years of service to Davenport and the Quad Cities, the old Municipal/John O'Donnell Stadium appears ready to serve the people of the Quad Cities for years to come.

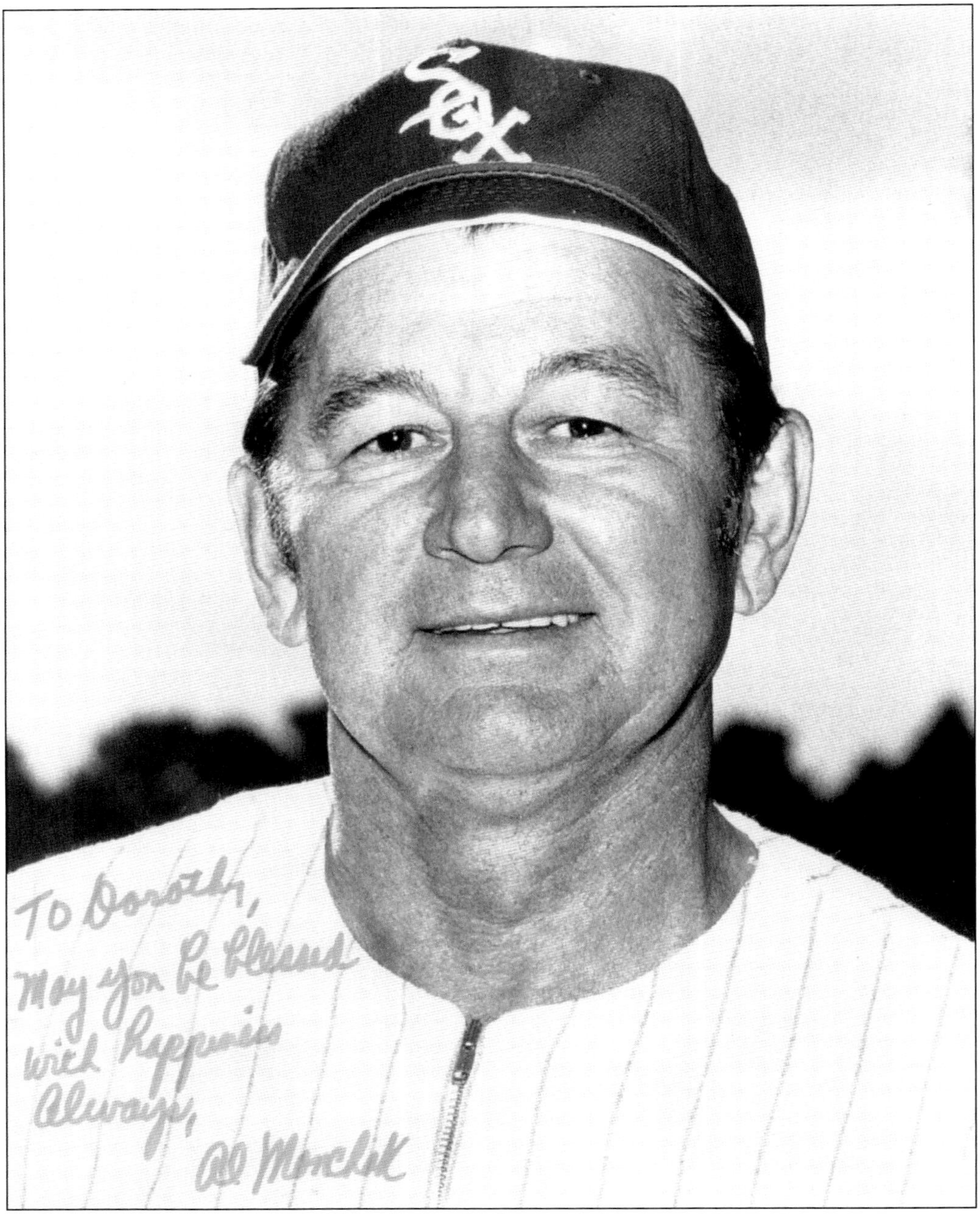

The manager of the 1961 Quad City Braves went on to a major league coaching career. While his Q.C. club didn't bring home a pennant, it did feature League Rookie of the Year Dennis Ribant, who thrilled a Sunday, July 2 Municipal Stadium crowd of over 10,000 by pitching a perfect game against Clinton.

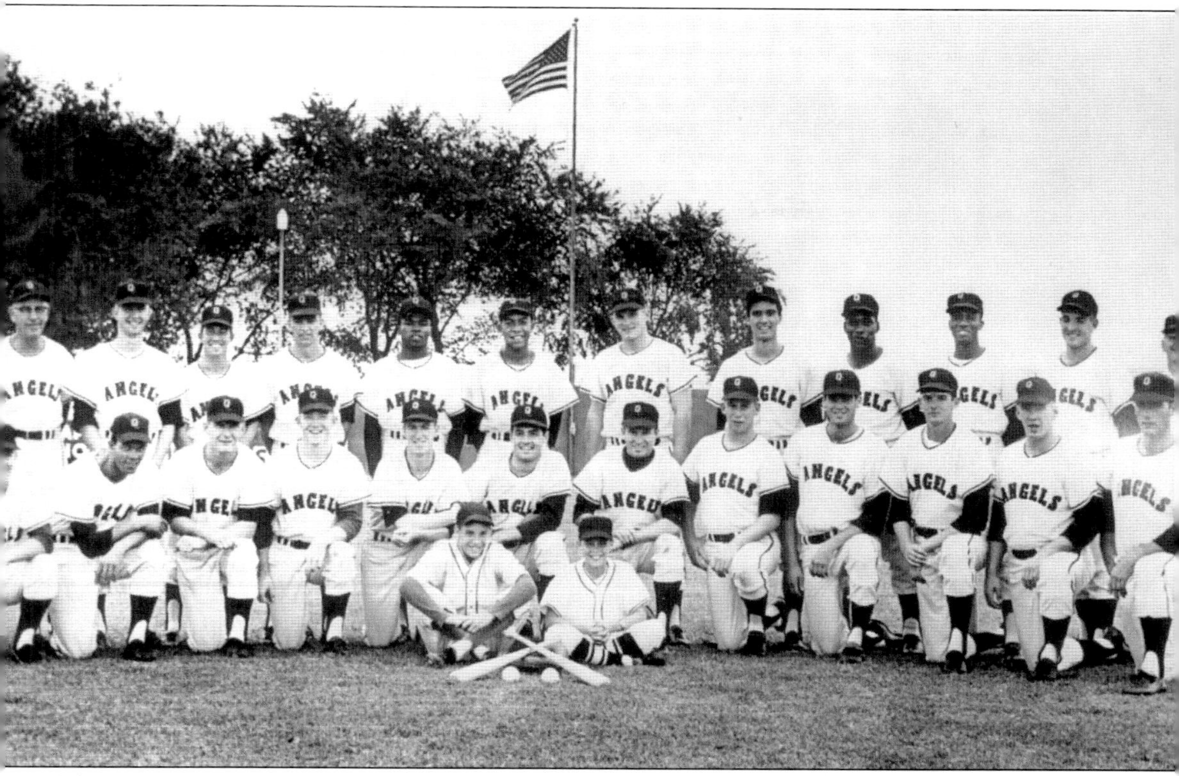

After two seasons as a Milwaukee Braves farm club, the Quad Cities began a 17-year affiliation with the Los Angeles (later California) Angels in 1962. Despite a second-half record of 40-27, Waterloo edged out the Angels for the second-half pennant by two games.

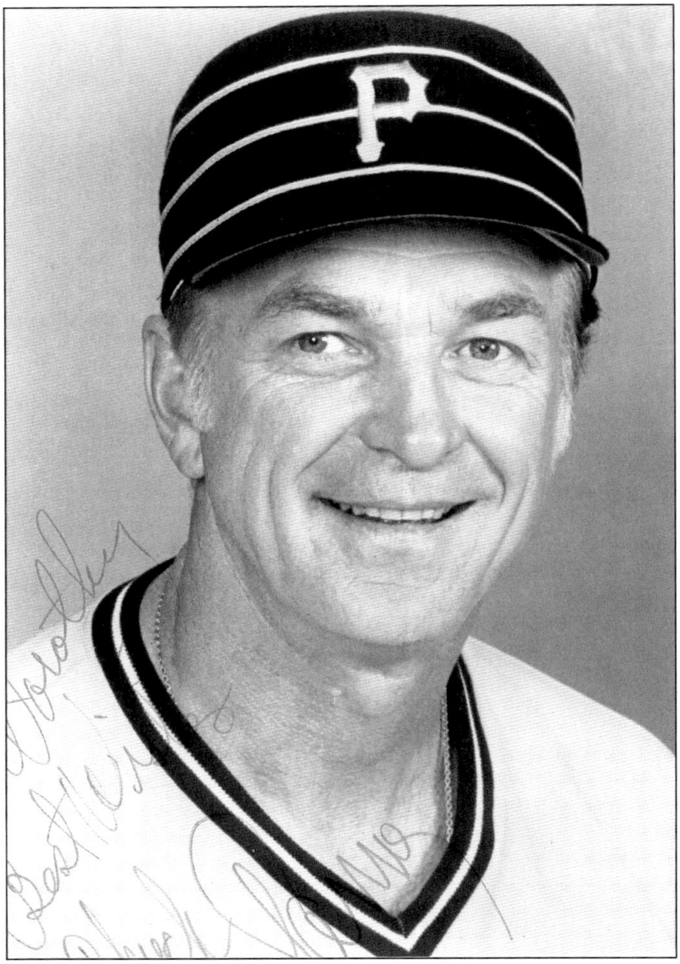

Future World Series champion managers have to start somewhere. Chuck Tanner, skipper of the 1979 "We Are Family" Pittsburgh Pirates, began his managerial career in 1963, guiding the Quad City Angels through two Midwest League campaigns.

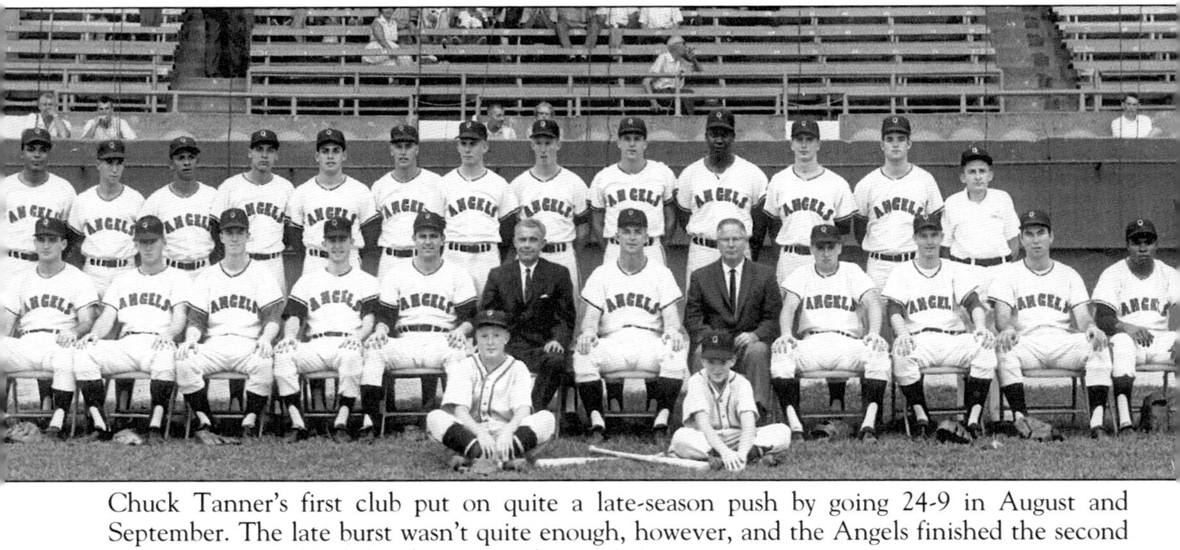

Chuck Tanner's first club put on quite a late-season push by going 24-9 in August and September. The late burst wasn't quite enough, however, and the Angels finished the second half two games behind the champion Clinton C-Sox.

The 1963 Angels finished 66-57 overall, thanks in large part to the pitching of Ken Turner, whose 18 wins led the league (accompanied by a sparkling 2.81 ERA and 170 strikeouts). Battery-mate Pete Gongola was a favorite among Quad City fans. Injuries limited him to 132 at-bats, but the clutch-hitting catcher socked 7 home runs and batted in 31 runs.

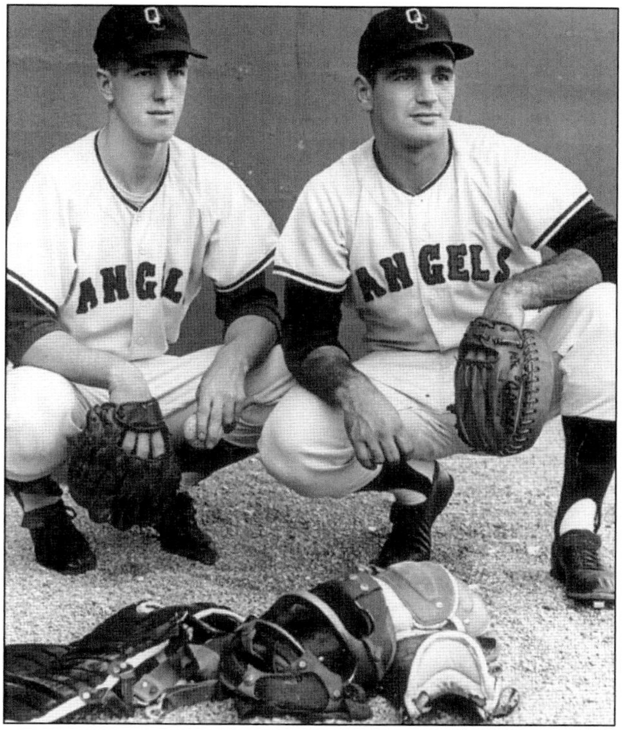

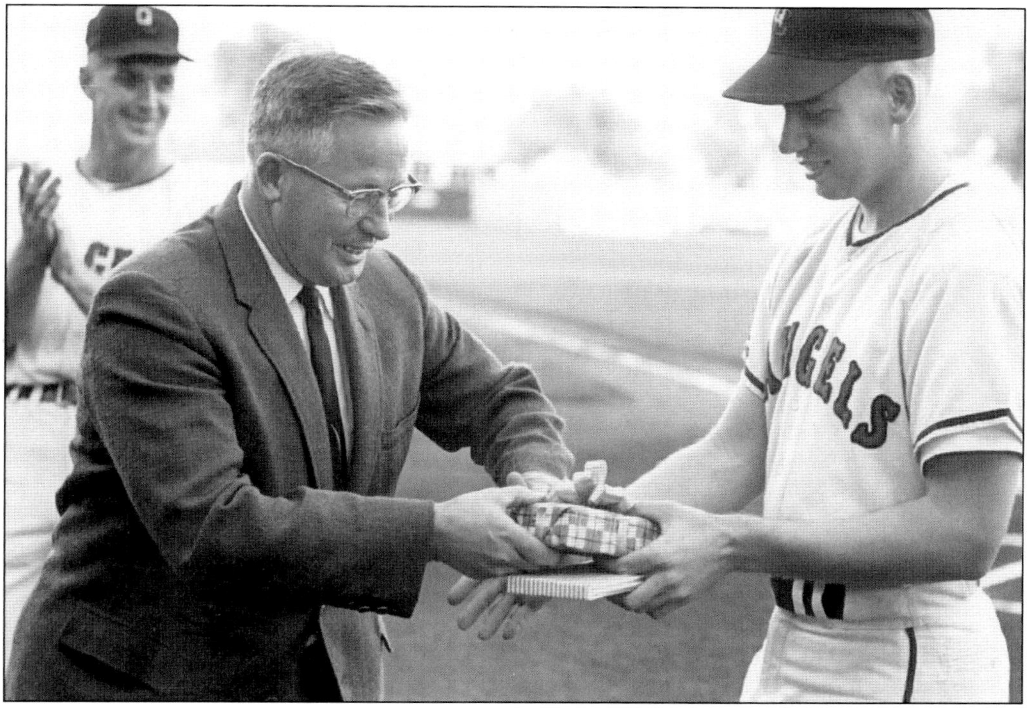

Who says fans only appreciate offensive players? Denny Meyer won the club MVP award for 1963, despite hitting just .268 with 5 homers and 49 RBI. However, the slick-fielding center fielder didn't miss an inning and was "Enemy Number 1 in the book of a flock of rival batters," according to John O'Donnell.

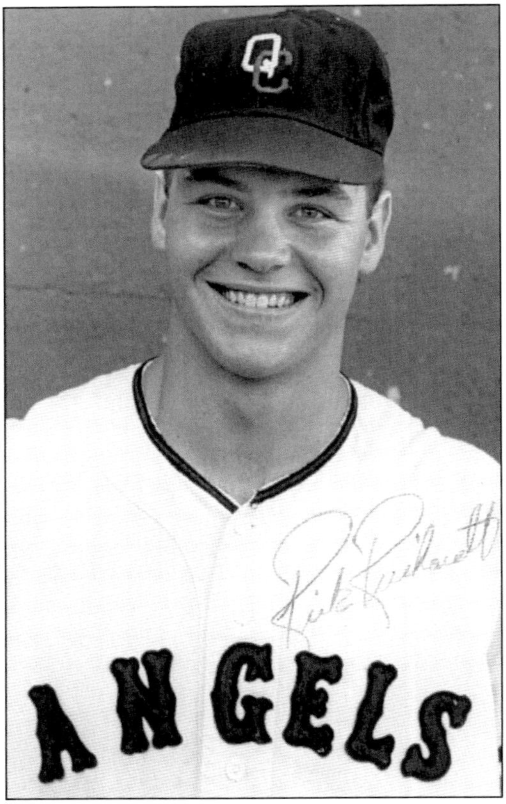

In June of 1964, the California Angels signed University of Wisconsin football and baseball star, Rick Reichardt, for a reported bonus of $100,000. Reichardt began a month-long stay in the Quad Cities on July 4th and made his major league debut September 1st.

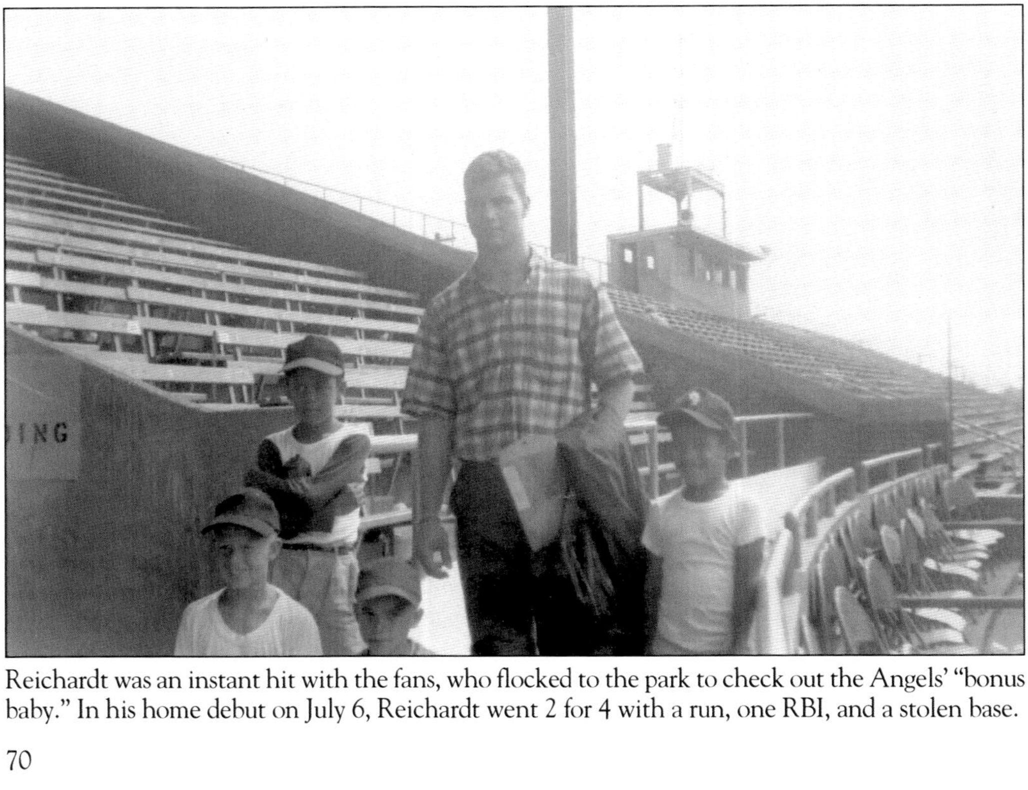

Reichardt was an instant hit with the fans, who flocked to the park to check out the Angels' "bonus baby." In his home debut on July 6, Reichardt went 2 for 4 with a run, one RBI, and a stolen base.

Reichardt was a big drawing card on the road as well, especially when the Angels traveled to the Midwest League's Wisconsin cities. In his professional debut, at Decatur, Reichardt tallied one of Quad Cities' five hits, although the Angels lost to the Commodores, 8-1.

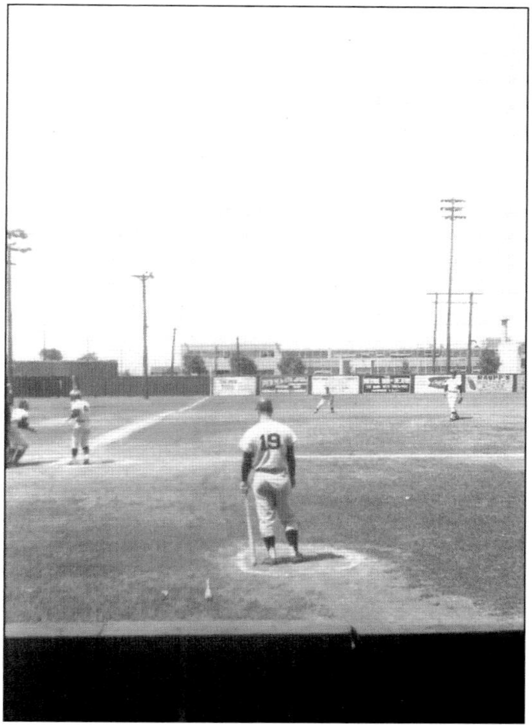

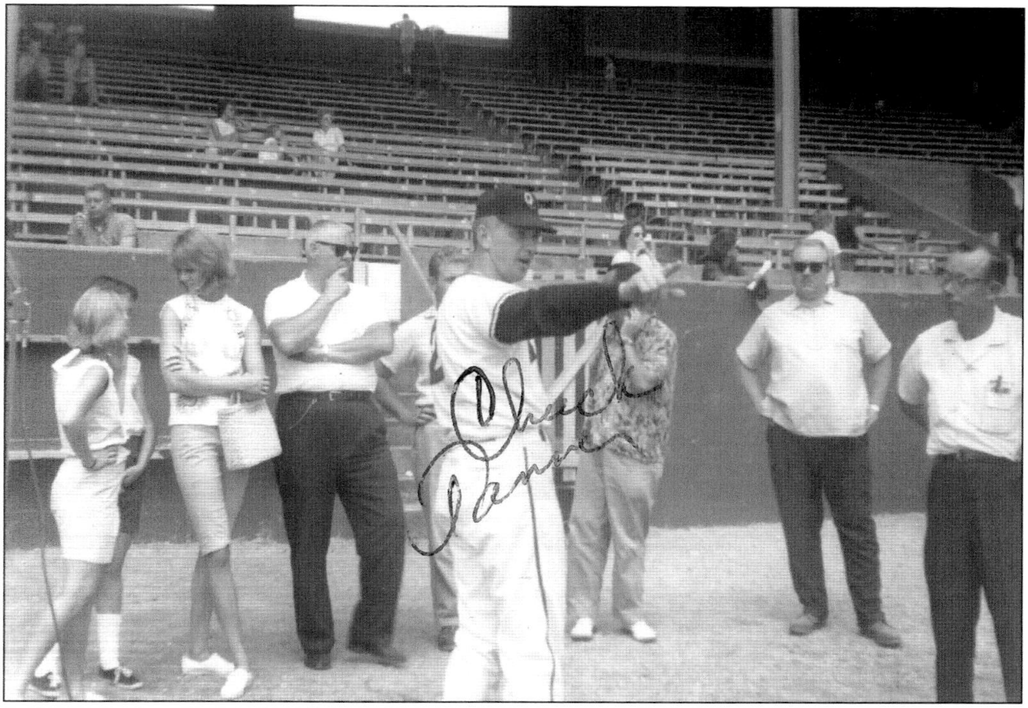

In his introduction to Quad City fans, Tanner quipped about his players, "They'll hustle or play for somebody else." The aggressive play of Tanner's clubs made the Quad City manager a popular figure with area fans.

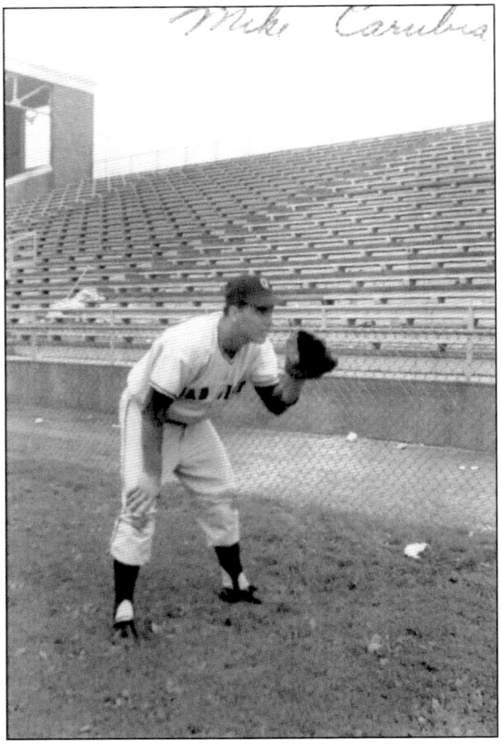

Michael Carubia led the 1964 Angels pitching staff with 15 wins (against 7 defeats) and posted a stellar earned run average of 1.69.

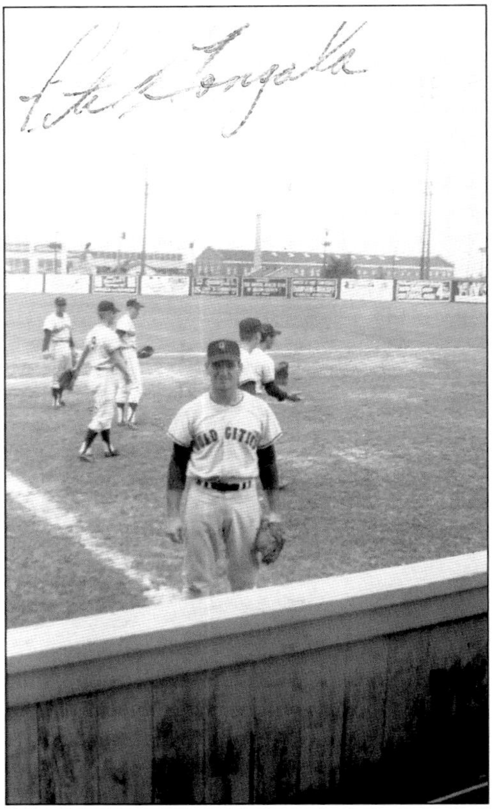

The "old man" of the '64 Angels, 25-year-old Pete Gongola played catcher, and would in later years serve as a coach. Fans respected his hustling style so much that Pete "could have run for mayor," according to long-time fan, Frank Wulf.

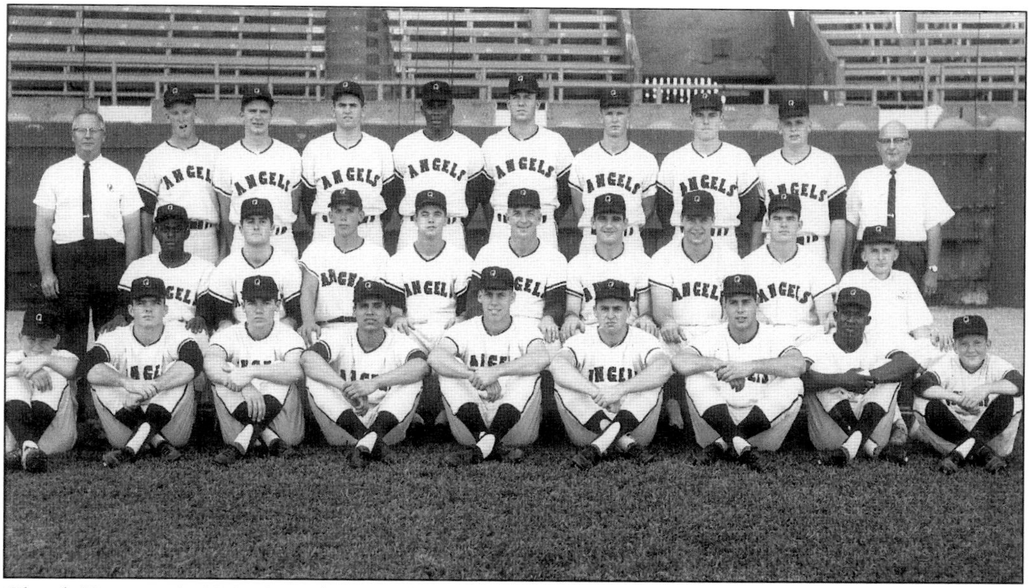

Chuck Tannner's 1964 Angels started slowly, finishing the first half of the season with a 24-31 record. In the second half, however, the club made a furious push for the pennant. Quad Cities posted a fine 38-25 record in the second half, but still finished two games behind eventual champion Fox Cities.

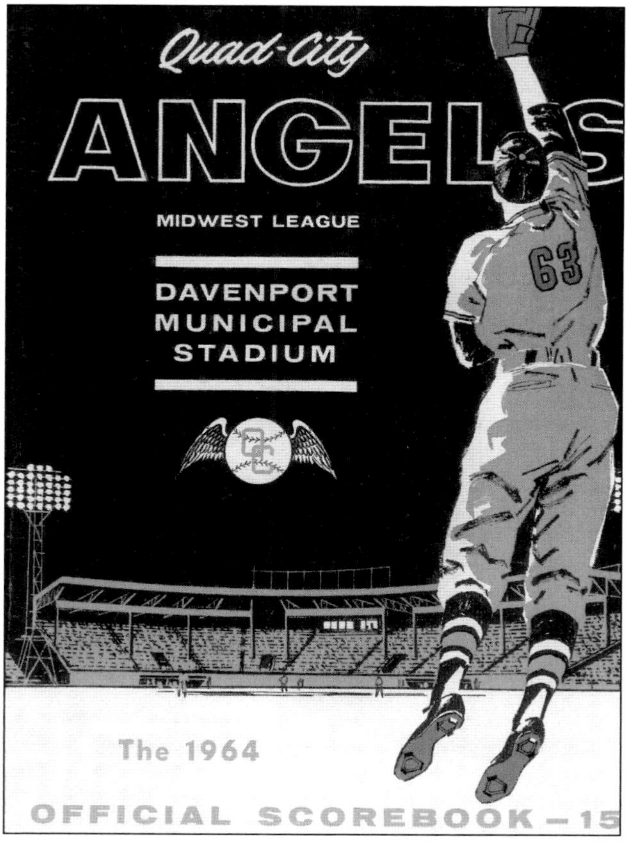

The 1964 Angels became the first Midwest League club to surpass the 100,000 mark in home attendance with 108,129 fans passing through the turnstiles. The mark bested the league record of 97,200, set by Dubuque in 1959.

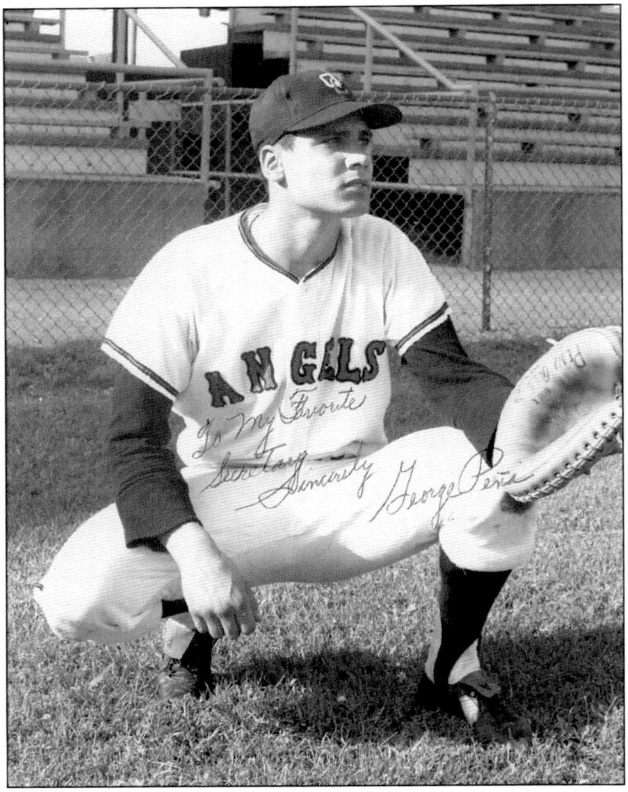

George Pena was a popular catcher for the 1963 and 1964 Angels. Pena made an encore appearance over a decade later, returning to John O'Donnell Stadium in 1975 as a member of the Iowa Oaks in an exhibition game against the Midwest League All-Stars. The Midwest League topped the Oaks, 6-2.

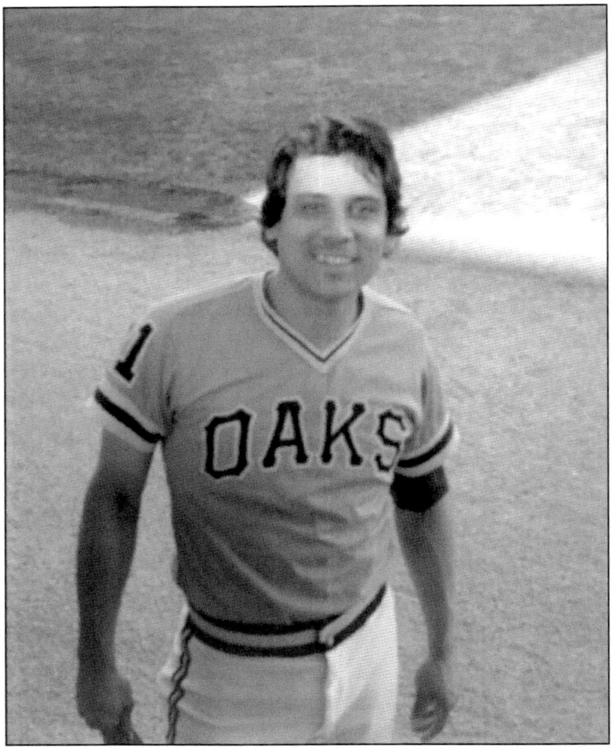

Pena went 0 for 4 in the Oaks loss to the Midwest League All-Stars in 1975. He did, however, tag out Quad City Angel Thad Bosley at the plate to prevent a run.

Dorothy Wulf was kept busy during the 1964 season in her Municipal Stadium office. "If you want to know anything about the business side of the Quad City Angels, call her," wrote John O'Donnell. "She'll give you the answer."

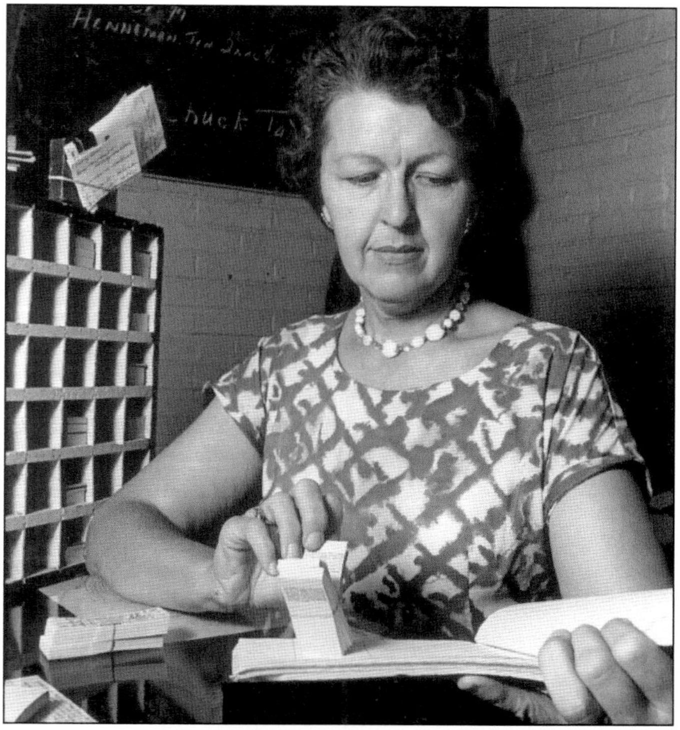

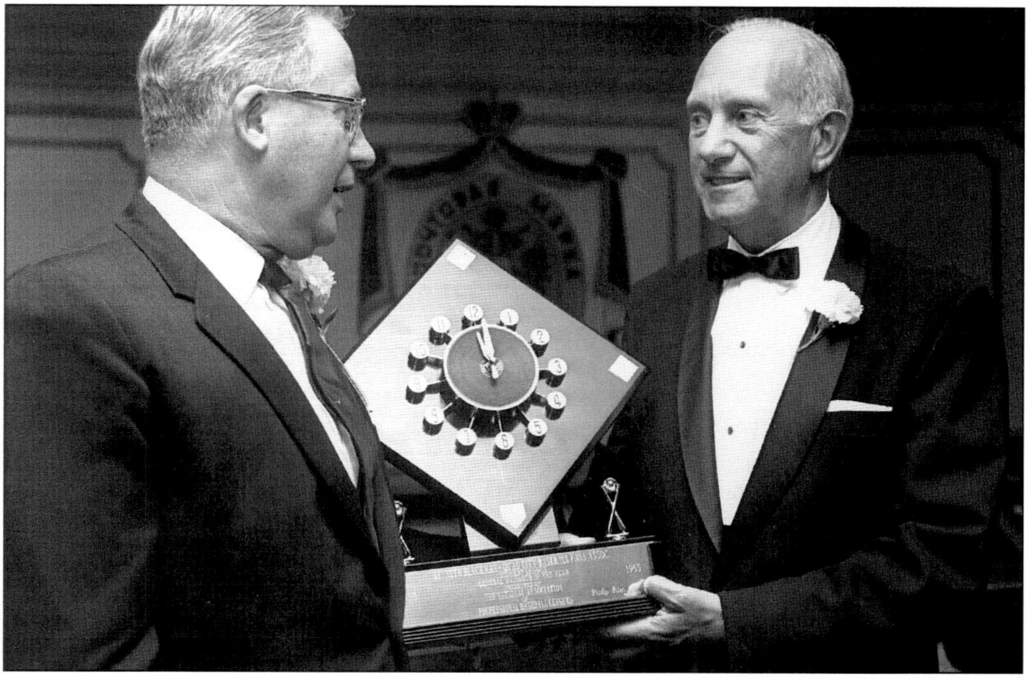

After setting a league attendance record one year, and enduring a flood the next, hard-working general manager Ken Blackman was honored by *The Sporting News* as "Class A Executive of the Year." "Behind the picture not seen by the fans there has to be a hard-working organization which is ready at all times to use elbow grease—and plenty of it," wrote John O'Donnell in a 1964 profile of Ken Blackman.

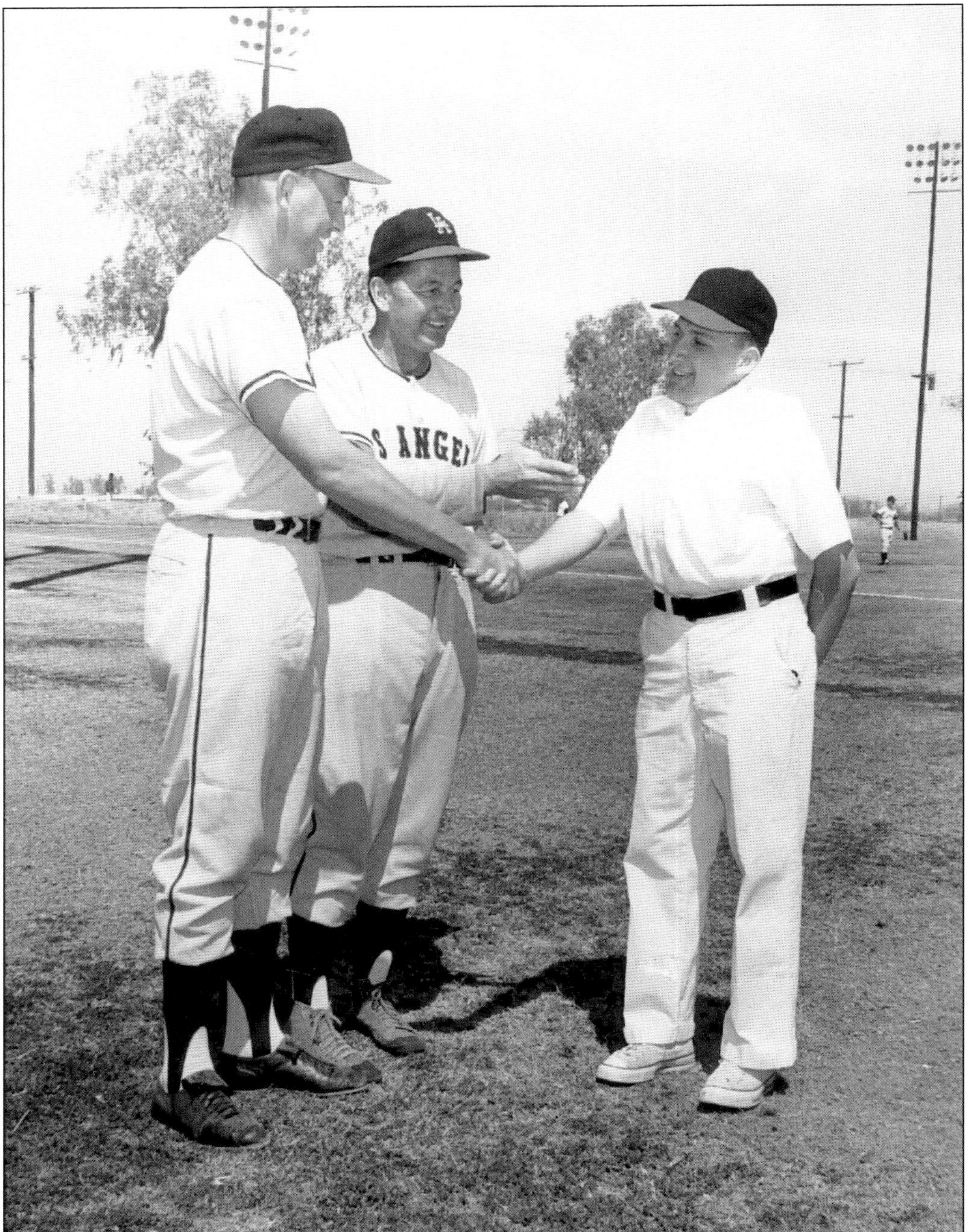

It isn't just players who dream of making the big leagues. St. Ambrose alumnus Don Bender (left) began his career as a trainer with the 1965 Angels. He would later move up to the same position with the parent California Angels. Here, former Quad Cities skipper Al Monchak introduces Bender to new manager Harry Dunlop during 1965 spring training.

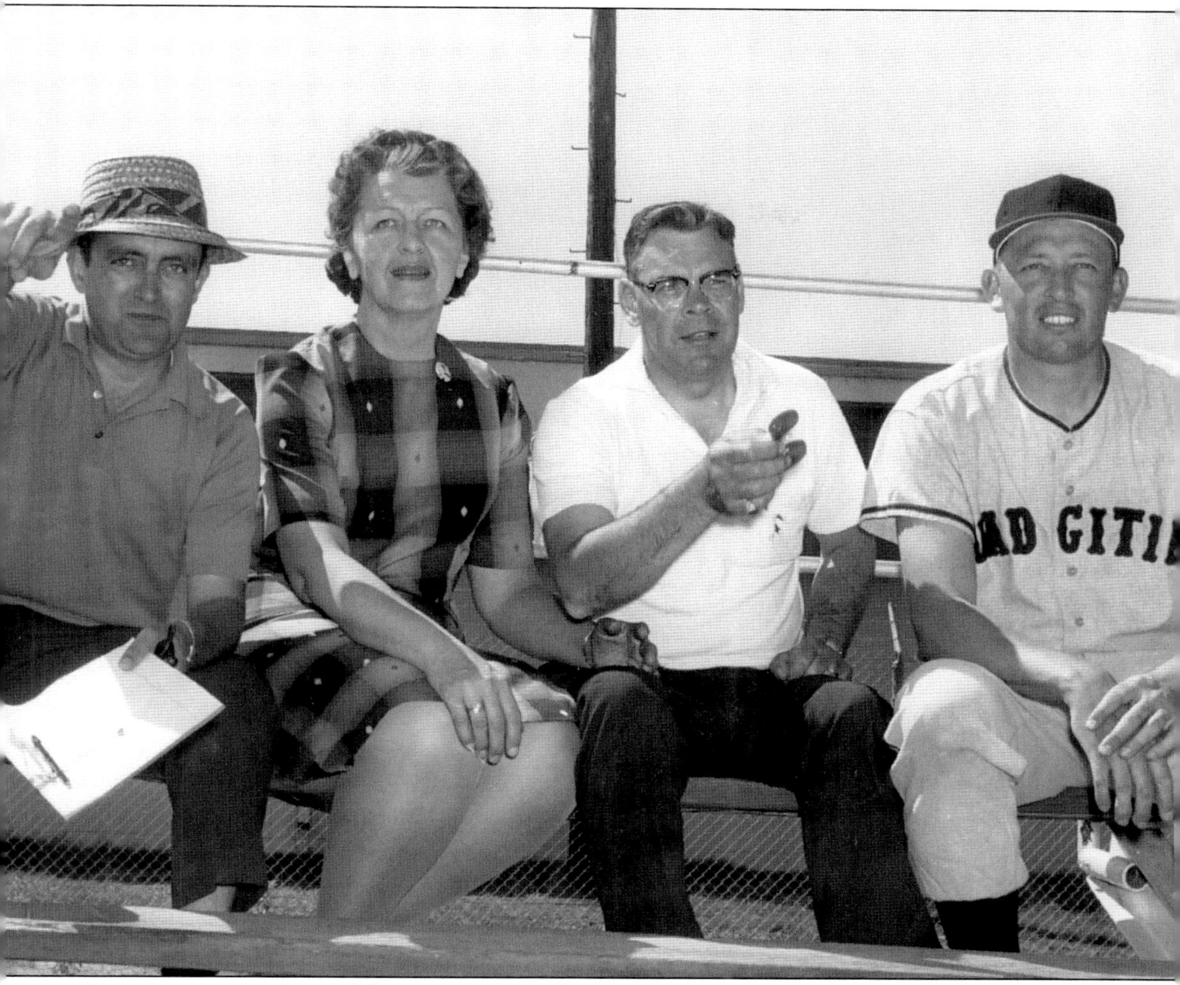

As farm director for the California Angels, Roland Hemond (left) became very familiar with Quad Cities baseball. "We, of course, like the facilities here in the Quad-Cities," Hemond told the *Times-Democrat* in 1970, "and we also like the weather, because we figure that by letting our younger men play in this type of climate [generally hot and humid], it'll separate the men from the boys, so to speak." Harry Dunlop (right) is seated next to Dorothy and Frank Wulf.

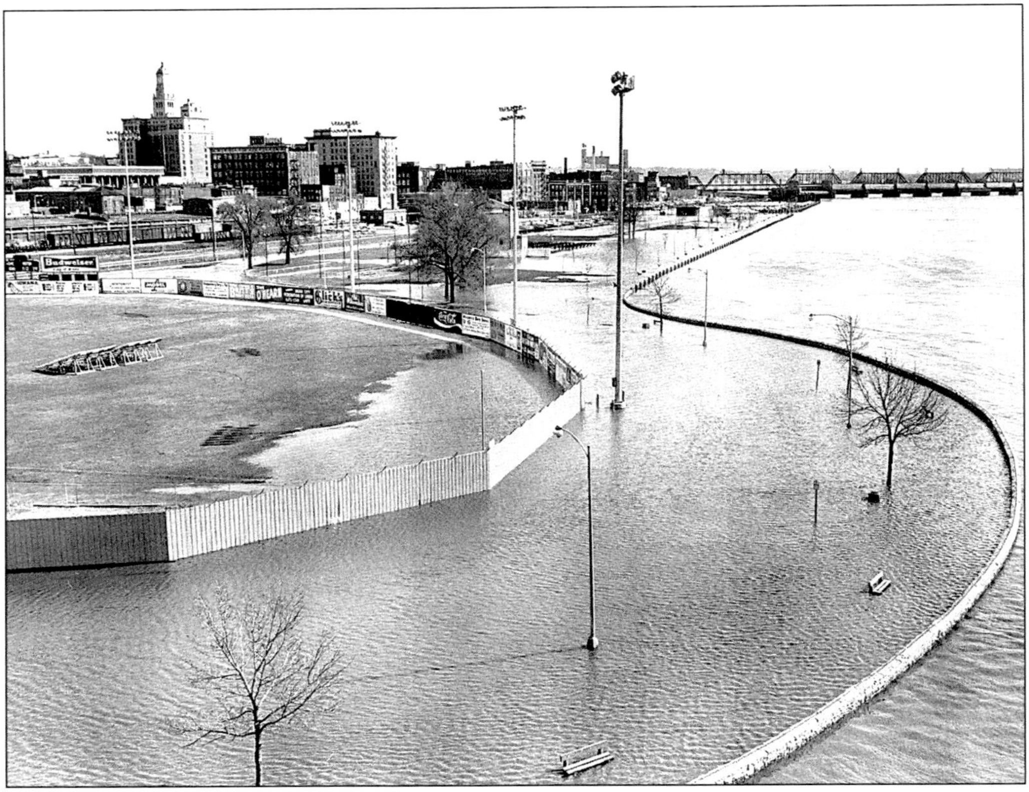

By 1973, Davenport was accustomed to fending off periodic floods. According to the *Times*, the flood of '73 barely even compared to the devastation of 1965. Still, the Angels were forced to open the season at Northwest Park in Davenport. They returned to the John O'Donnell on May 19, and beat Clinton 9-4 in their delayed home opener. Before 1993, Quad City residents remembered 1965 as the most devastating year for Mississippi River flooding. In 1965 (and in 1969, 1993, and 2001) the stadium fell victim to flood waters.

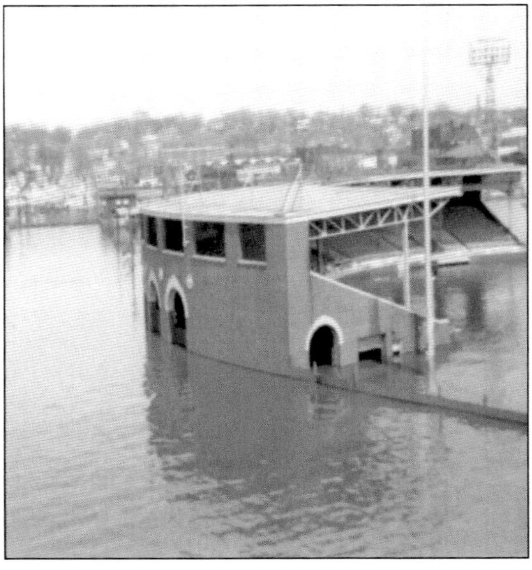

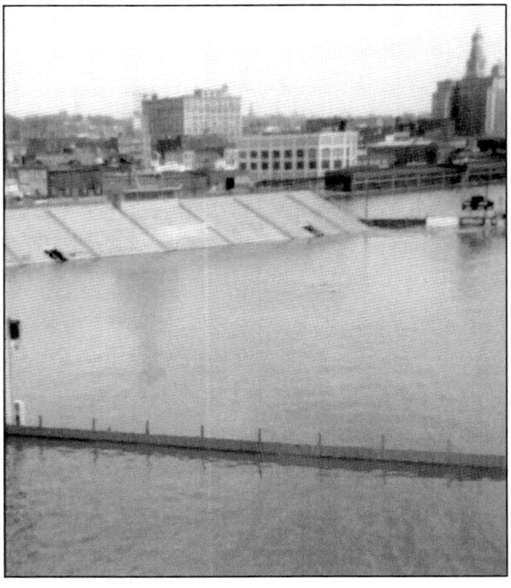

This view from Centennial Bridge shows the Muny completely engulfed by floodwaters. Prior to the 1965 season, torrential rains caused devastating floods throughout the Mississippi River Valley. Flooding at Municipal Stadium forced the Angels to move their first twelve home games to Rock Island. Few at the time thought the park would be ready before July 4, but the Angels played their first game at Municipal Stadium on May 16. Despite the lost home dates, Quad City drew 80,391 fans in the course of the year.

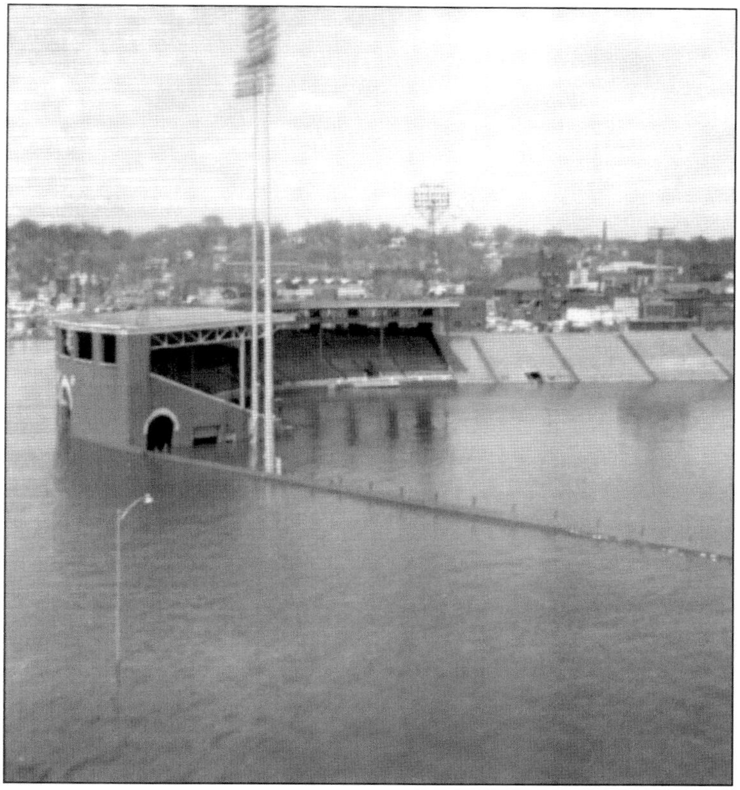

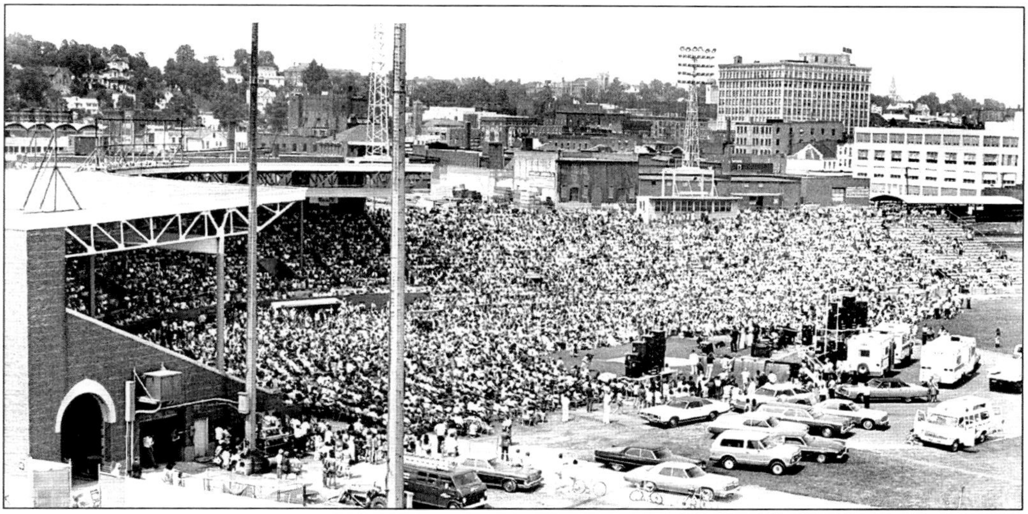

Is it the same ballpark? In this scene from almost a decade later, when country music legend Johnny Cash came to play to a jammed stadium, the '65 flood is all but forgotten.

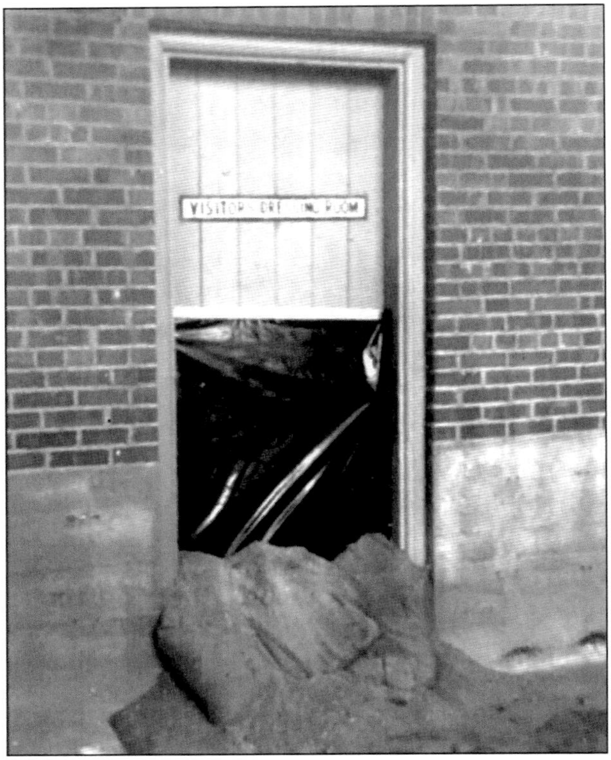

Sandbags protect the locker room door outside Municipal Stadium.

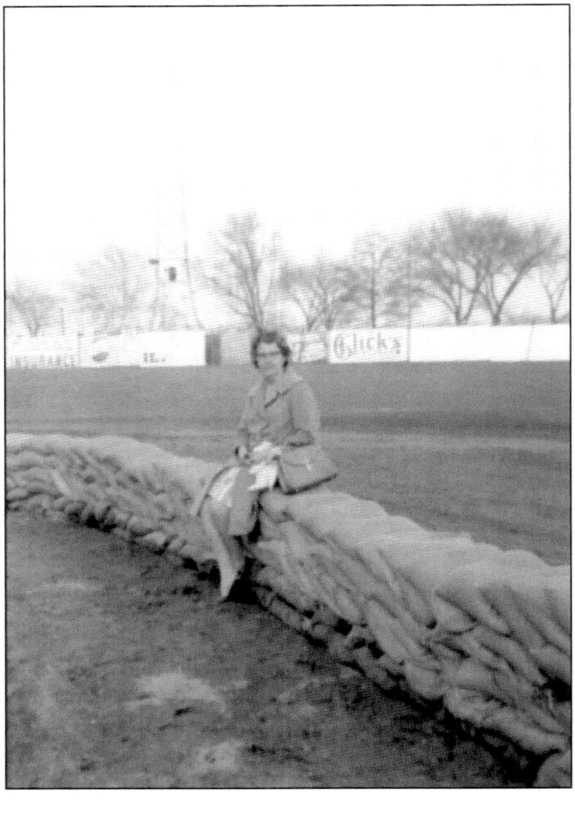

Dorothy Wulf appears confident that the sandbags around the infield will keep her safe from the dangers threatened by the Mississippi.

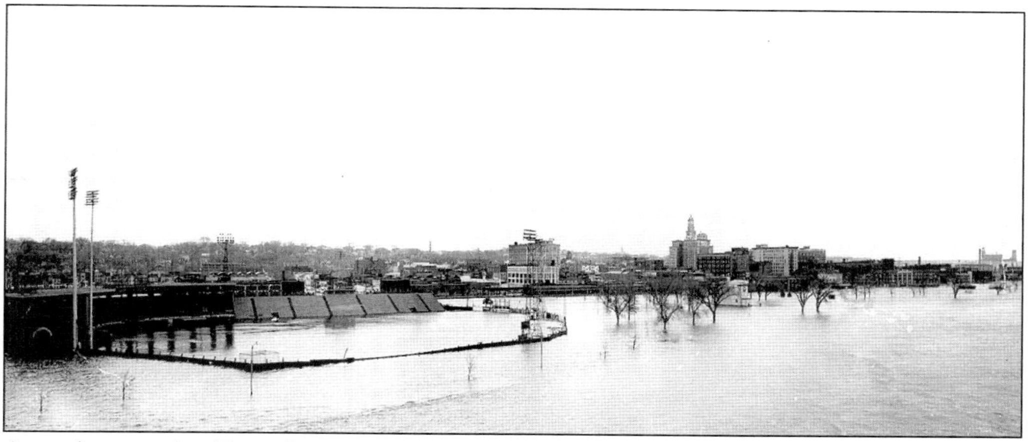

According to the *Times-Democrat,* Municipal Stadium became a "fisherman's and surfer's paradise" in March of '69, as flood waters once again engulfed the field. Although the Angels had to play a few early season games at Northwest Park, the stadium suffered no lasting damage to its brand new light towers or plumbing.

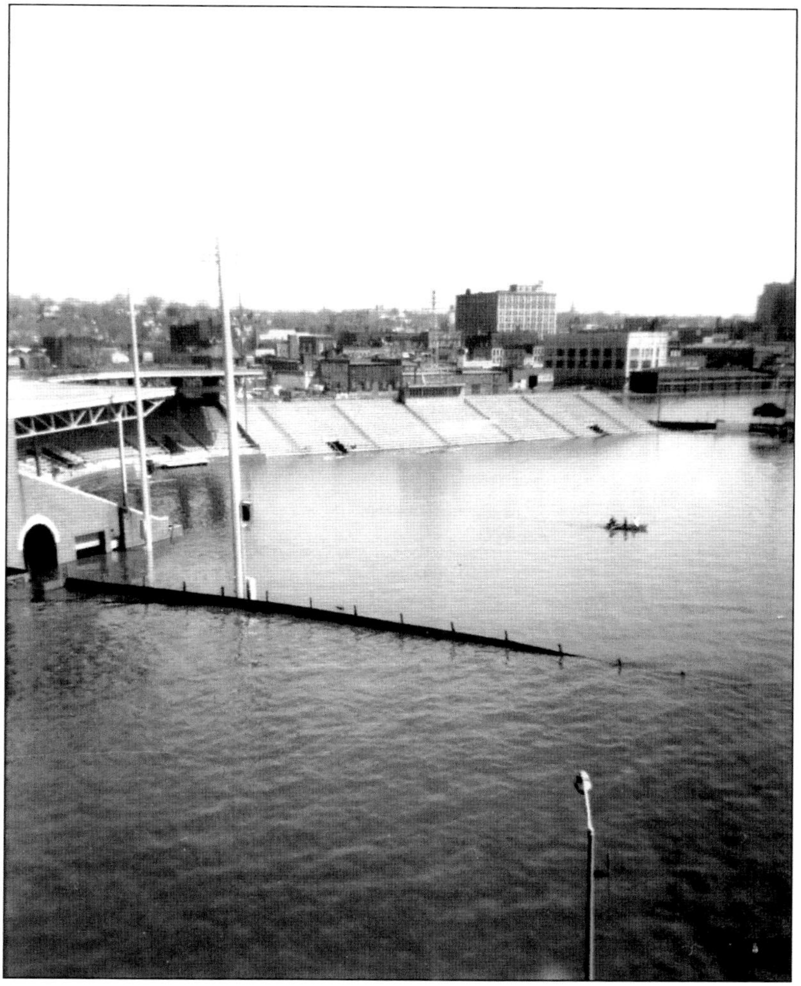

A small fishing boat heads for home plate from center field. Hopefully, the improvements to John O'Donnell scheduled for 2004 will make such scenes of "John O'Donnell Island" a thing of the past.

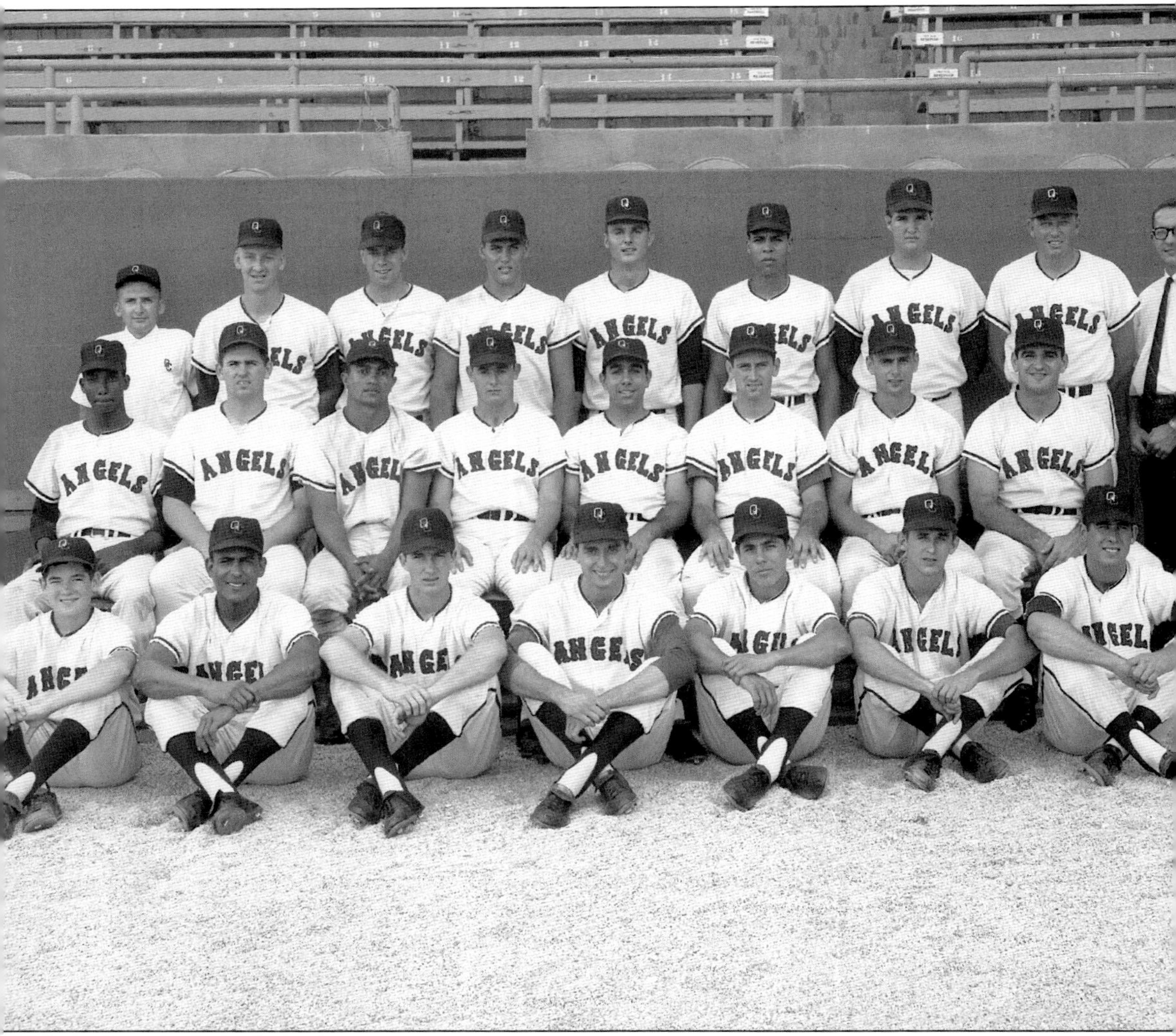

The Angels crept back above the .500 mark in 1966, finishing 63-61. The highlight of the year was Vern Geishart's May 6 no-hitter against Appleton.

Koenig arrived in 1967 for a three-year hitch as the Angels' manager. Koenig's clubs compiled a record of 198-158. John O'Donnell contrasted the style of Koenig with that of 1930's skipper Cletus Dixon: "I don't think [Dixon] ever knew a first name of his players. He, like Casey Stengel, would point to 'that fellow over there.' Fred Koenig was on the ball in regards to names. Maybe that is the new breed of managers."

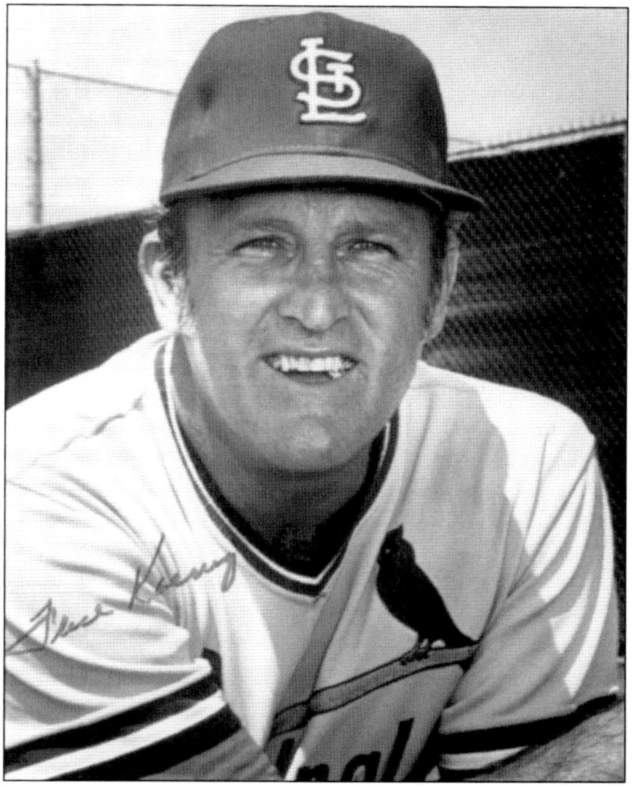

On opening day, April 30, 1968, Dorothy Wulf threw out the opening pitch on behalf of her boss, Mayor John Jebens. The Angels shut out Dubuque, 3-0, before a crowd of 1,346.

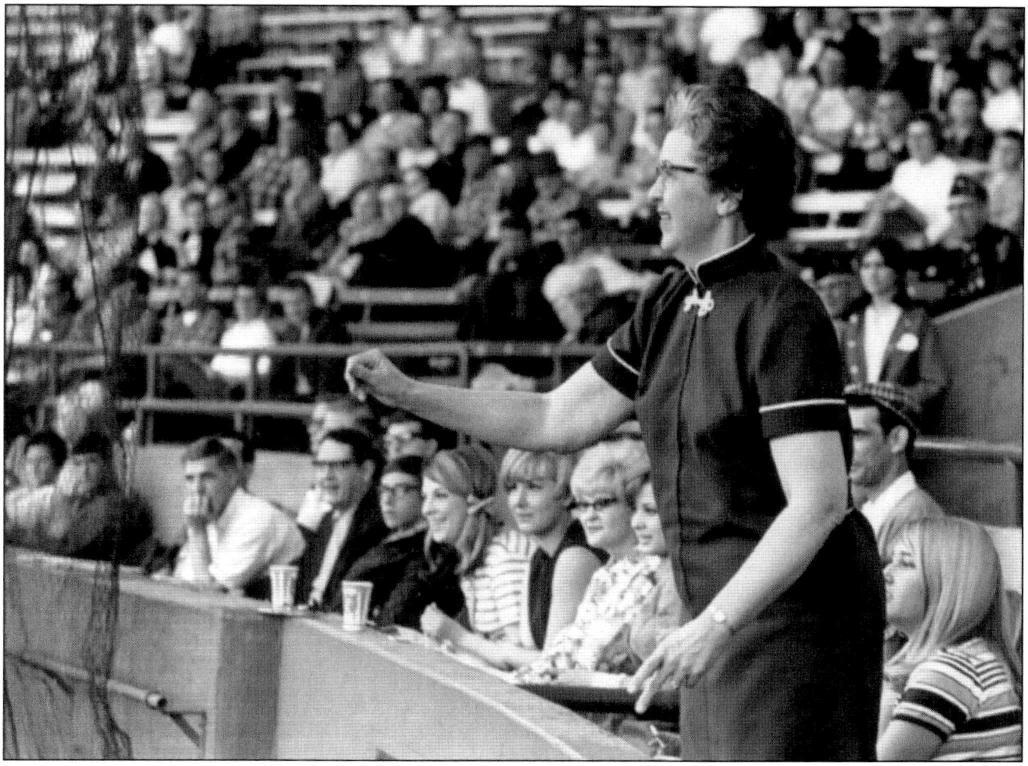

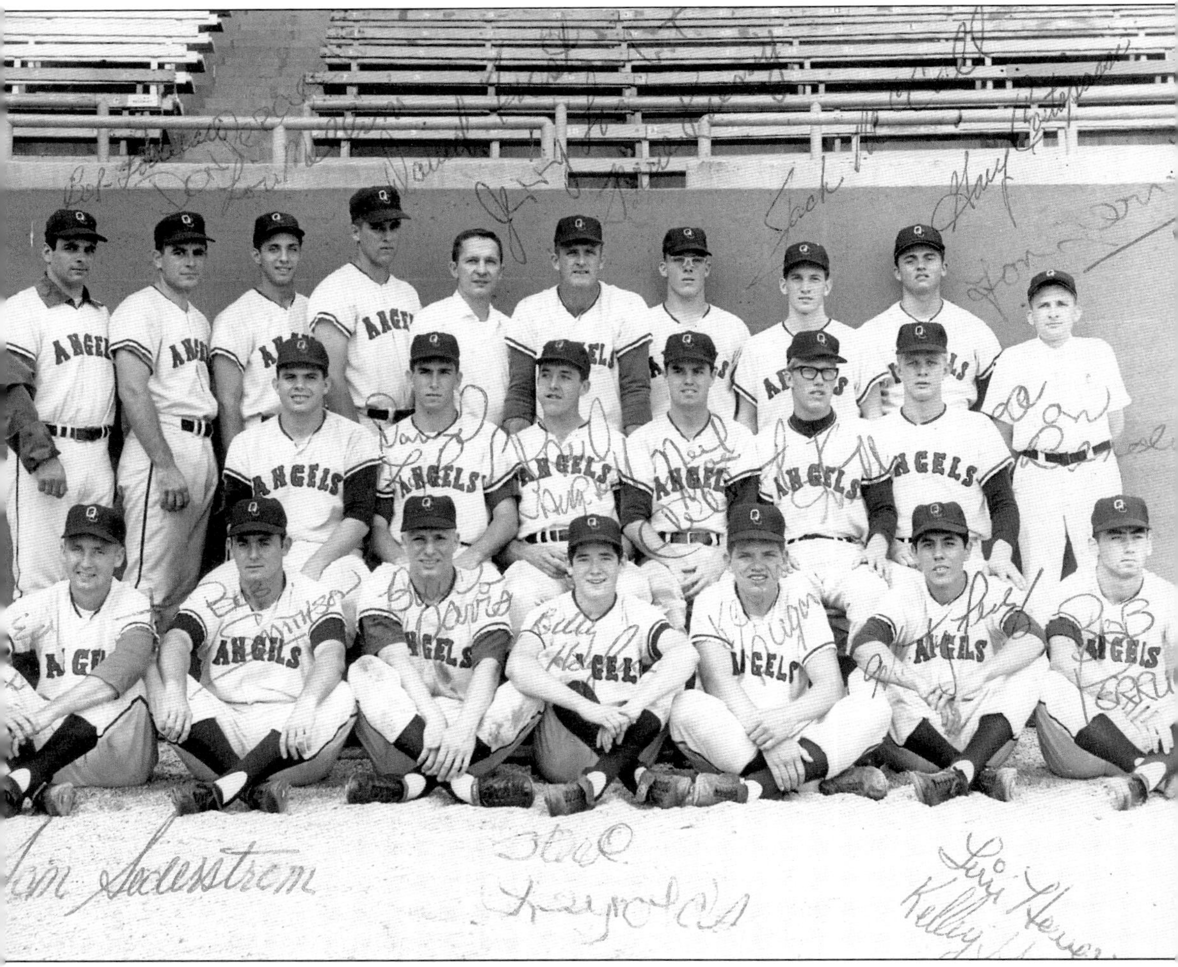

Fred Koenig's first Quad Cities club finished the 1967 season in third place overall, with a record of 69 wins and 59 losses. "I think the season was a success," Koenig told John O'Donnell. "I particularly liked the improvement shown by our players. I can readily say that they tried hard to learn the game of baseball, and they put out to the best of their ability."

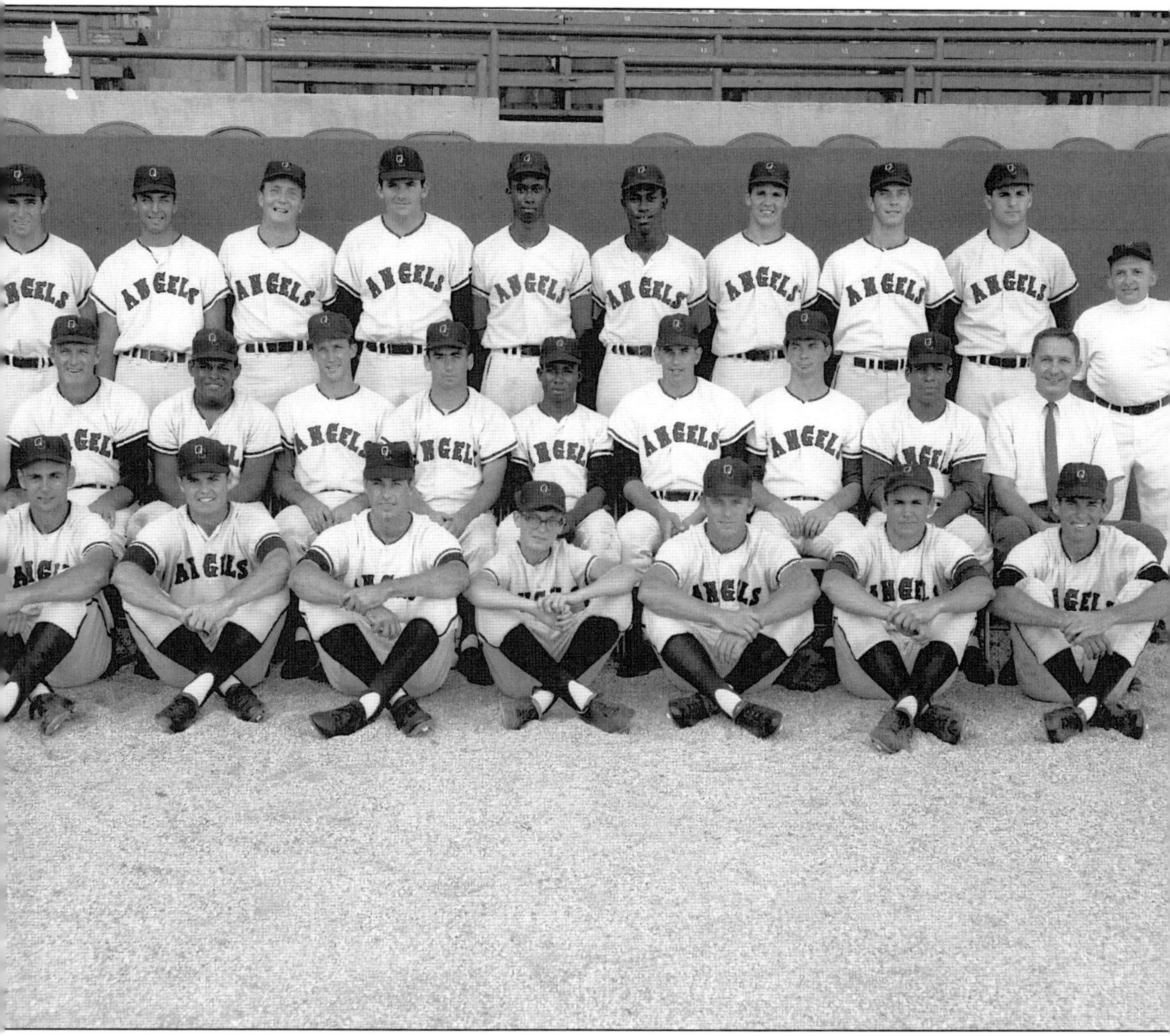

Since joining the Midwest League in 1960, Quad Cities hadn't even won a divisional title. The club finally broke through in 1968, winning the first-half title, then besting Decatur, two games to one, in the Midwest League Championship.

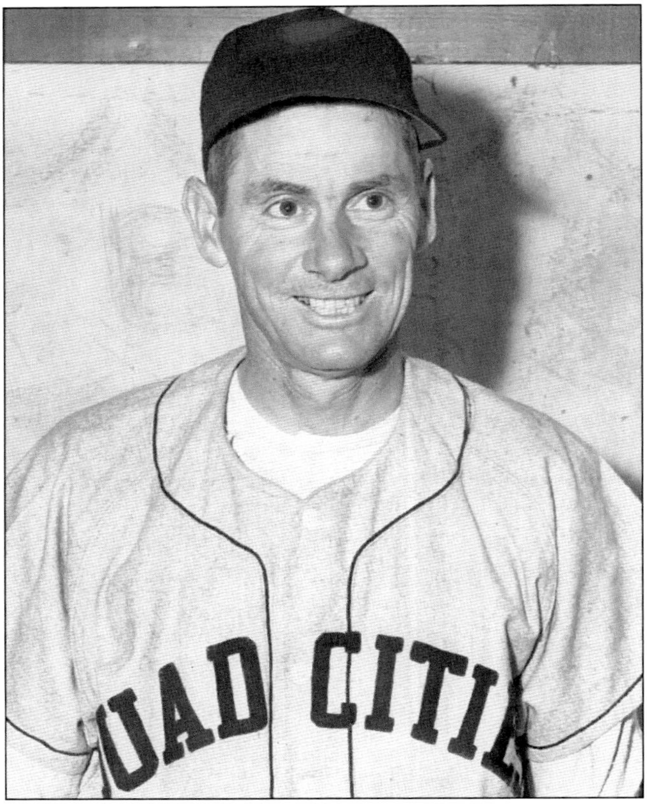

The idea of inviting players over for a meal after a winning streak originated with manager Marv Olson (1950-51). Olson and his wife would invite seven players to dinner every time the team had a 7-game winning streak (unfortunately, the club had only one such streak during his tenure).

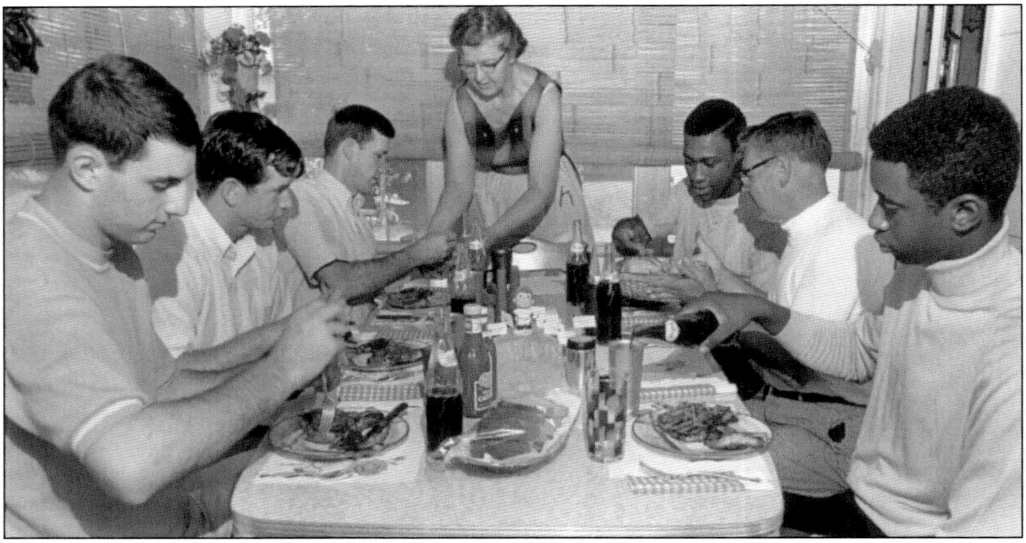

Dorothy and Frank Wulf picked up the tradition, although they only required the team to win five games to earn the meal. Pitchers Marty Pavlik and Don Richards, along with third baseman Steve Schneider, right fielder Don Cunnigan, and first baseman Dayle Campbell enjoy some home cooking.

A one-pound T-bone steak was the main course of the Wulf's cookouts—definitely a special treat for players on a limited budget.

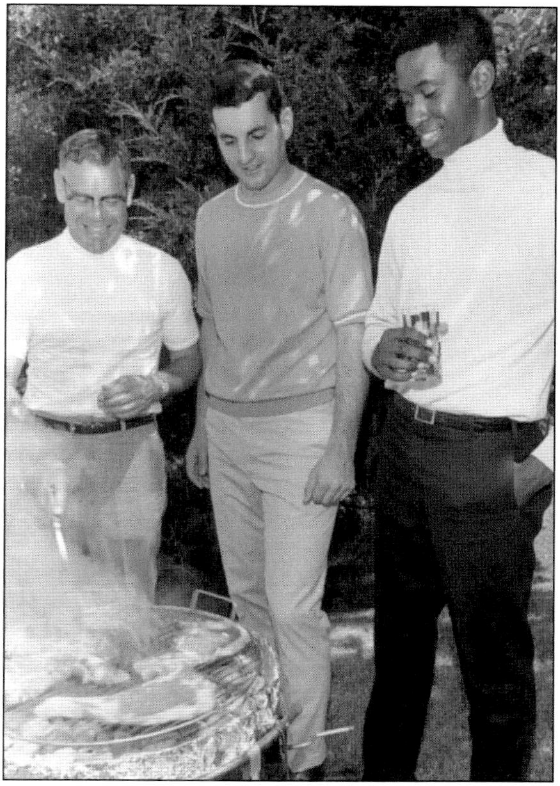

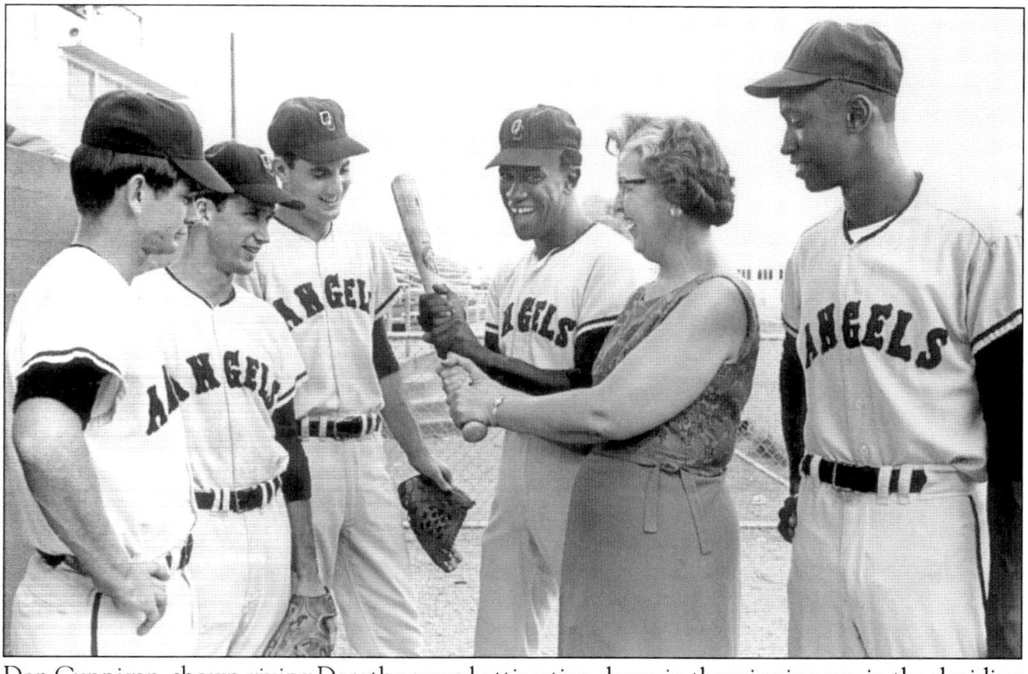

Don Cunnigan, shown giving Dorothy some batting tips, drove in the winning run in the deciding game of the league championship series. Don Richards (far left) picked up the win in relief as the Angels topped Decatur 3-1 to claim Quad Cities first Midwest League Playoff Title.

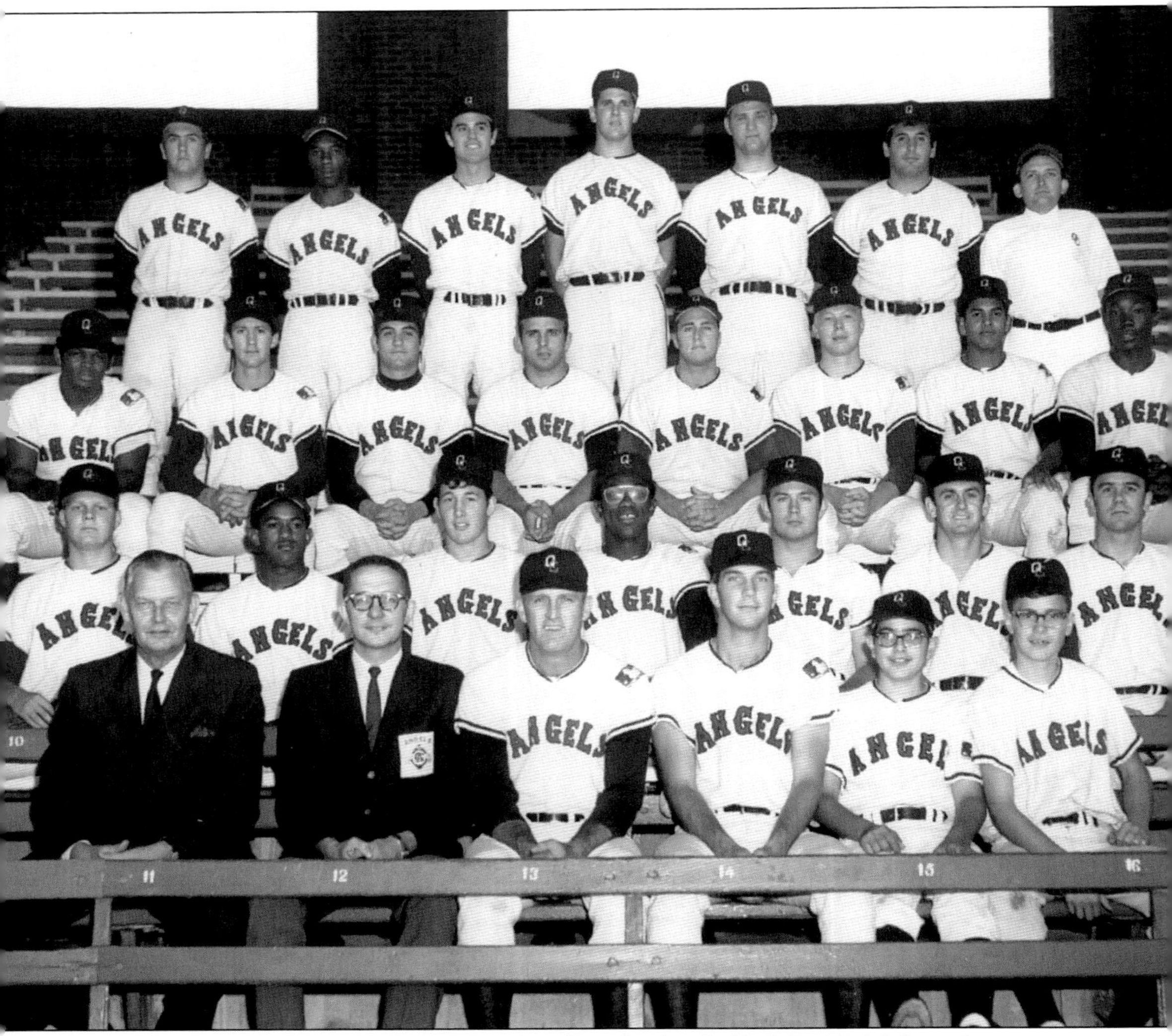

Fred Koenig's last Angels squad played well in the first half of the '69 Midwest League season, finishing in a first-place tie with Appleton. To break the deadlock, the first second-half meeting between Quad Cities and Appleton on July 16 doubled as a first-half tiebreaker. The teams battled for 16 innings in Appleton, with the Foxes finally pulling out a 4-3 win over the Angels.

In an annual promotion, the club gave away a car, with the manager drawing the winning ticket. Dorothy Wulf once won a Buick when Chuck Tanner drew her name. Here, Fred Koenig announces the winner at the 1969 home finale.

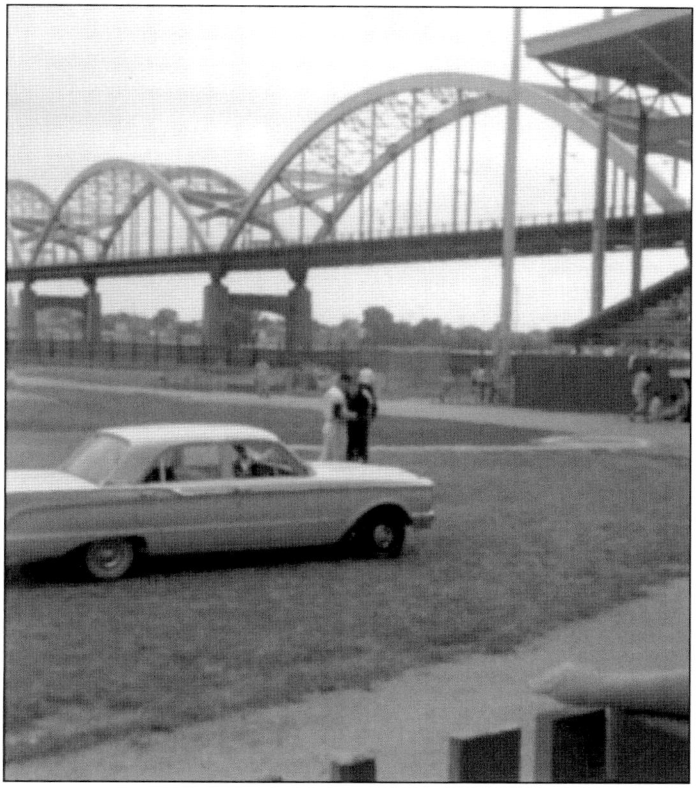

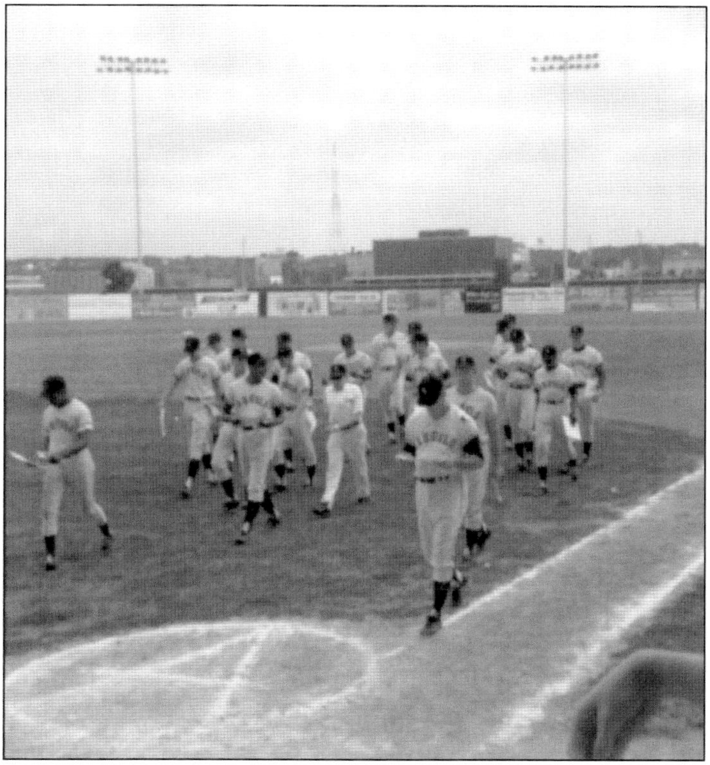

The members of the '69 Angels are made "honorary citizens" of the Quad Cities at the home finale.

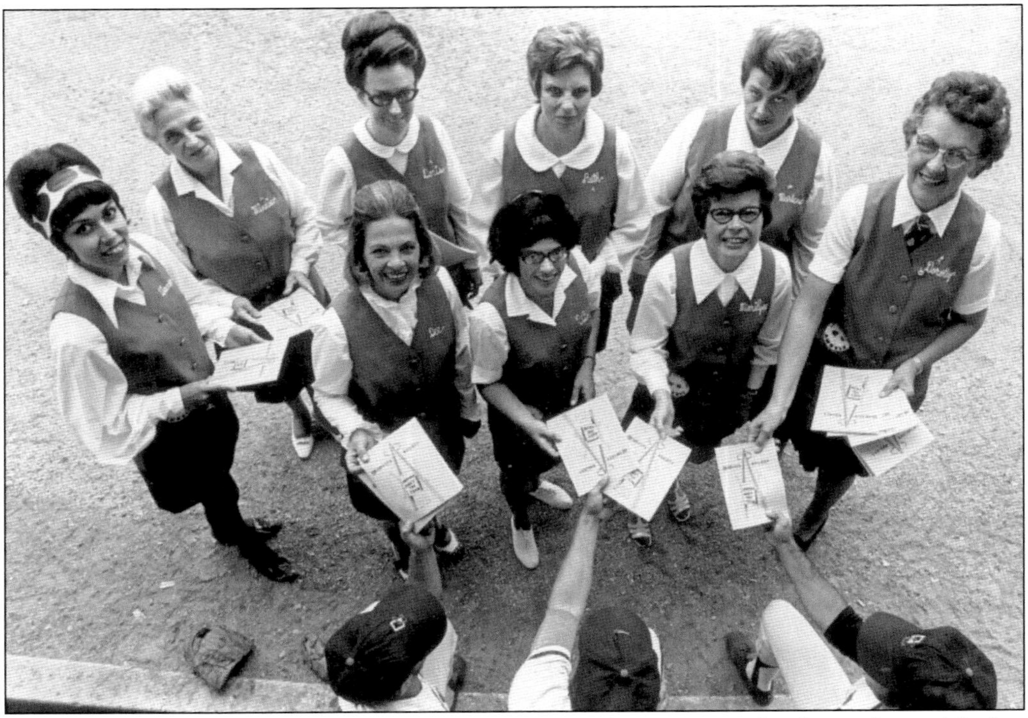

Formed in 1965, the Ladies Night Committee organized promotions for the traditional Ladies Night on Tuesdays at the Stadium. In addition, the committee also acted as "ministering angels" to the young ballplayers and their wives.

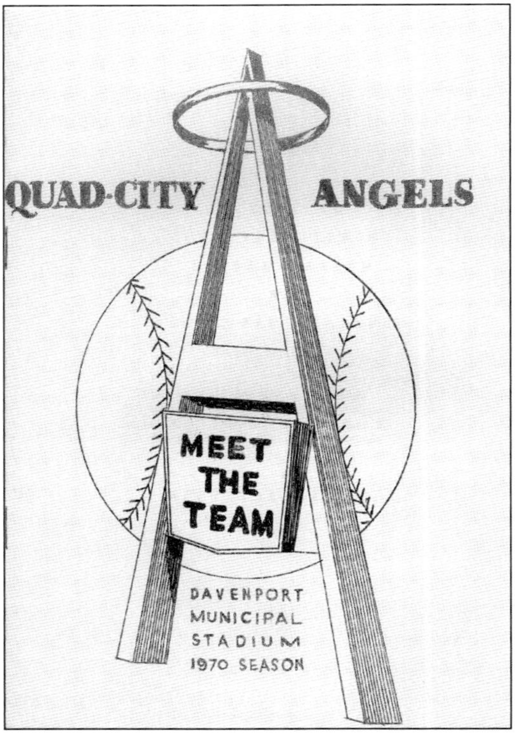

A special project of the 1970 Ladies Night Committee was a book of player bios, free to anyone who requested it.

Players' wives are pictured here with the Ladys Night Committee. A cookbook was a popular project of the Ladies Night Committee. It contained recipes like Ranger's Potato Casserole.

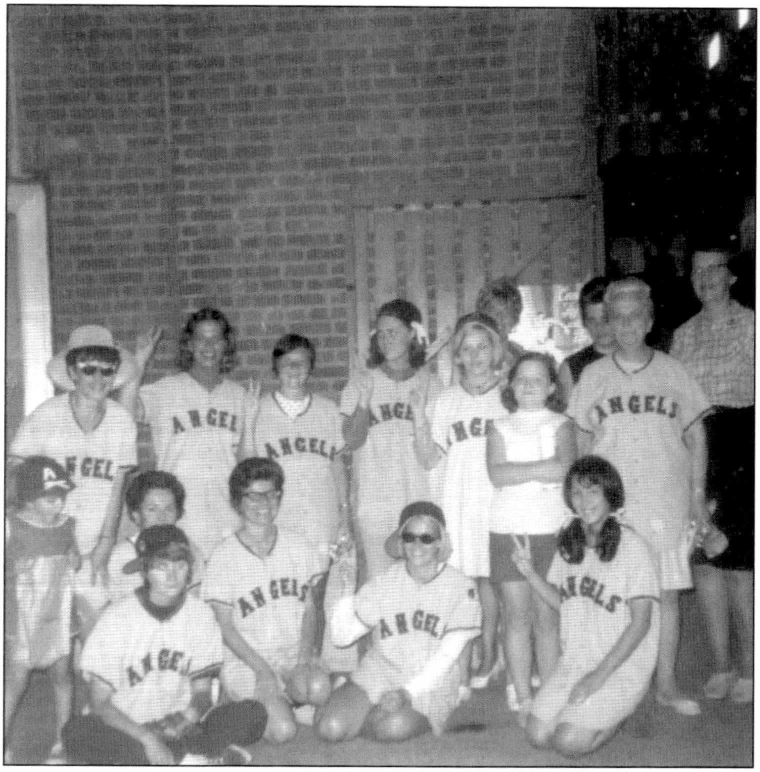

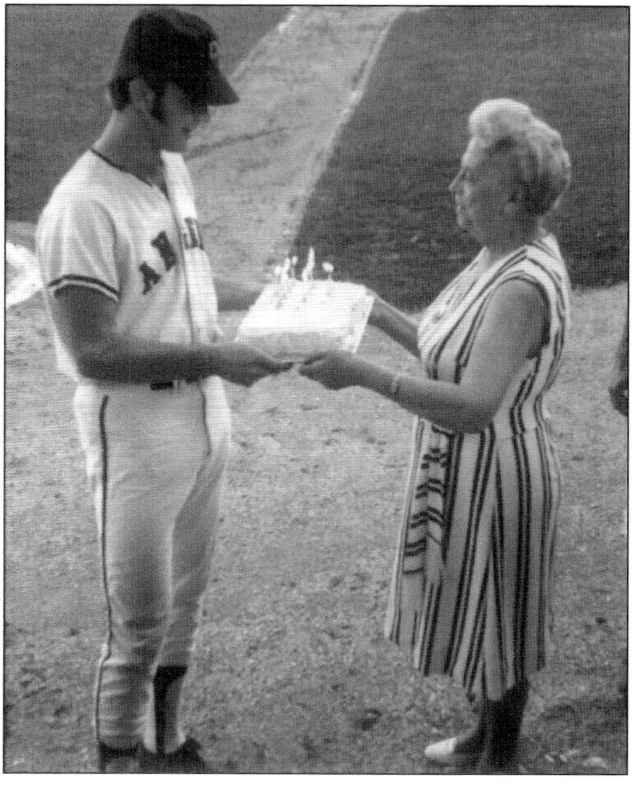

Ladies Committee member Minnie Nuest presents pitcher Jeff Pryor with a birthday cake, July 30, 1970.

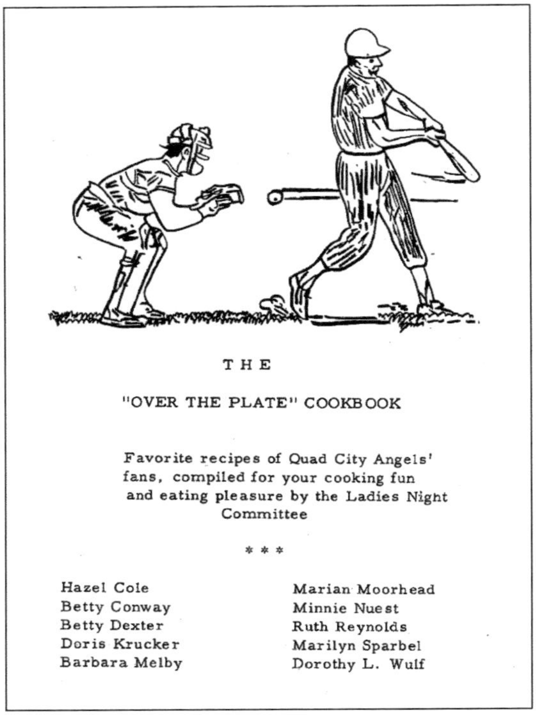

THE

"OVER THE PLATE" COOKBOOK

Favorite recipes of Quad City Angels' fans, compiled for your cooking fun and eating pleasure by the Ladies Night Committee

* * *

Hazel Cole	Marian Moorhead
Betty Conway	Minnie Nuest
Betty Dexter	Ruth Reynolds
Doris Krucker	Marilyn Sparbel
Barbara Melby	Dorothy L. Wulf

A baseball theme (naturally) ran through the recipes of the cookbook, titled *Over the Plate*.

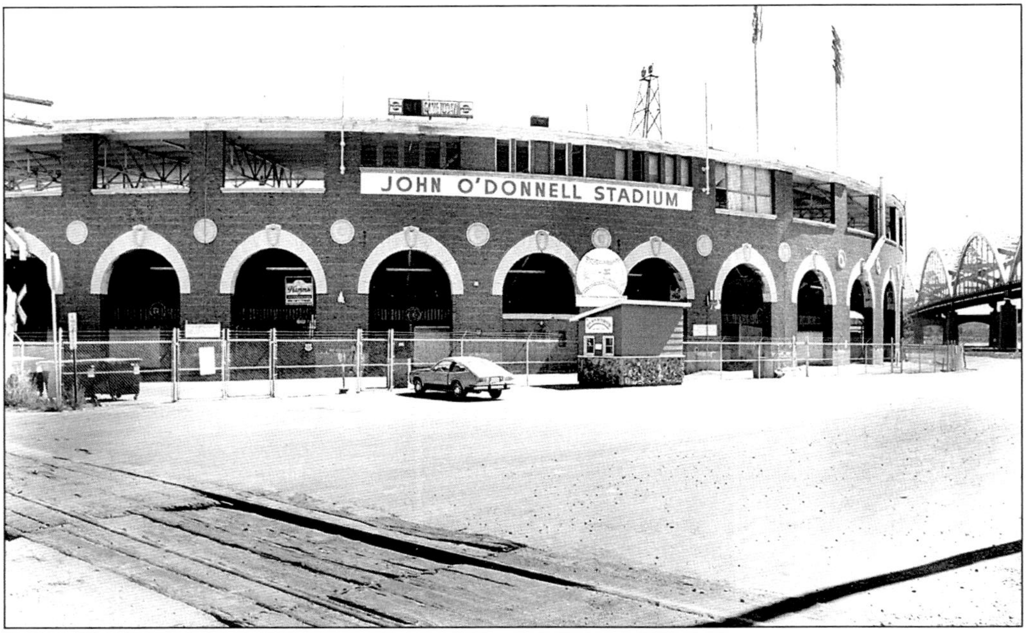

On May 26, 1971, the "Municipal Stadium" sign outside the ballpark was replaced by a new sign proclaiming "John O'Donnell Stadium," in honor of the longtime local sports editor who passed away just before the start of the 1970 season.

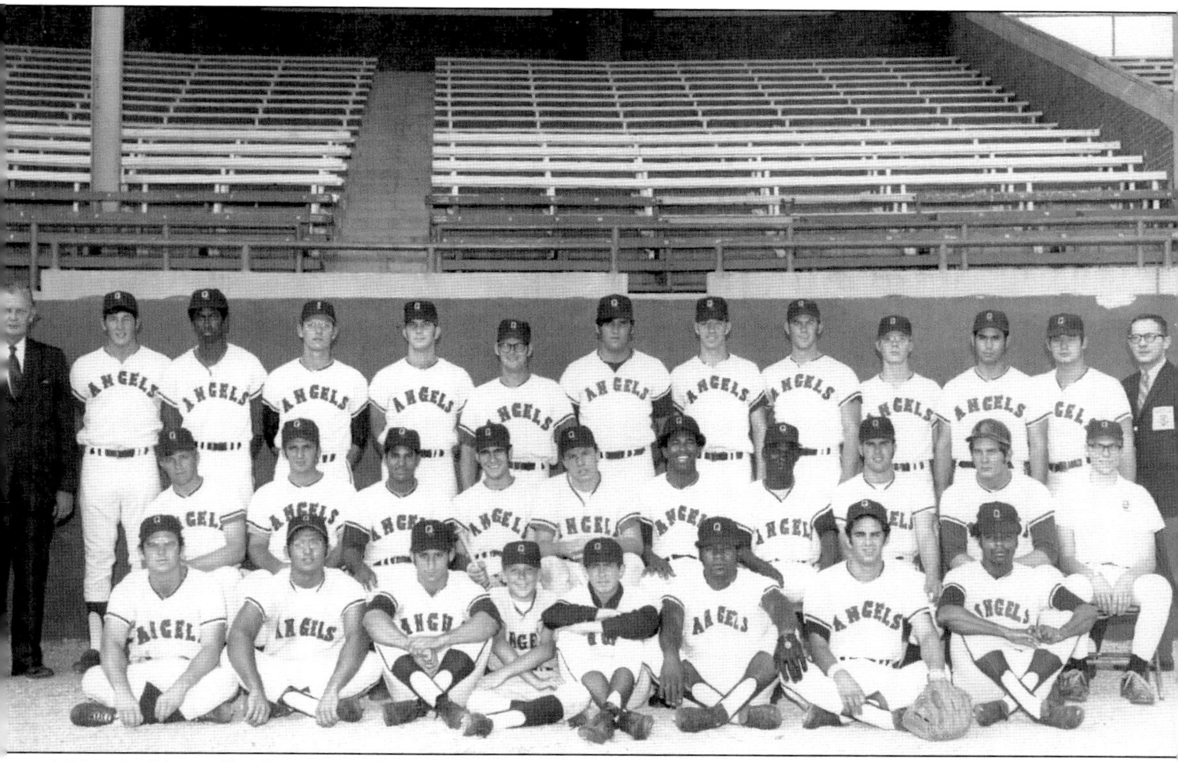

Mike Stubbins (back row, sixth from left) came on board as manager of the 1970 Angels. The club engaged in a thrilling duel with Decatur for the second-half pennant, and the two teams finished with identical 36-26 records at the end of the half. Quad Cities won the one-game playoff, 8-5, to advance to the finals against Quincy, where the first-half champs dispatched the Angels, two games to none.

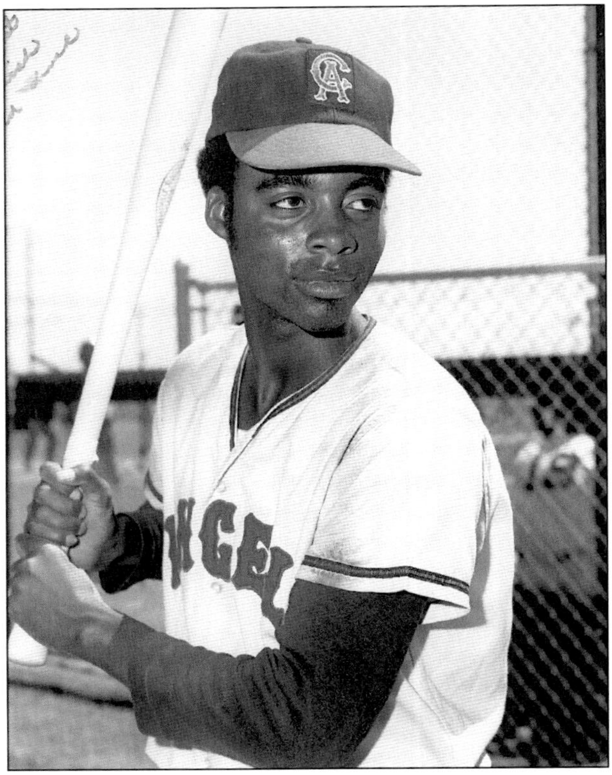

As an outfielder for the 1970 Angels, Roger Minor led the league with 65 stolen bases, despite a batting average of only .206. Midway through the '71 season, the Angels converted Minor to shortstop, and he returned to Quad Cities, improving his batting average to .306.

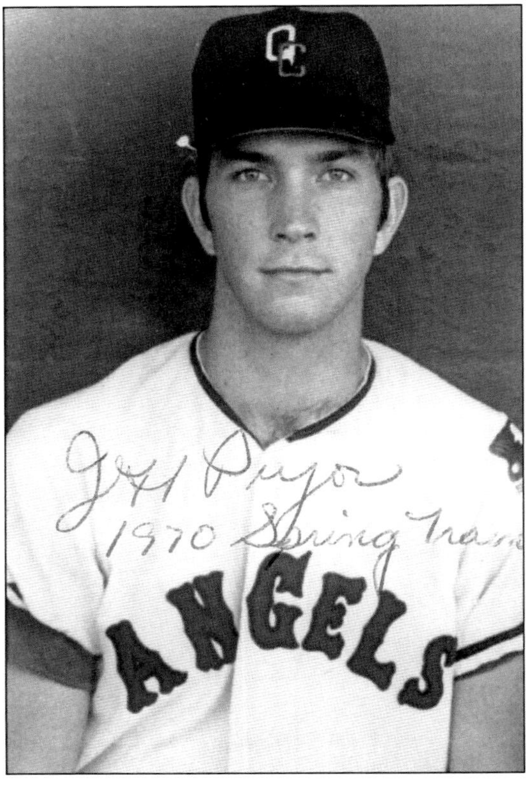

Jeff Pryor pitched for the Angels in 1969 and 1970. After leading the league with 98 striketouts in the first half of the 1970 season, Pryor was named to the Midwest League All-Star team.

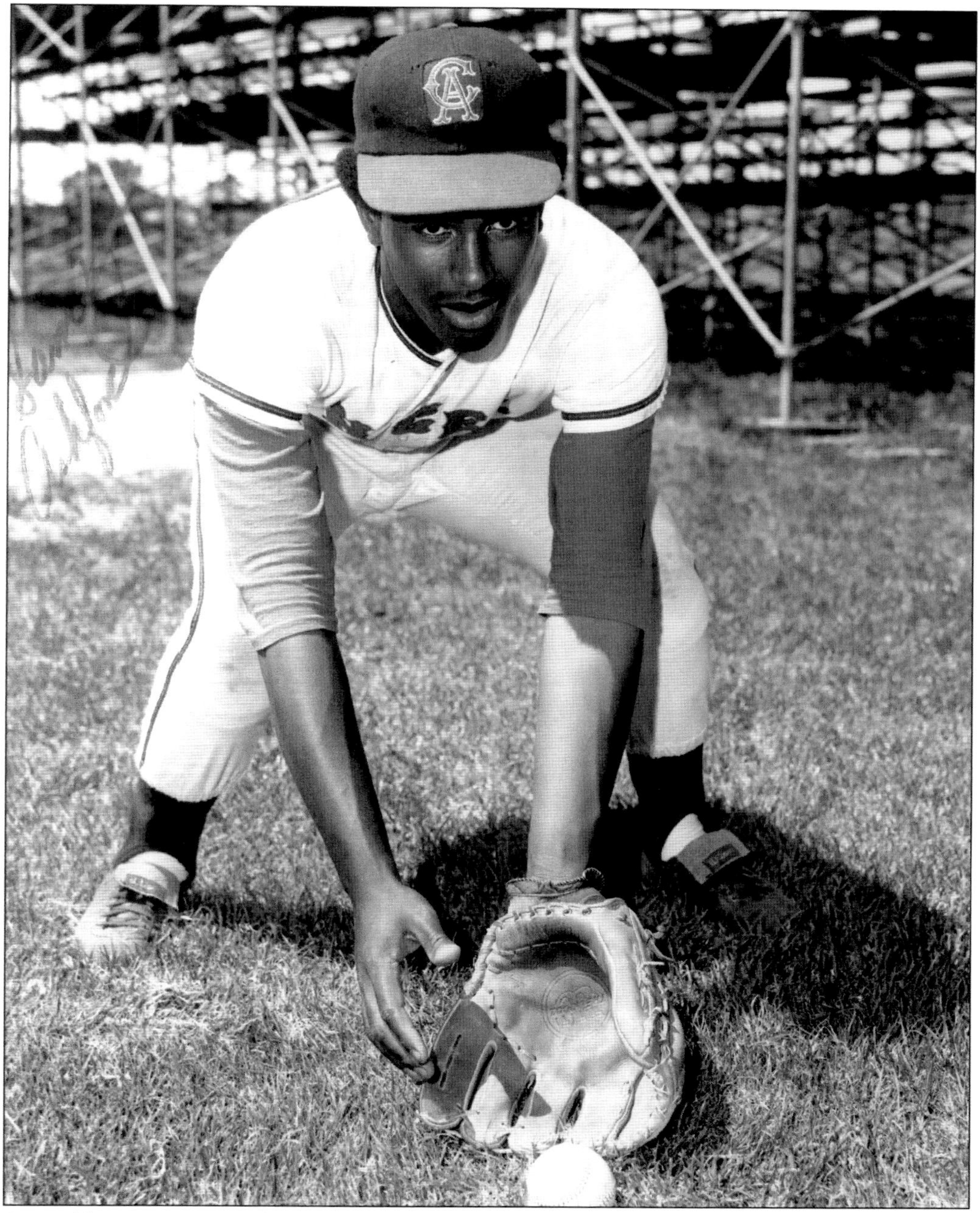

Second baseman Sam Ashford was a fixture on the 1970 and 1971 Quad Cities playoff teams. He was named the Midwest League's top second baseman in 1970, batting .270 with 8 home runs and 57 RBI. Ashford did not make the All-Star team in 1971, but his 17 home runs and team-leading 74 RBI helped the Angels to a Midwest League title.

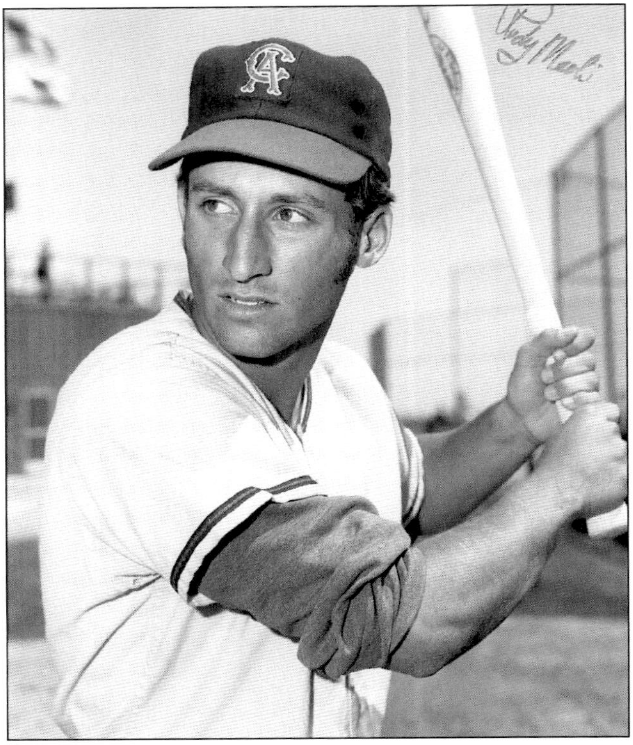

Shortstop Rudy Meoli led the Midwest League with 11 triples in 1970. In six seasons with the California Angels, Chicago Cubs, and Philadephia Phillies, Meoli hit just four three-baggers.

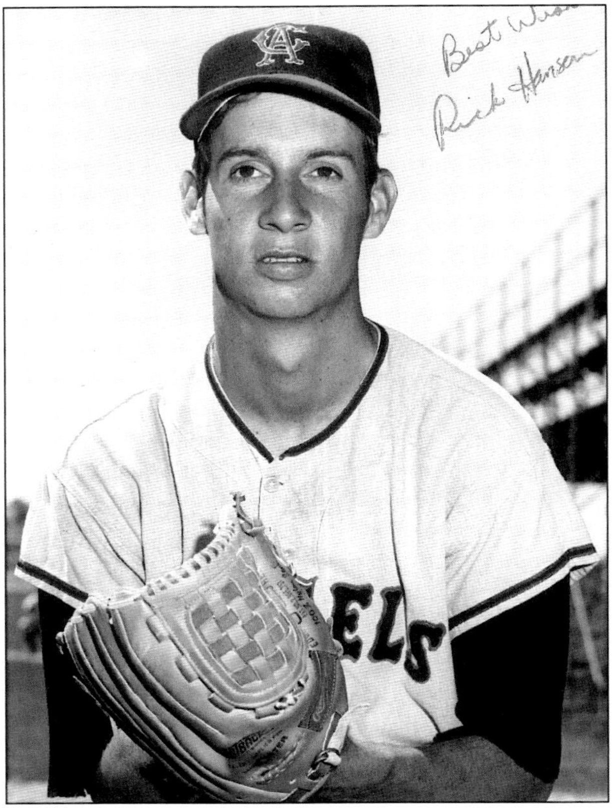

As in the major leagues during the same era, pitching was the name of the game in the Midwest League in 1970. Rick Young's record was only 4-4, despite an ERA of 2.54, while teammate Rick Hanson managed just a 5-4 record with a 2.70 ERA.

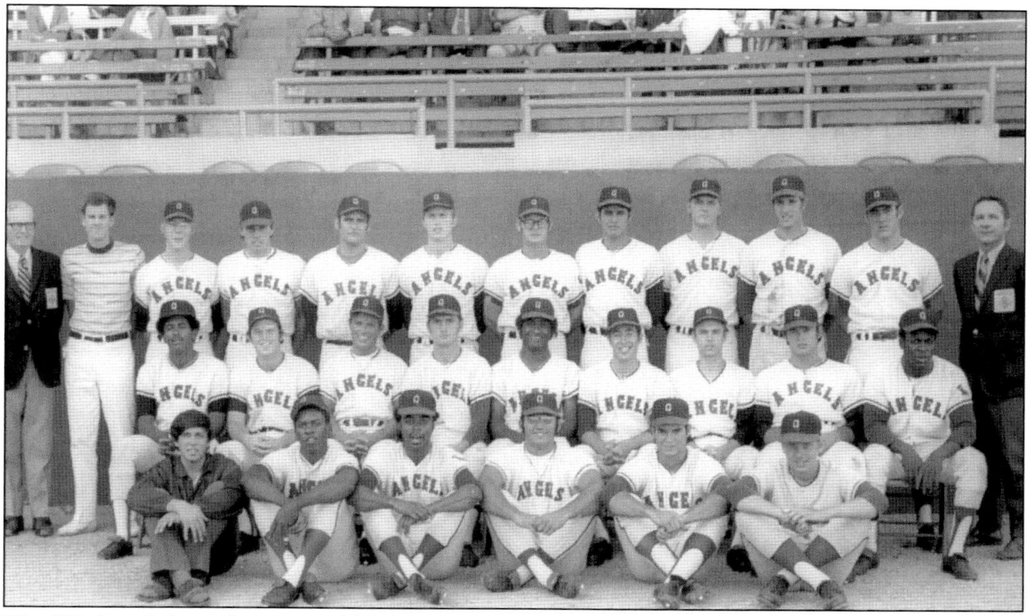

The '71 Angels brought a second Midwest League pennant to the Quad Cities and turned in some outstanding pitching performances along the way. On May 4, Sid Monge (back row, fifth from right) struck out 11 on the way to a no-hitter at Cedar Rapids. The following night, starter Larry Dierks (back row, fifth from left) and two relievers joined forces in a one-hitter against Clinton.

In a pregame ceremony on May 26, 1971, Davenport's mayor, John Jebens, officially rechristened the ballpark in honor of John O'Donnell. O'Donnell's son, John, and widow, Virgenette, accepted the proclamation from Mayor Jebens. "John witnessed more sports events, either as a writer or an official, than any other person in this stadium which now bears his name," wrote *Times-Democrat* colleague, Jerry Jurgens.

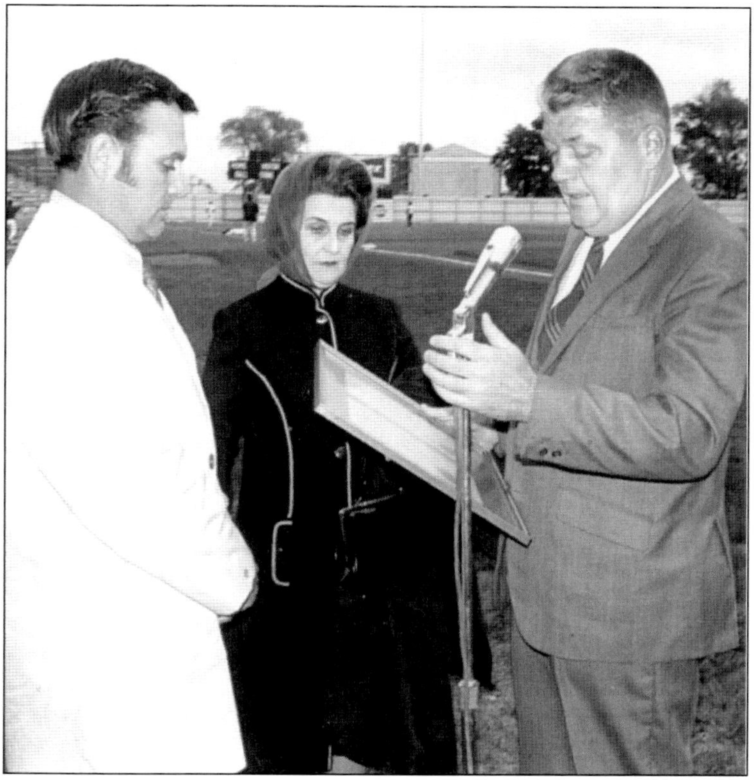

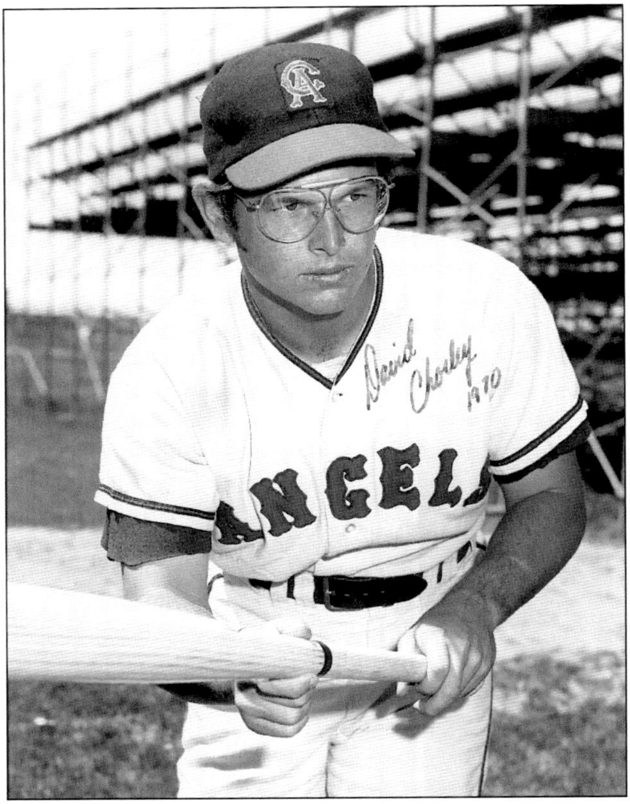

First baseman Dave Chorley was the hero of the 1971 Midwest League Finals. His home run in the sixth inning of the third game gave Quad Cities the lead, and his leaping grab of a line drive for the final out sealed a 3-2 win over Appleton.

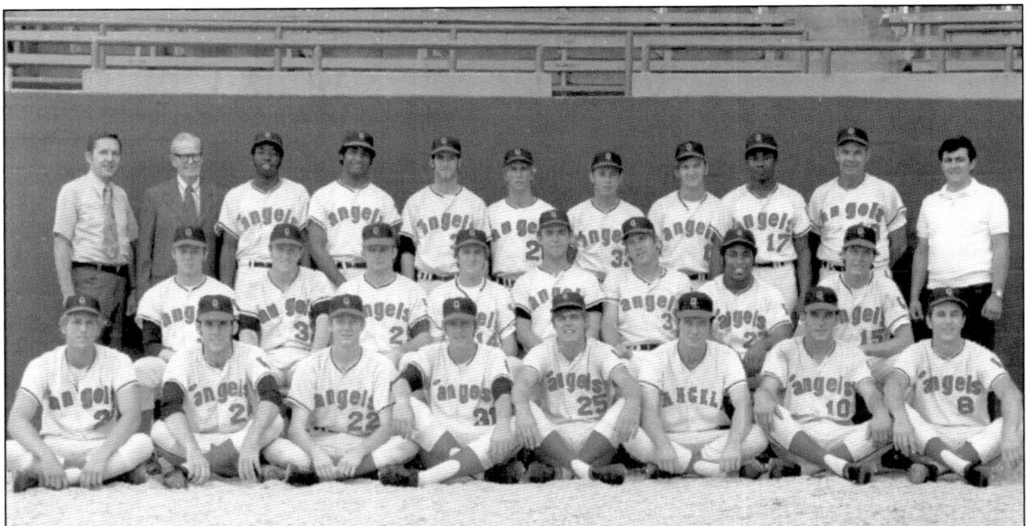

Cold, wet weather in the early part of the season led to low attendance figures in 1972: only 67,108 turned out to see the Angels. The club posted a respectable overall record of 69-59, but failed to make the playoffs for the first time since 1967. One bright spot was the pitching of young Frank Tanana (#25, front row, fourth from right) who posted a 7-2 record with 2.83 ERA. He would make his major league debut the following year and go on to win 240 games in 21 big league seasons.

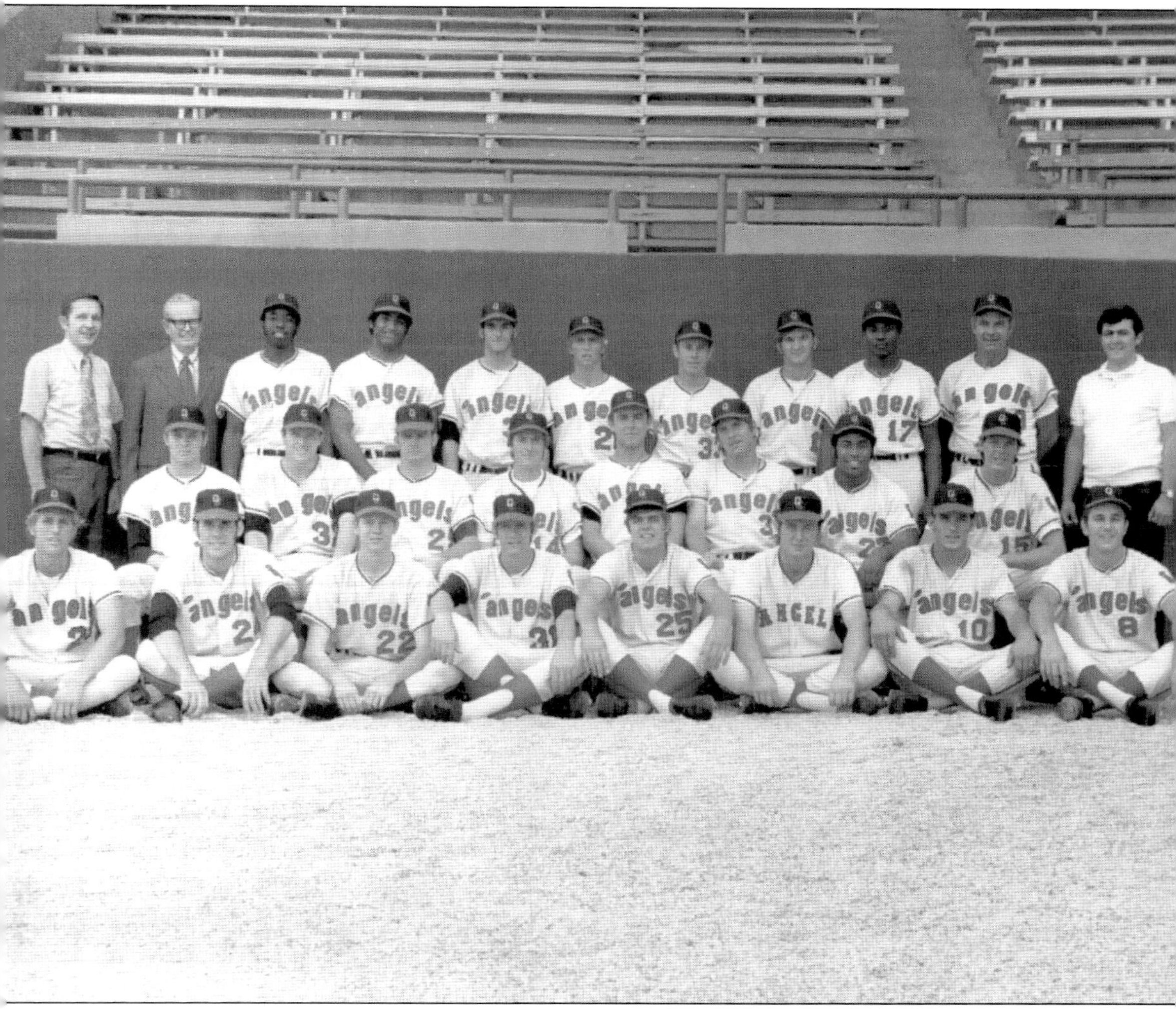

The 1973 season was not particularly memorable for either the Angels or for John O'Donnell Stadium. Floodwaters from the Mississippi forced some games to be moved to Northwest Park in Davenport, while other games were played in JOD with a temporary fence set up in right field to block the rising waters. Jerry Remy (front, third from left) was the Angels brightest star—the second baseman led the Midwest League with a .335 batting average. Remy's accomplishment was the first batting title for a Quad City player since the club became a member of the Midwest League in 1960.

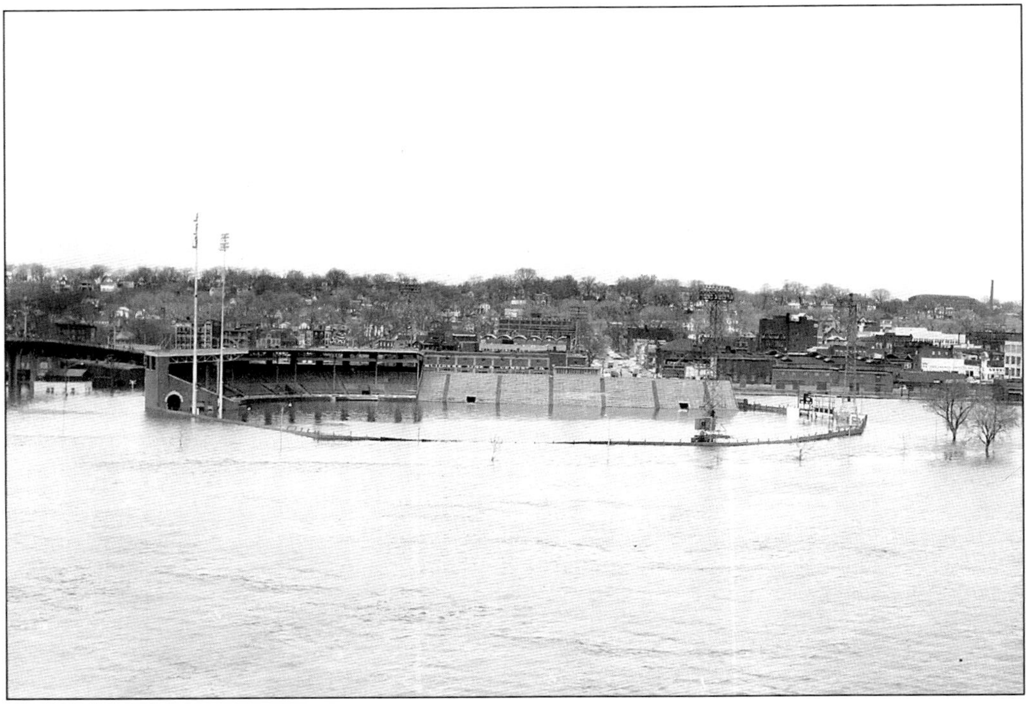

Davenport was growing accustomed to spring flooding at the historic ballpark.

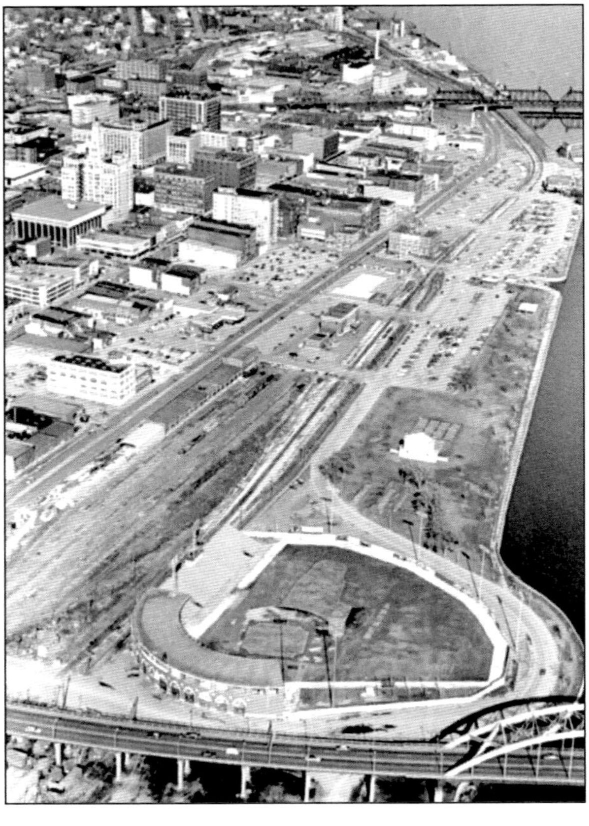

Viewed from the air, John O'Donnell Stadium has always been a jewel of the Davenport riverfront. With Centennial Bridge in the foreground and downtown Davenport in the background, the stadium is an attractive landmark for both residents and visitors.

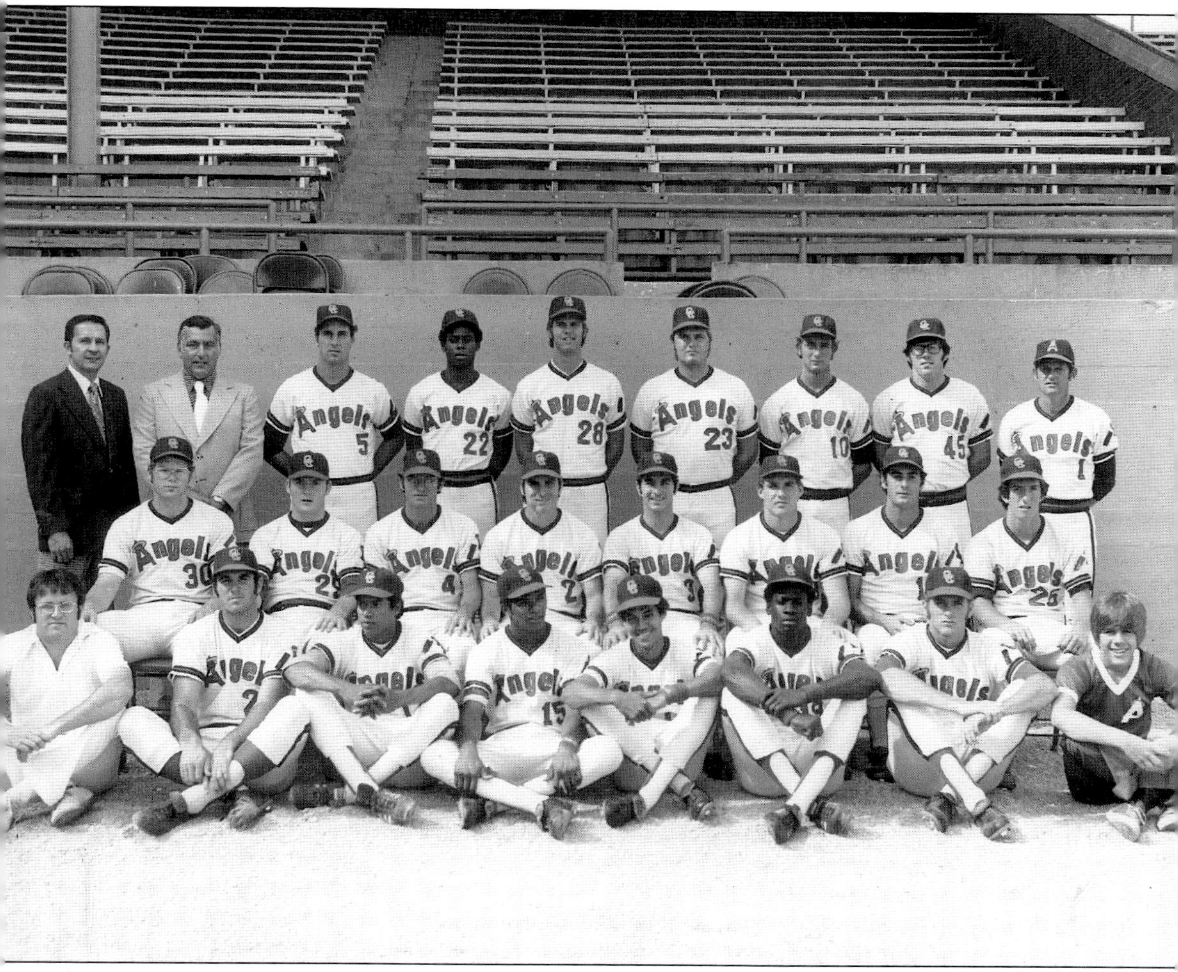

The Angels returned to the Midwest League playoffs in 1974 by winning a first-half title in the South Division. After splitting the first two games with Danville in the divisional playoffs, the Angels dropped a heartbreaker in the rubber game. Starter Steve Lacki (#5, standing, third from left) allowed only one hit, but Danville scratched out a run in the ninth to advance to the finals, 1-0.

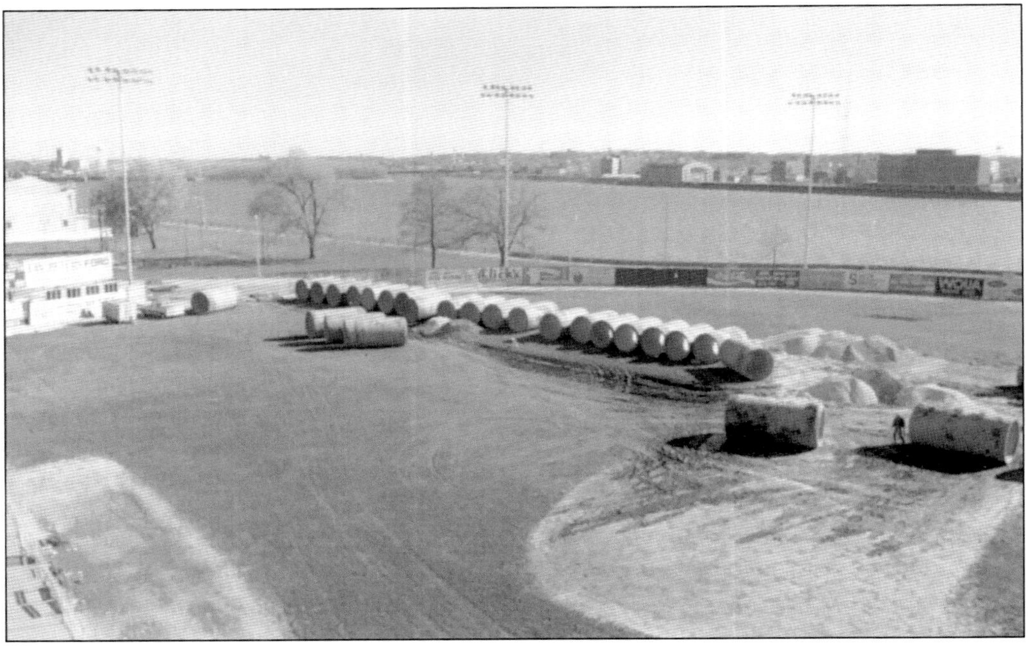

Flooding may have been a periodic problem for John O'Donnell Stadium, but in 1976, the opening of Quad Cities' home season was delayed by sewer line work that tore up the field. After shifting the scheduled home opener on April 17 to Clinton, the Angels were slated to kick off the home schedule on April 26. Pictured here, above and below, is the work in progress as the new sewer line is laid beneath the playing field.

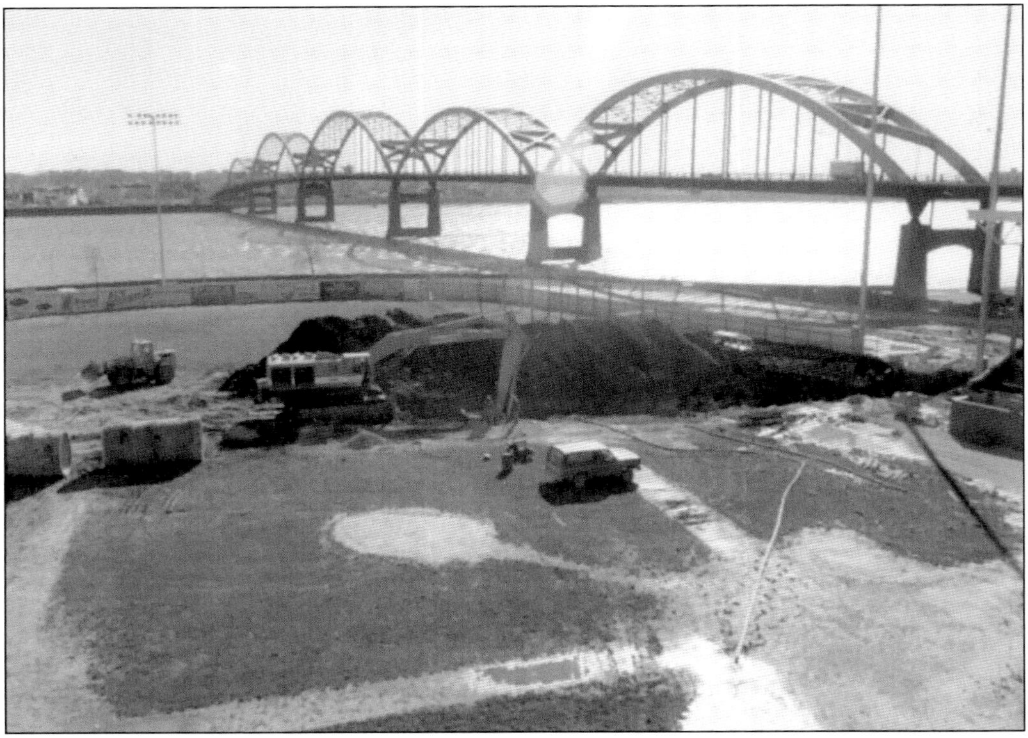

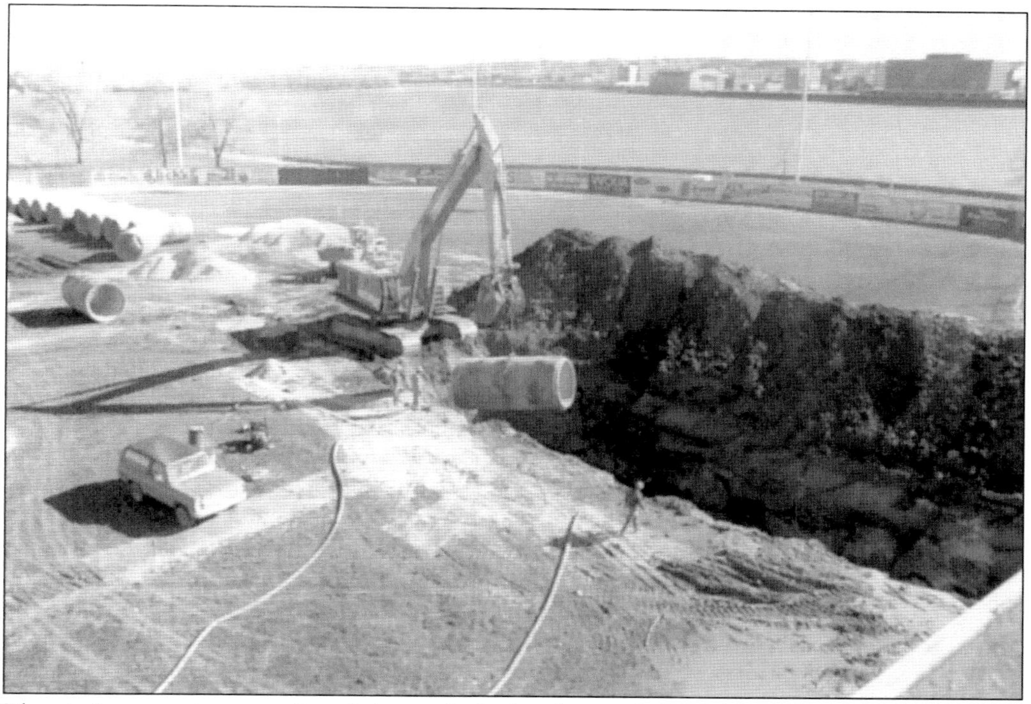

The city's sewer pipe runs directly beneath the baseline path from first to second base.

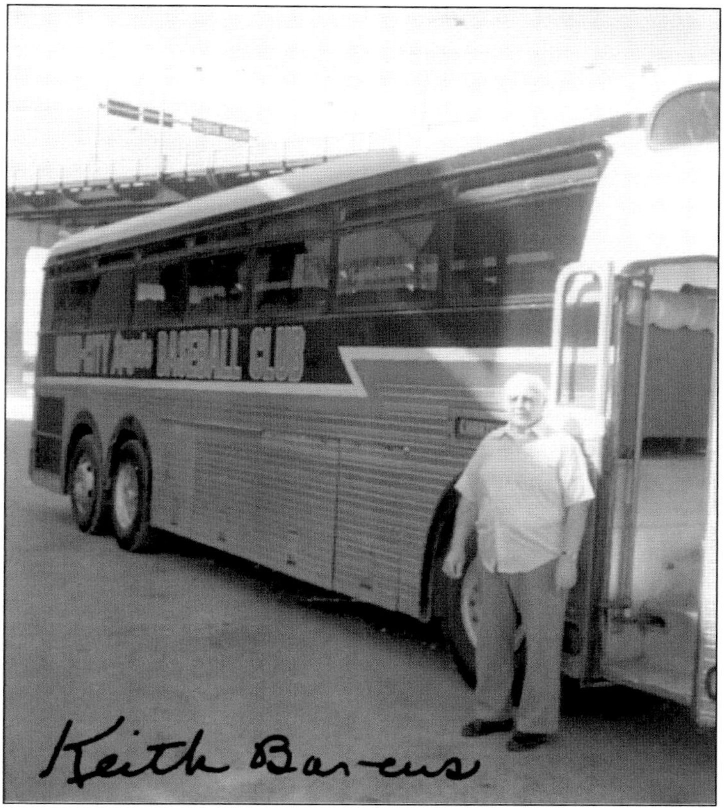

One thing never changes in the low minor leagues—the bus ride from town to town.

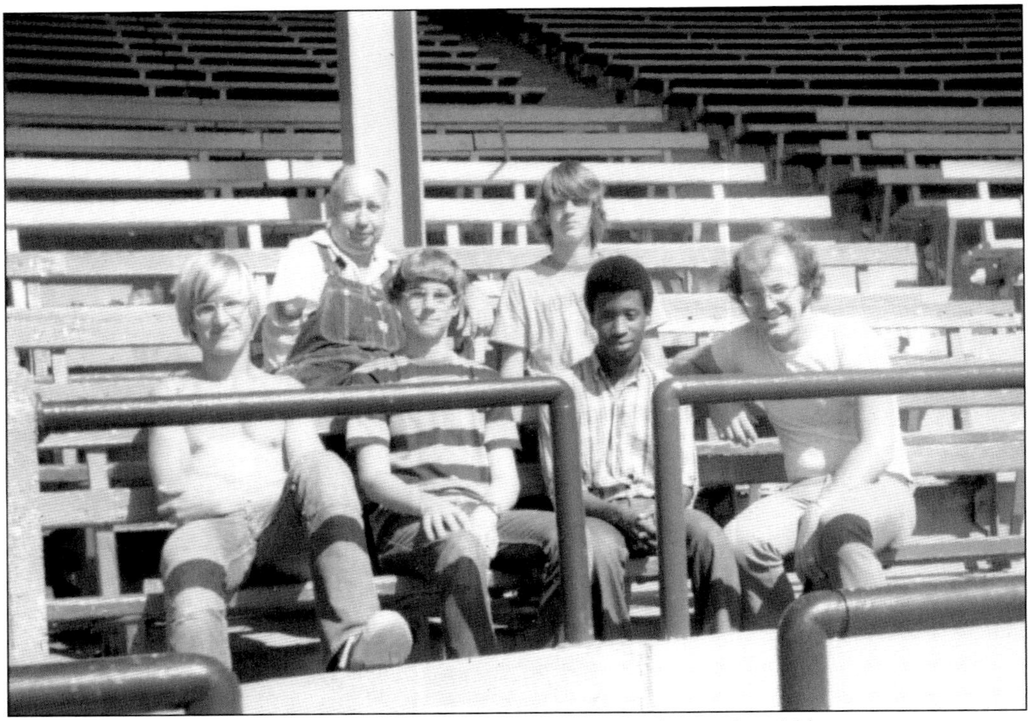

A 1976 John O'Donnell Stadium crew takes a moment to relax in the old box seats.

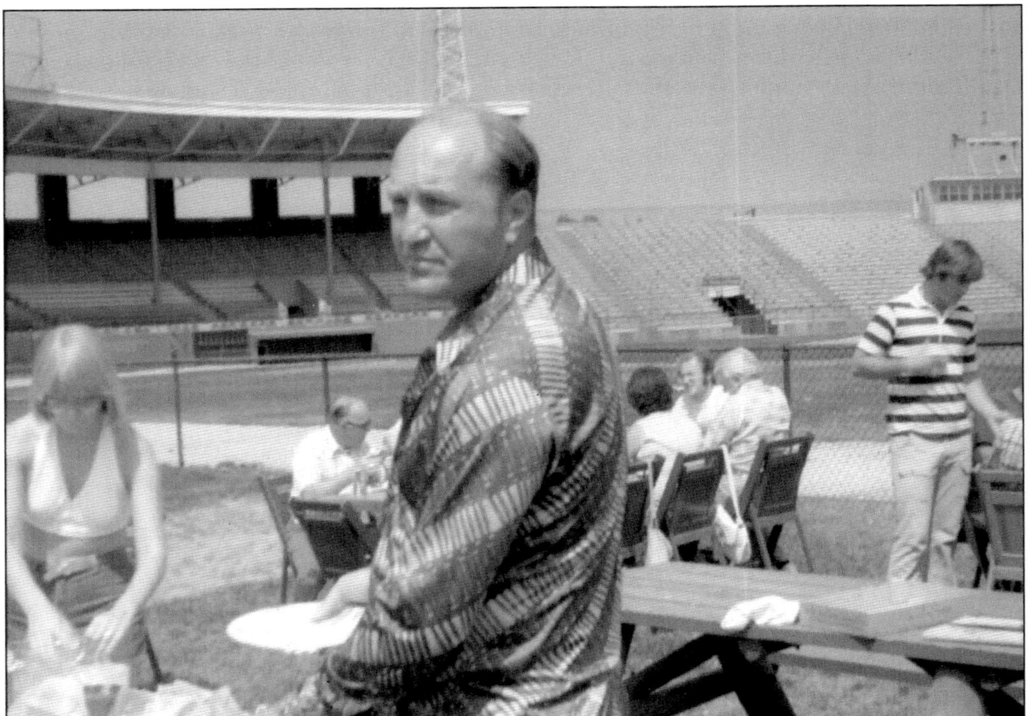

Manager Moose Stubing enjoys some Quad Cities hospitality at a post-game picnic. Over his right shoulder is the old structure of the left field stands, with the football press box at upper right.

The bicentennial-year season of the Quad City Angels started slowly; they finished the first half under .500 at 30-31, seven games behind Cedar Rapids. In the second half, the Angels dueled Cedar Rapids to a draw; both clubs posted 41-28 marks. Then the Angels beat Cedar Rapids 7-6 in the tiebreaker to decide a second-half Southern Division champion, and then blanked the Giants in a one-game divisional playoff, 6-0. In a rematch of the previous year's final, the Waterloo Royals again swept the Angels, with Dan Quisenberry beating Quad City in the deciding game.

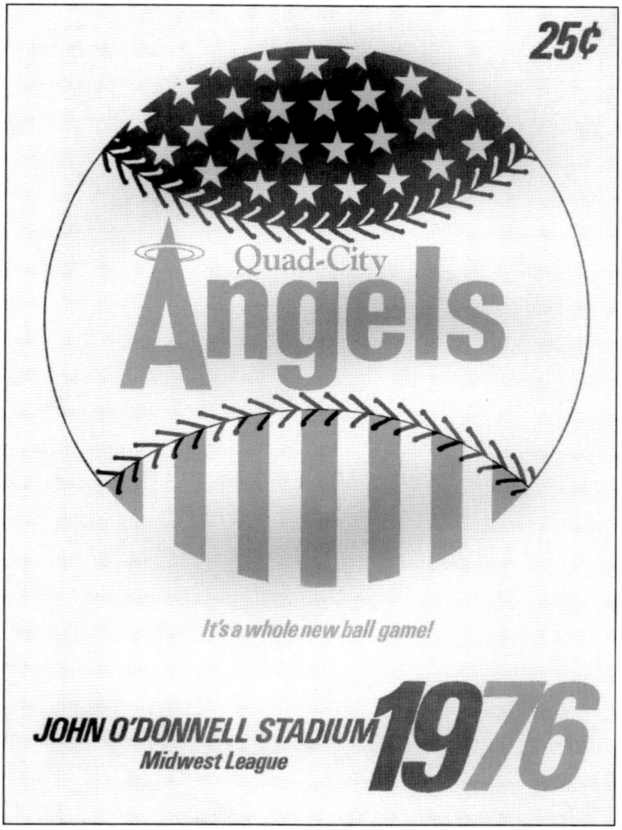

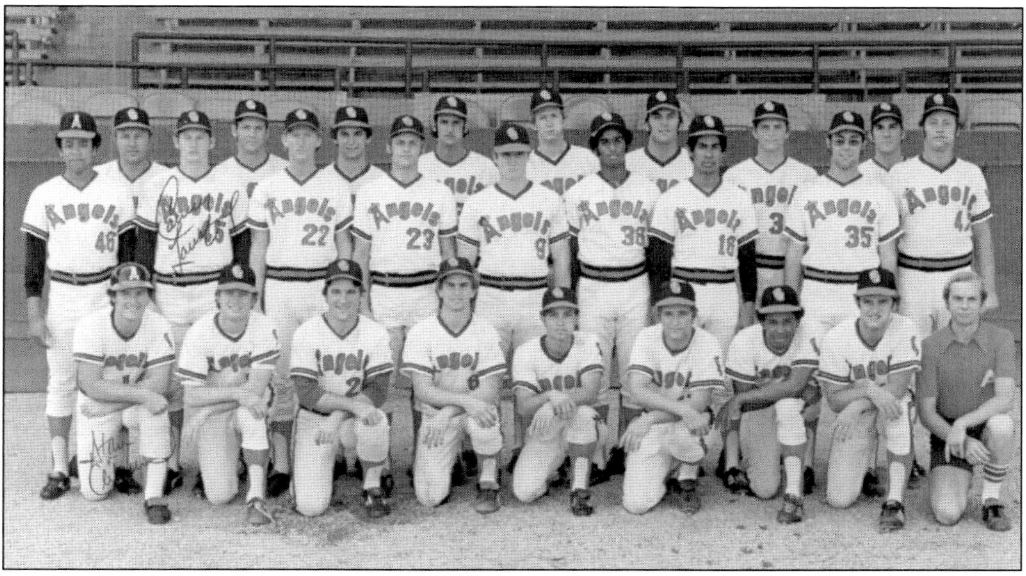

The 1976 Angels were keyed by the strong batting of Scott Moffit, Carney Lansford, and Dickie Thon, but the club's pitching staff also provided some highlights. Don Mraz (back row, third from right) no-hit the Wisconsin Rapids in a seven-inning game on May 31. United Township alumnus Scott Eddy (back row, third from left), the first Quad City native to play for the Angels in 15 years, also pitched on the '76 staff.

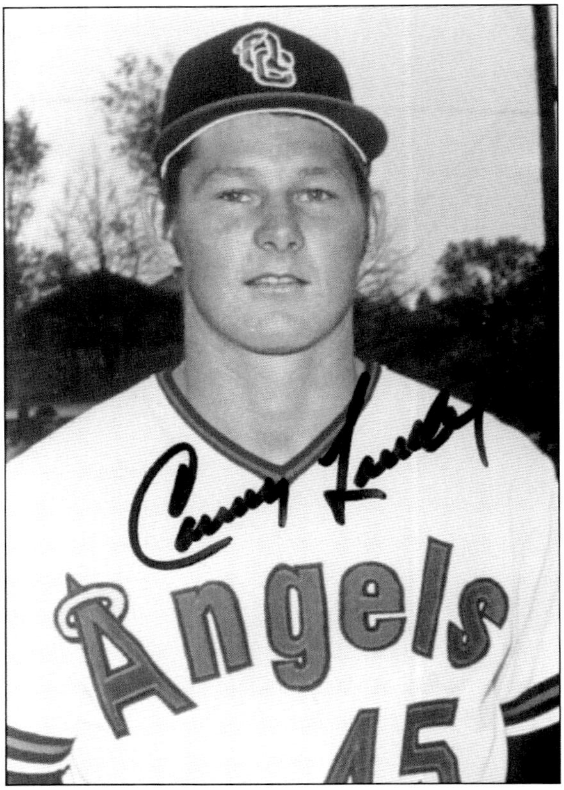

Lansford was a versatile member of the '76 Angels, spending time at both shortstop and third base. The future major league star had one streak of 8 consecutive at-bats with a hit, along with a 19-game hitting streak. He finished the year hitting .287 with 14 homers, 86 RBI, and 26 stolen bases.

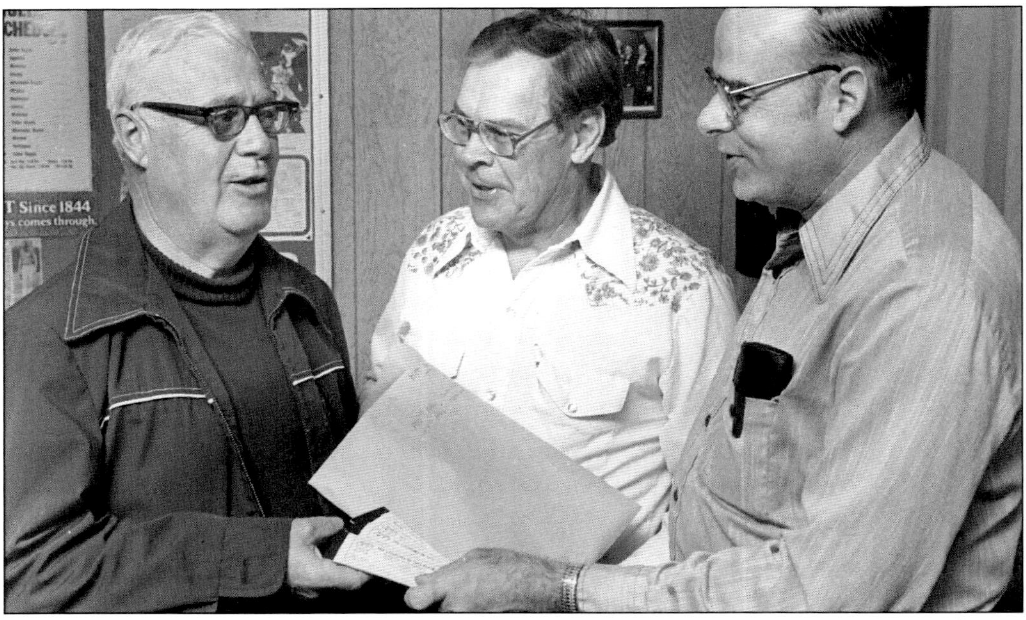

Despite a national trend of declining minor league attendance, the Quad City club posted some impressive ticket sales. Prior to the 1977 season, G.M. Harry Pells and the Quad City Board of Directors boosted preseason sales by one-third over the previous season. Club director William R. Montgomery receives the first block from Co-chairman Frank Wulf and Angels president Bob Mast. The Angels 1977 attendance of 108,662 easily topped the Midwest League.

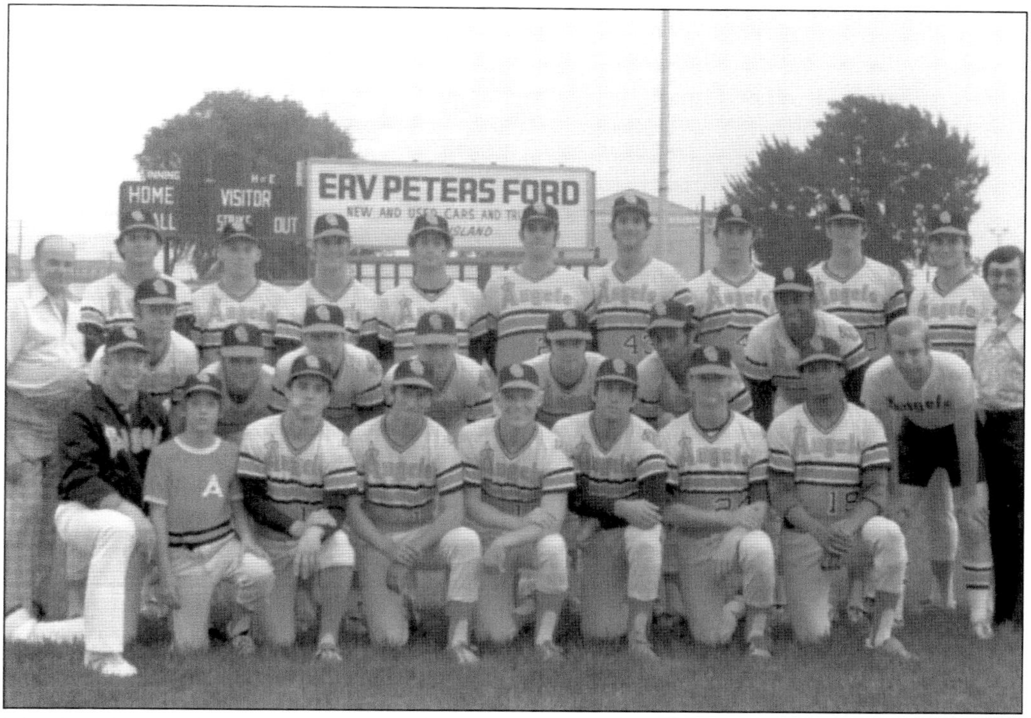

The '77 Angels failed to make the playoffs, but still played winning baseball. Pitcher Joel Crisler (top row, third from left) threw a seven-inning no-hitter in the second game of a July 9 doubleheader. The no-hitter was unusual, in that a third inning hit was changed to an error after the official scorer Marc Nesseler conferred with the umpires after the game. When asked later about his gem, Crisler remarked, "I didn't feel any pressure, because I didn't think I had a no-hitter going."

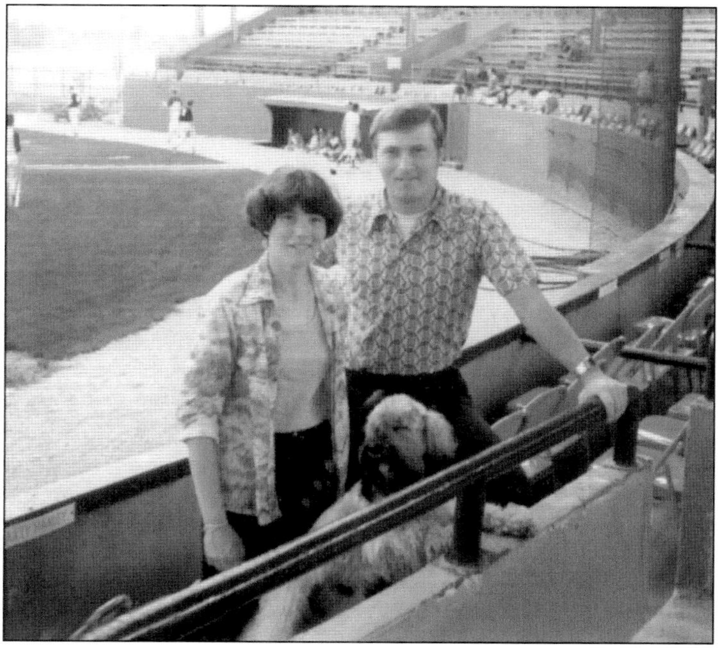

Chris Wren (left) was one of the first women to umpire in the minor leagues. She and umpiring partner Gerry Davis pose in John O'Donnell Stadium, 1977.

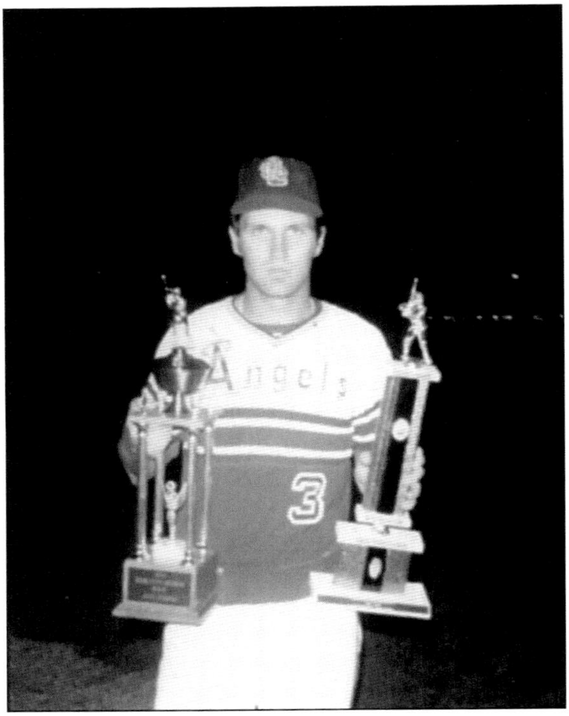

The Most Valuable Angel award for 1977 went to John Harris, who hit .318, and tied the QC Angels record for home runs (23) and RBI (93).

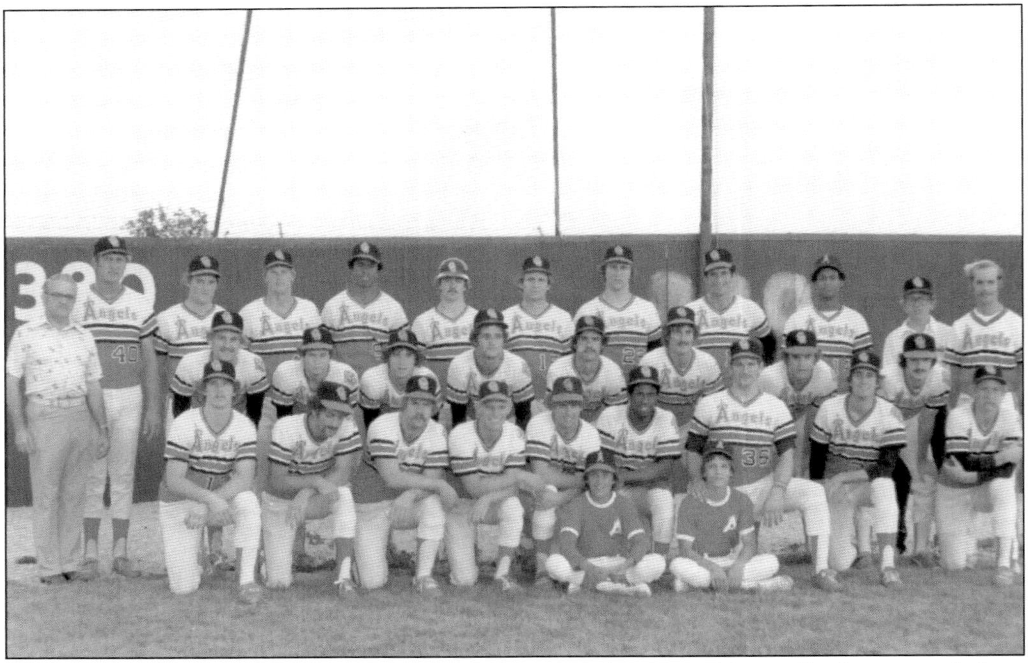

Only one year after John Harris' fine offensive year, catcher Brian Harper (back row, sixth from left) rewrote the local record book by hitting .293 with 24 home runs and 101 RBI. The 24 homers remains the Quad City record, while Harper's RBI total stood as the local benchmark until 1999, when Michael Restovich drove in 107. Cotton Nash's (back row, second from right) charges won the first-half title in the South Division, but Q.C. was eliminated in the first round of the playoffs by the Burlington Bees.

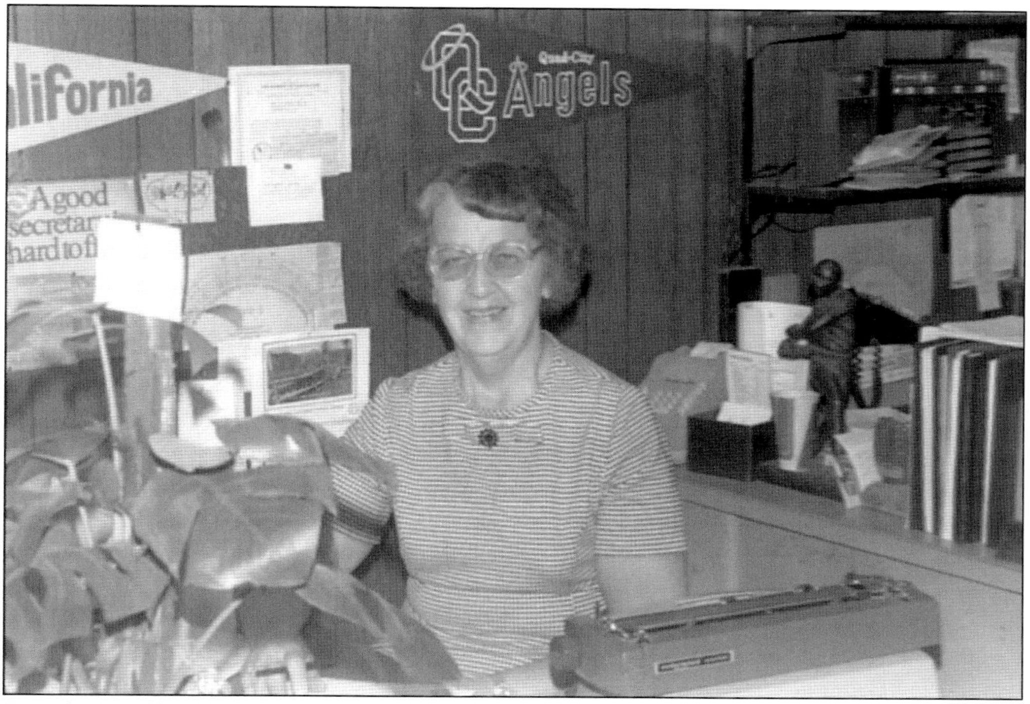

Dorothy Wulf works in the 1978 front office, decorated with Angels pennants. After the season, the pennants would come down, as California ended its 17-year affiliation with the Quad Cities.

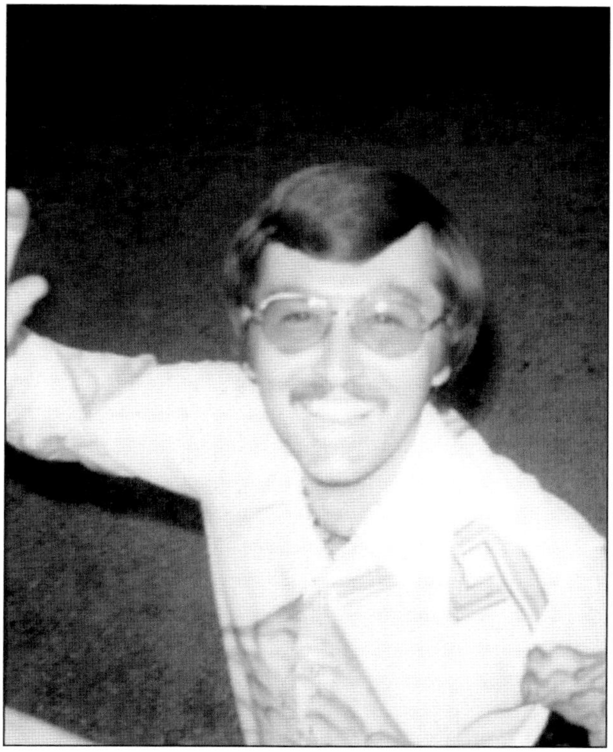

Hired by the local club in 1975, this former Rock Island insurance salesman, Harry Pells, quickly set about increasing the Angels attendance by staging numerous promotional events at the ballpark. His efforts paid off for both the club and himself, as *The Sporting News* tapped Pells as their "Class A Executive of the Year" for 1977.

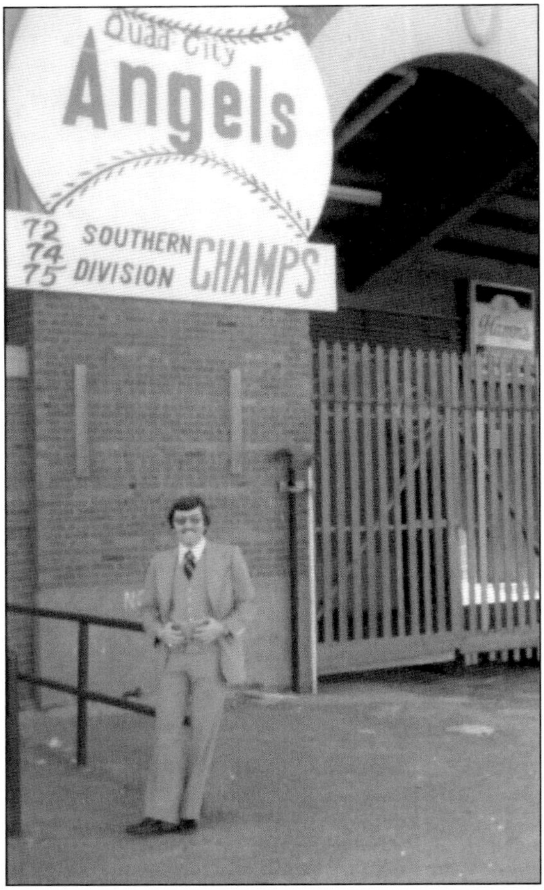

Harry Pells wasn't alone at the stadium gates too often. The young general manager helped the Quad City Angels set league attendance records in 1977 and 1978. Pells renewed a focus on attracting children to the ballpark, reaching out to youth baseball teams, and with promotions like the "Angel of the Day" title, given to a young fan.

Unfortunately, not every one of Pells' promotions turned out as planned. A pregame wedding ceremony exacerbated tensions between Pells and manager Cotton Nash. In the ensuing controversy, Pells stepped down as general manager.

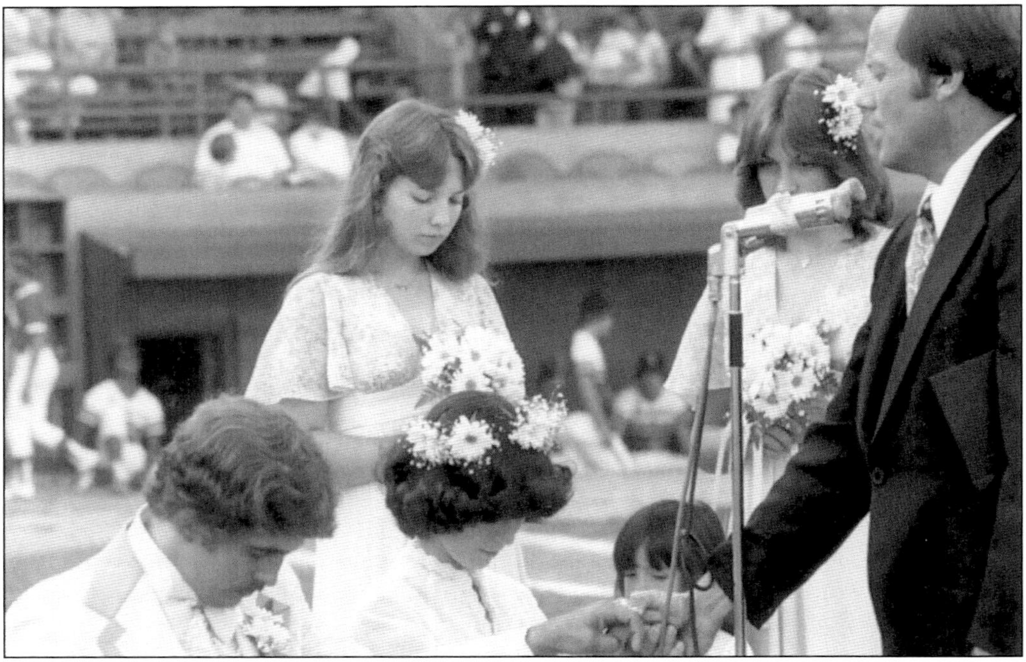

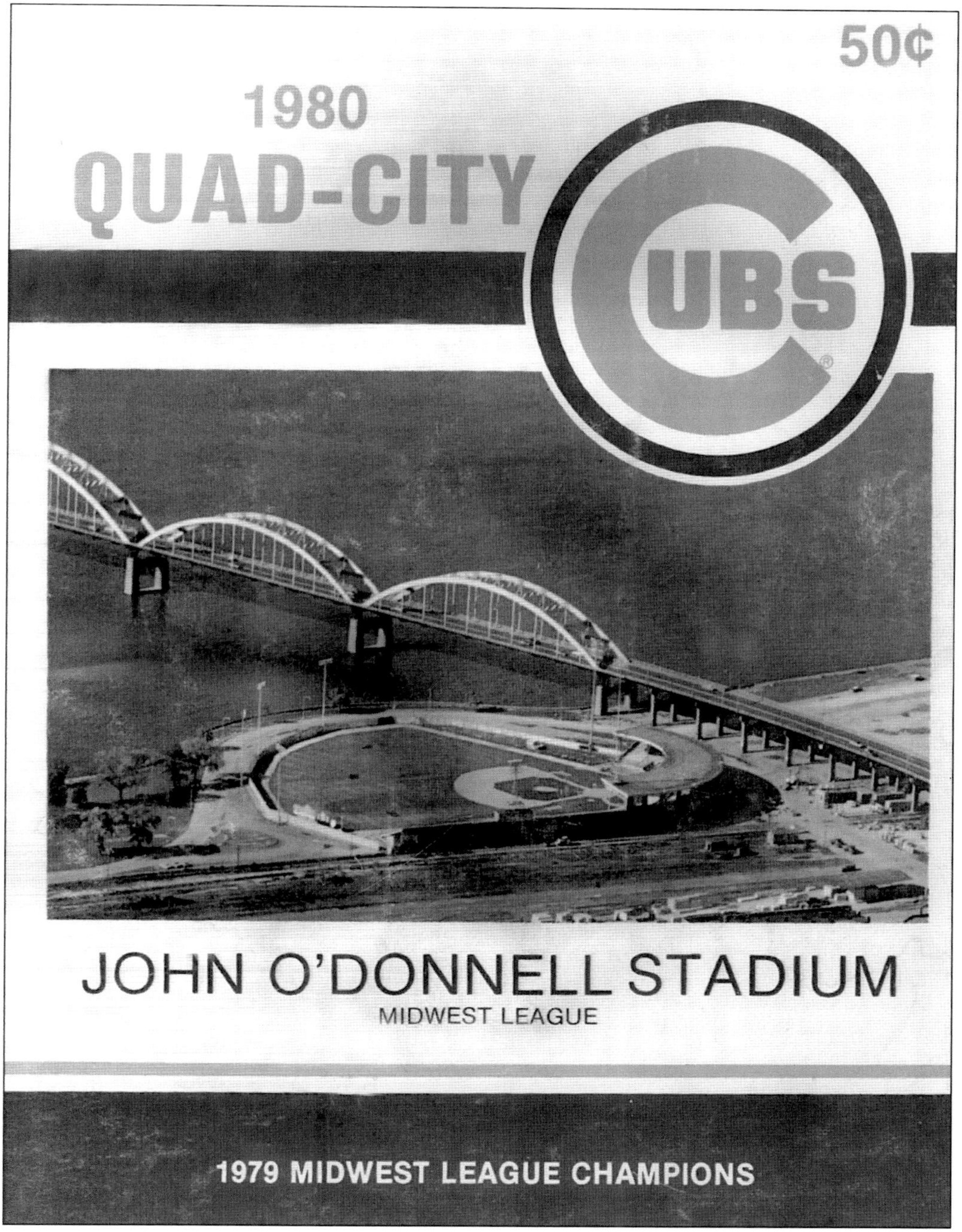

From 1979 to 1984, Quad City was an affiliate of the Chicago Cubs. The first three Quad City Cubs teams would reach the Midwest League finals, with the '79 club winning the championship. The most prominent player during the six seasons was shortstop Shawon Dunston, who batted .310 with 58 stolen bases in 1983.

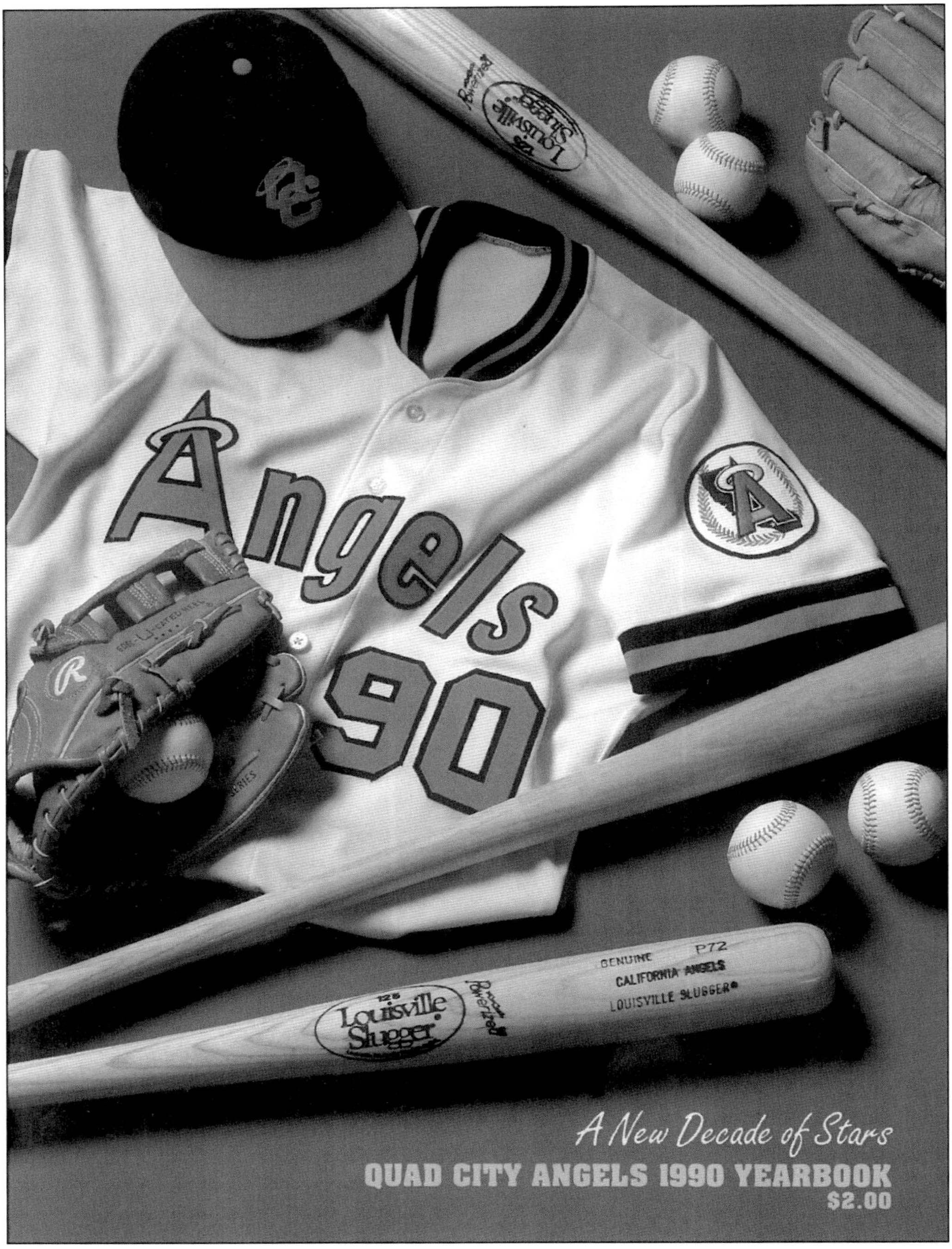

In 1990, the Angels brought home a Midwest League title, the third for an Angels affiliate and the fourth Quad City championship in the Midwest League.

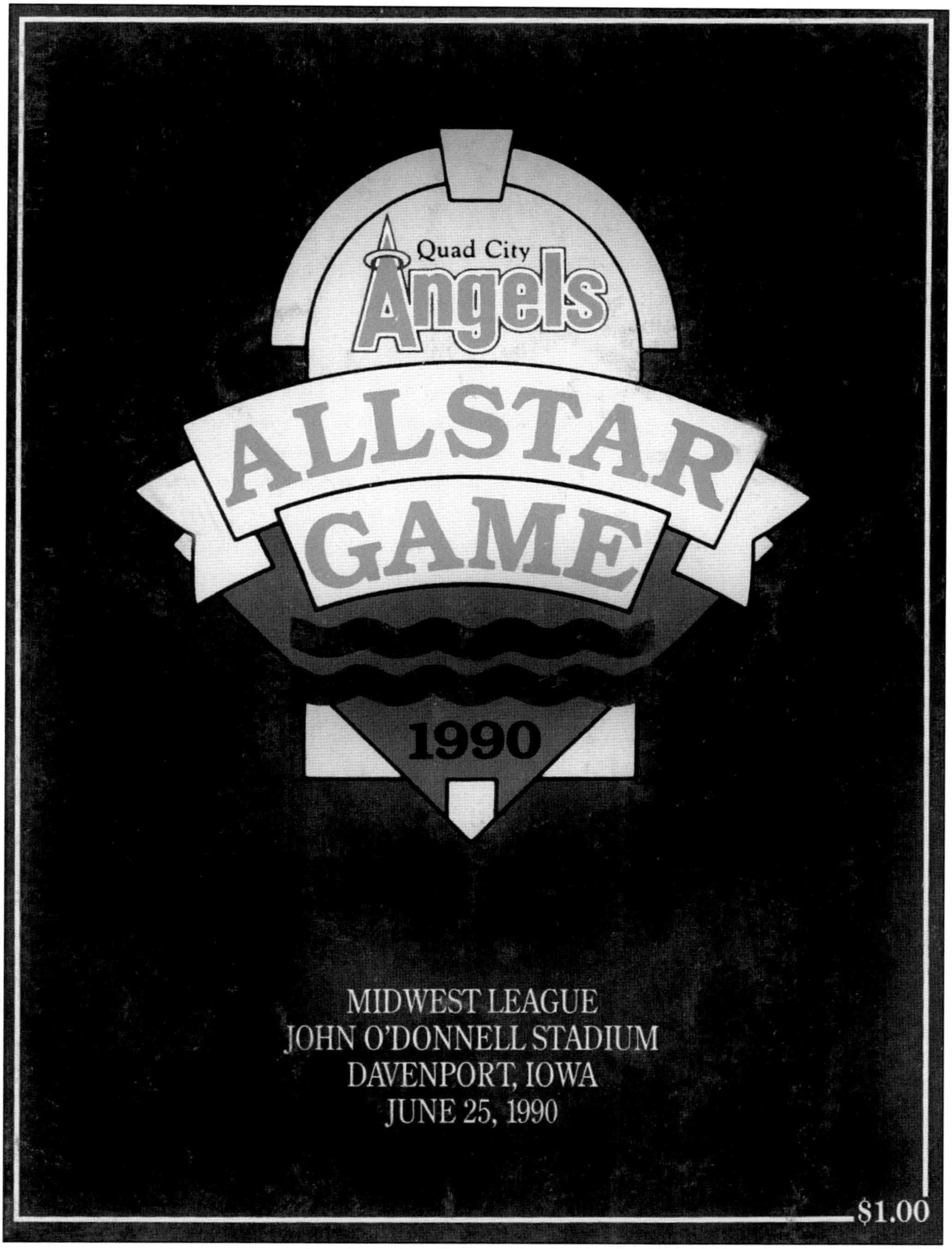

The last time John O'Donnell hosted the Midwest League All-Star Game was in 1990. The Southern Division Stars took advantage of eight Northern Division errors to cruise to a 10-5 win. Clinton's Roger Miller took MVP honors, while Cedar Rapids Red's star Reggie Sanders wowed fans by claiming the home run derby. Other Midwest League All-Star Games played in John O'Donnell were: 1964 (South 6, North 3); 1968 (MWL Stars 5, Quad Cities 1); 1975 (MWL Stars 6, Iowa Oaks 2); 1980 (North 6, South 1); and 1982 (North 4, South 2).

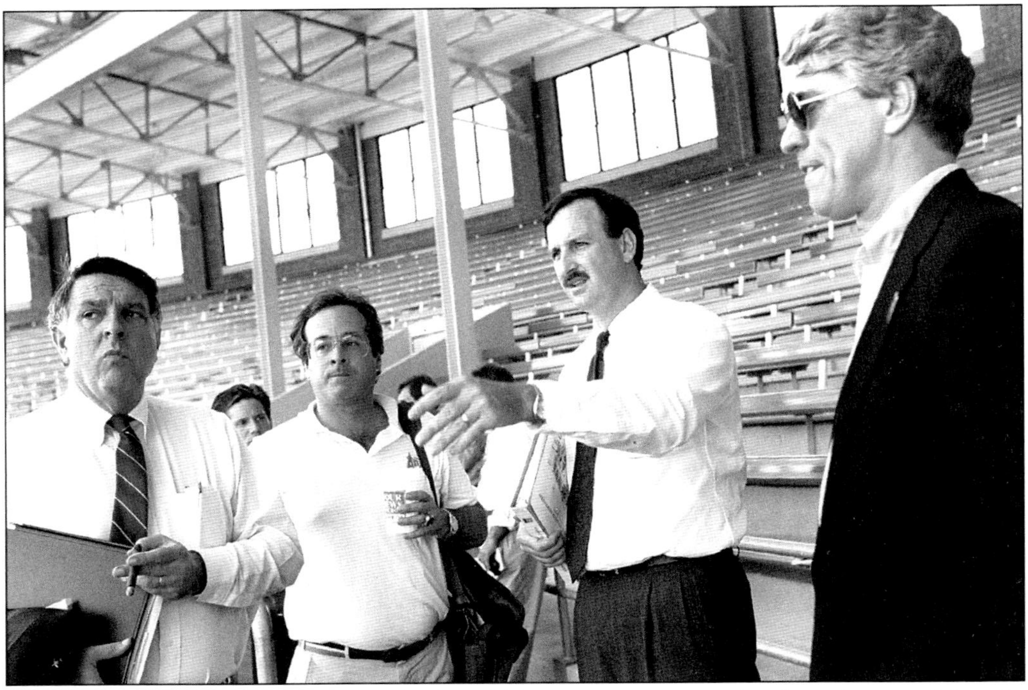

Although it may seem strange now, the Quad Cities was once considered a prime candidate for a Triple-A ballclub. When major league baseball prepared to add the Rockies and the Marlins in 1991, the minor leagues expanded also. This photo shows team owner Rich Holtzman (second from left) guiding memebrs of the Triple-A Exapnsion Committee on a tour of the stadium.

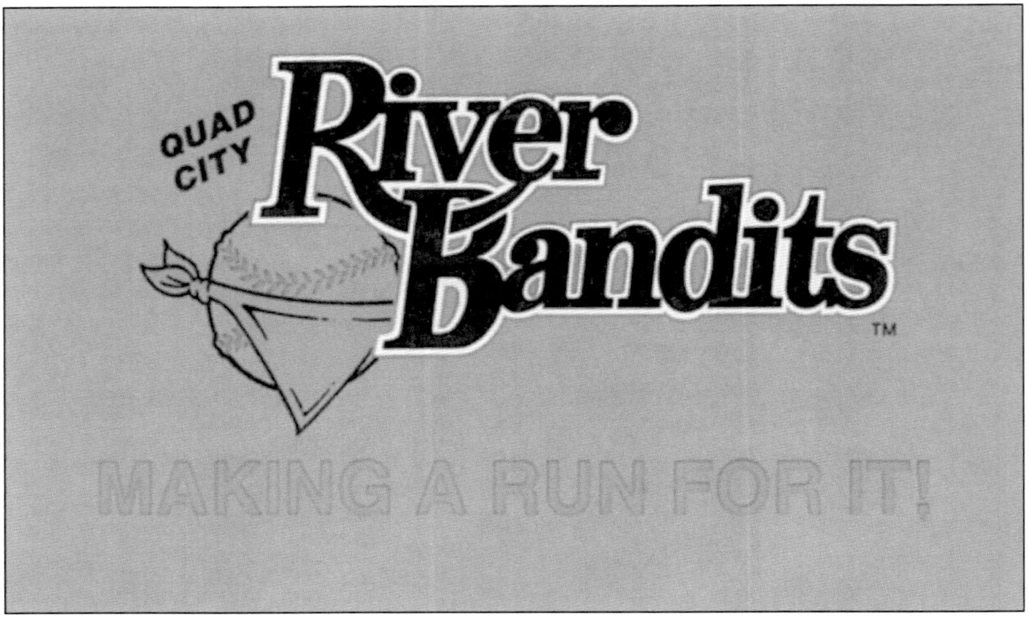

In the early 1990s, a growing number of minor league clubs created unique nicknames to set themselves apart from their major league patrons. In 1992, Quad Cities joined the movement with the new name, River Bandits.

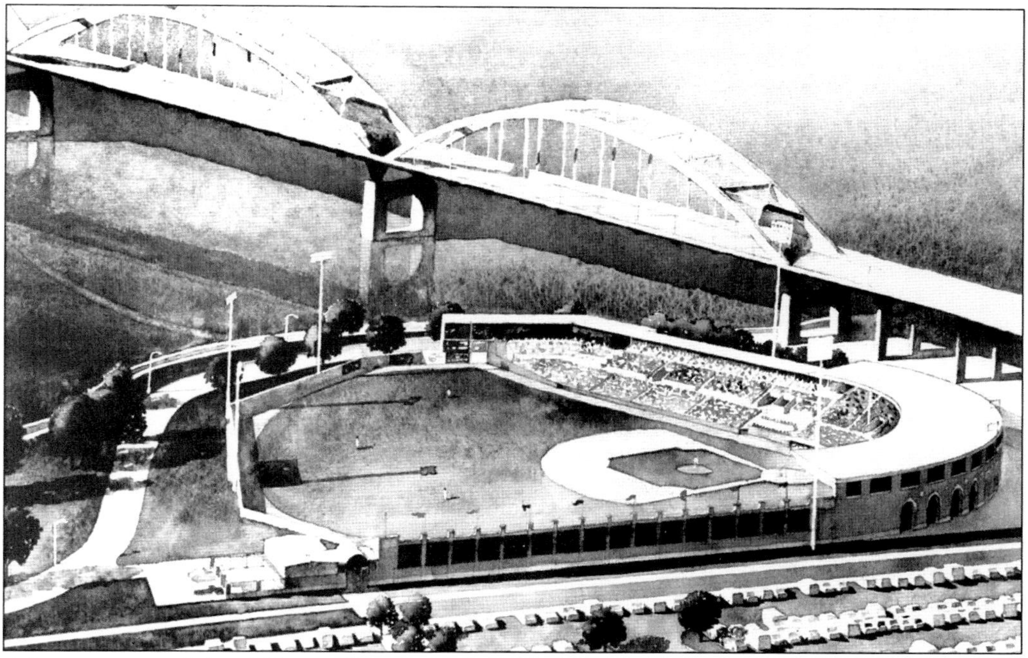

After improving John O'Donnell Stadium in the late 1980s, further plans were drafted to make the ballpark suitable for a Triple-A franchise. This image depicts an artist's sketch of what a AAA-caliber JOD might have looked like.

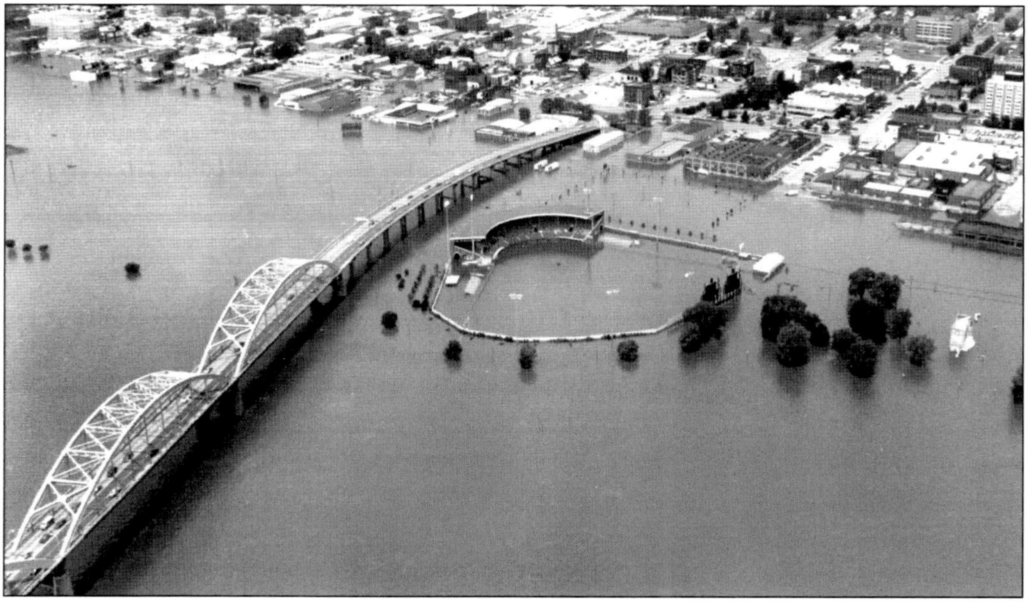

Recurrent scenes like this did not help the Quad Cites' bid for a Triple-A team. By far the most devastating flooding occurred in 1993. For much of the season the baseball field became a part of the Mississppi River. This view shows a totally inudated stadium.

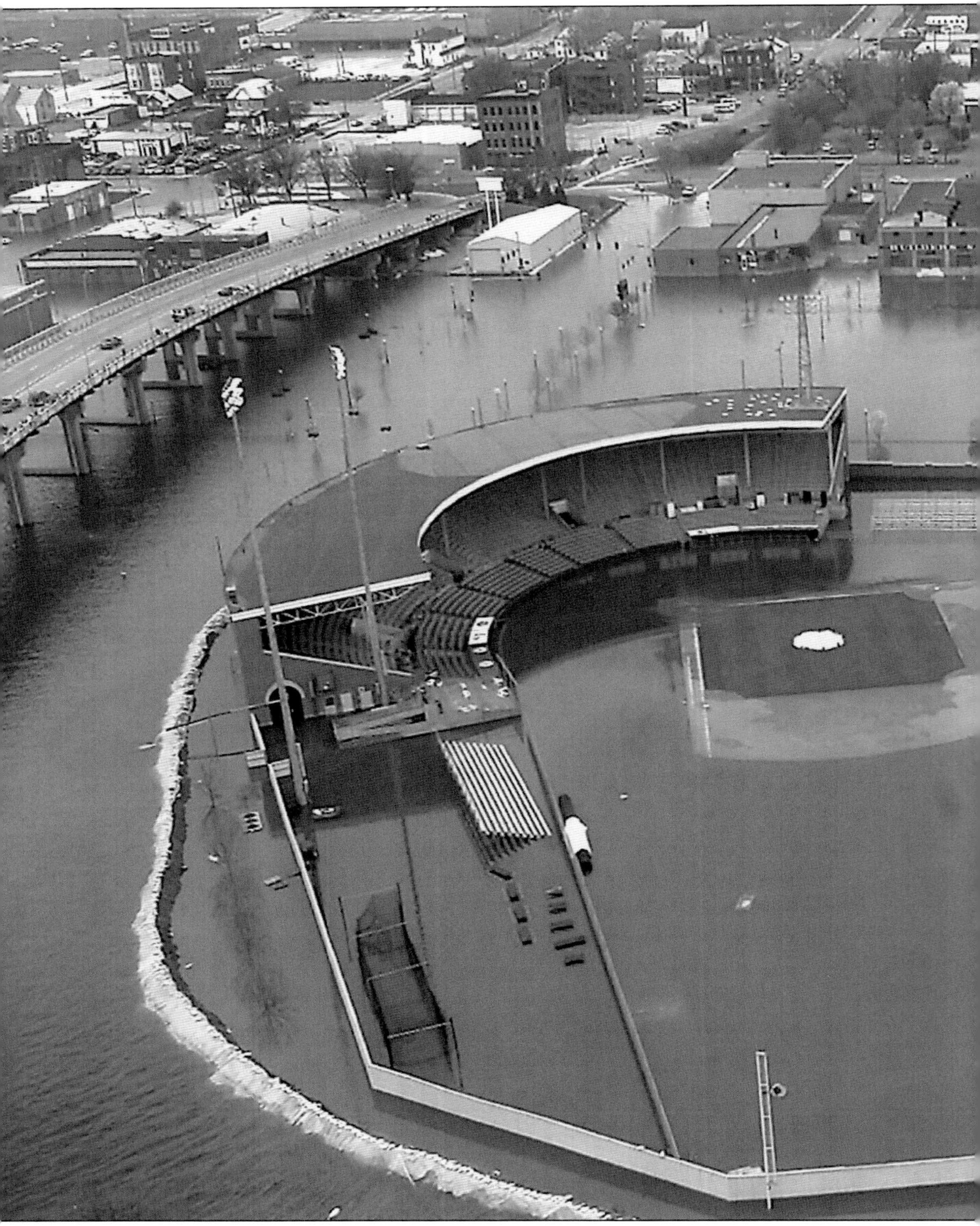

When floodwaters once again inundated the field in April of 2001, the River Bandits were prevented from playing at their home ballpark for 77 days, until they were able to return on July 2. During that tumultuous season, team owner Kevin Krause explored moving the team to Eastlake, Ohio, or

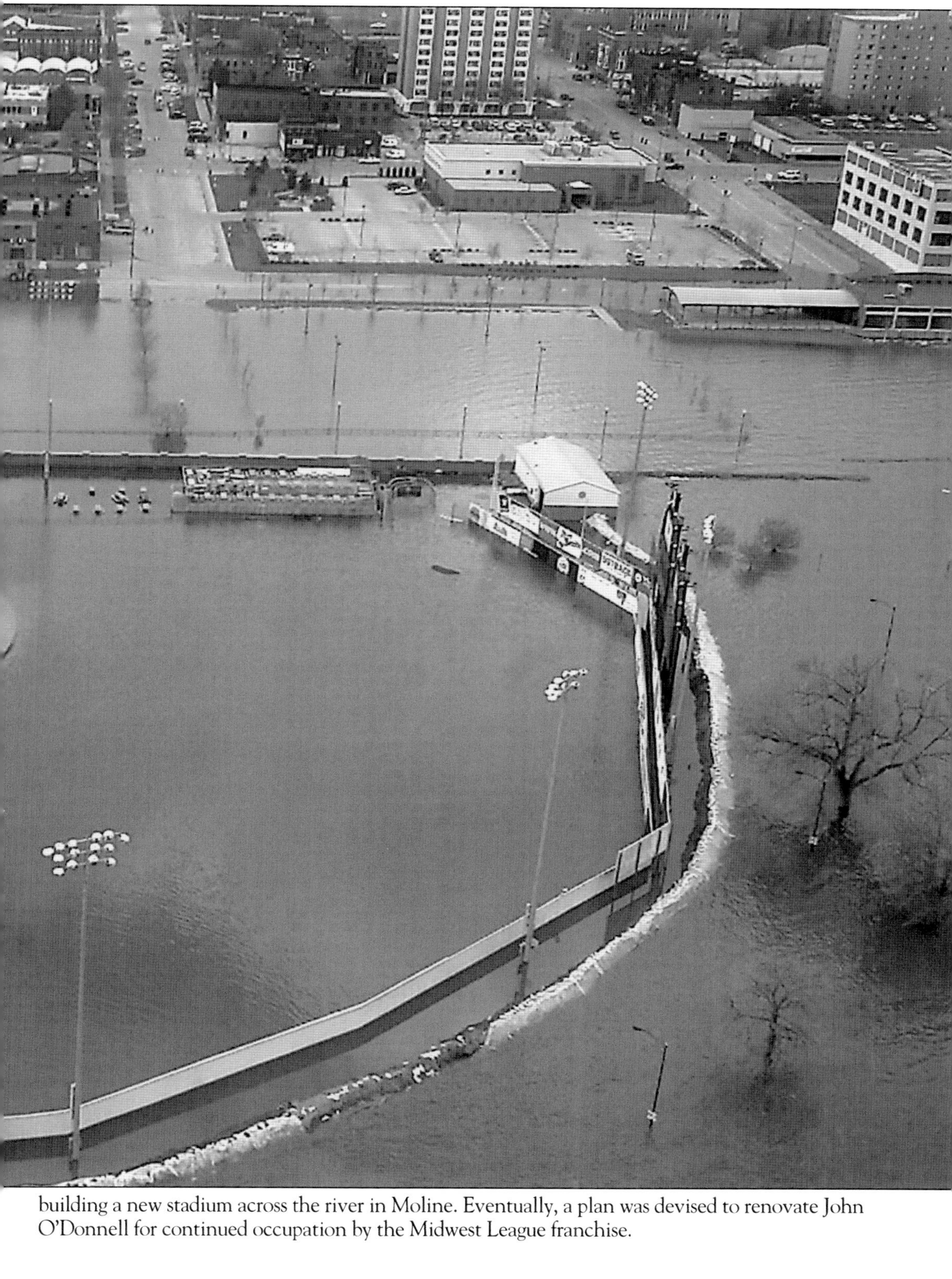

building a new stadium across the river in Moline. Eventually, a plan was devised to renovate John O'Donnell for continued occupation by the Midwest League franchise.

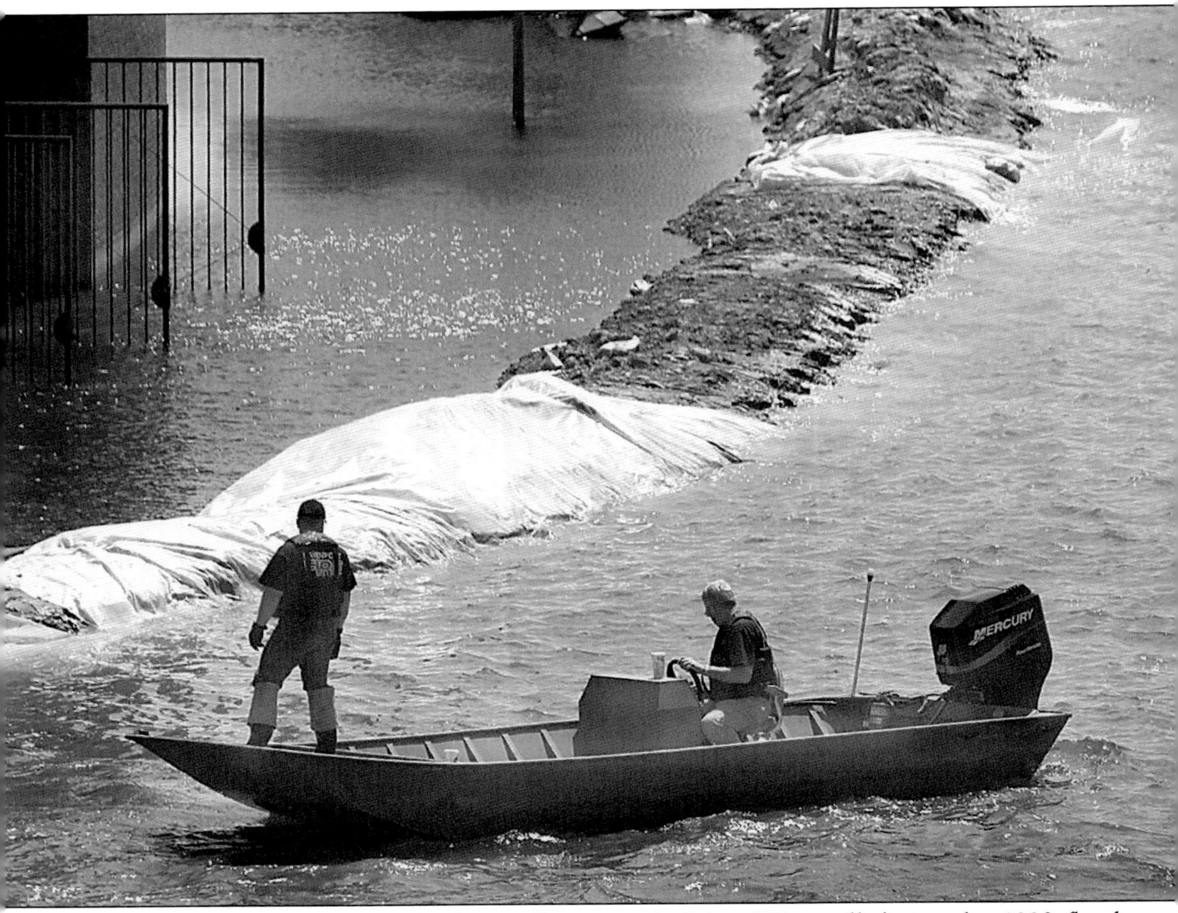

Davenport fire fighters check the sandbags outside John O'Donnell during the 1993 flood. The improvised levee failed to hold back the Mississippi, forcing the River Bandits out of the ballpark for most of the season.

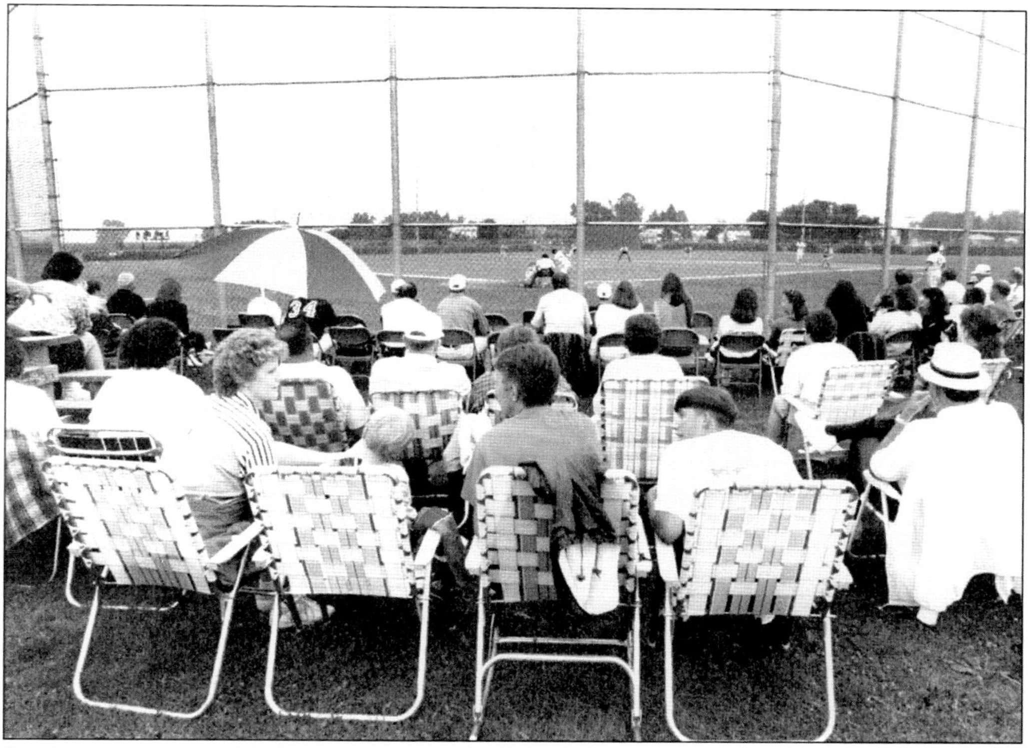

Finals-season action, 2003.

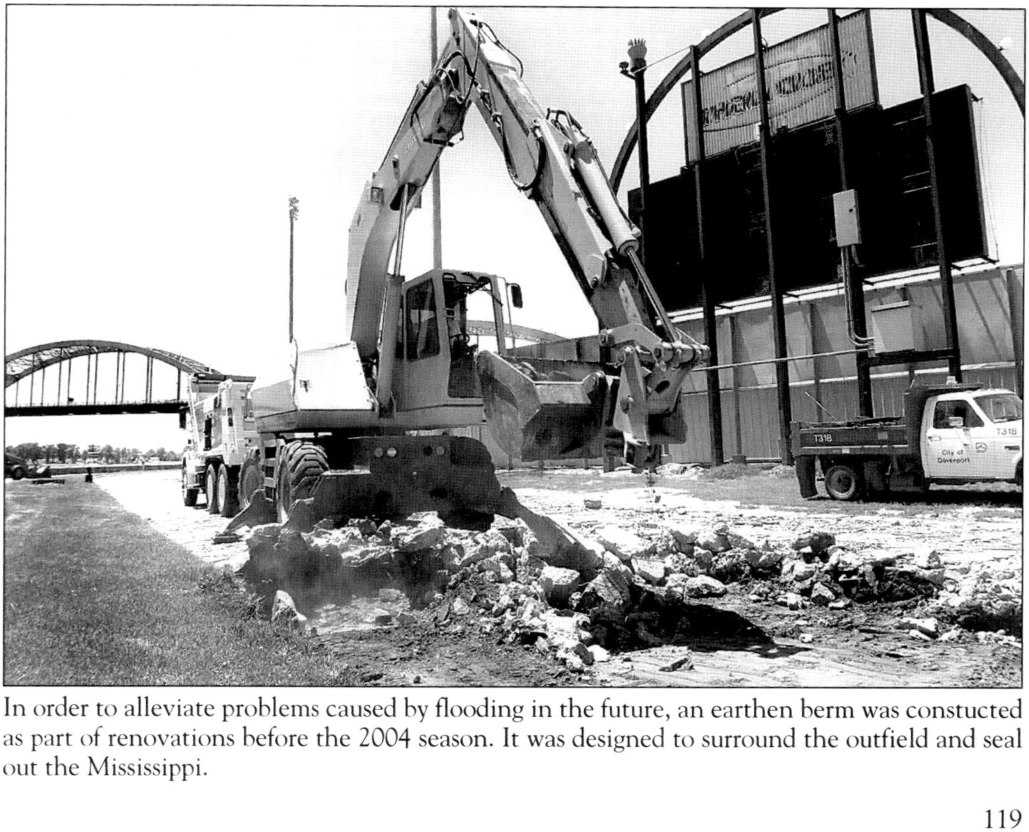

In order to alleviate problems caused by flooding in the future, an earthen berm was constucted as part of renovations before the 2004 season. It was designed to surround the outfield and seal out the Mississippi.

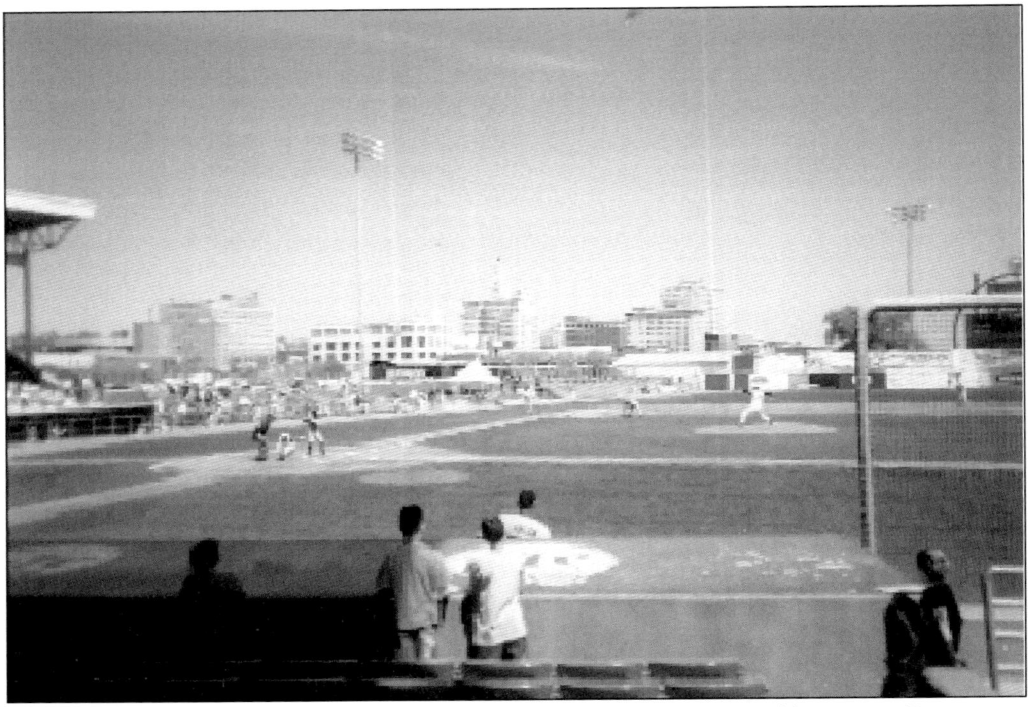

Fans who sit along the first base line at John O'Donnell get a clear view of downtown Davenport. Here fans enjoy the action during a May 2003 contest.

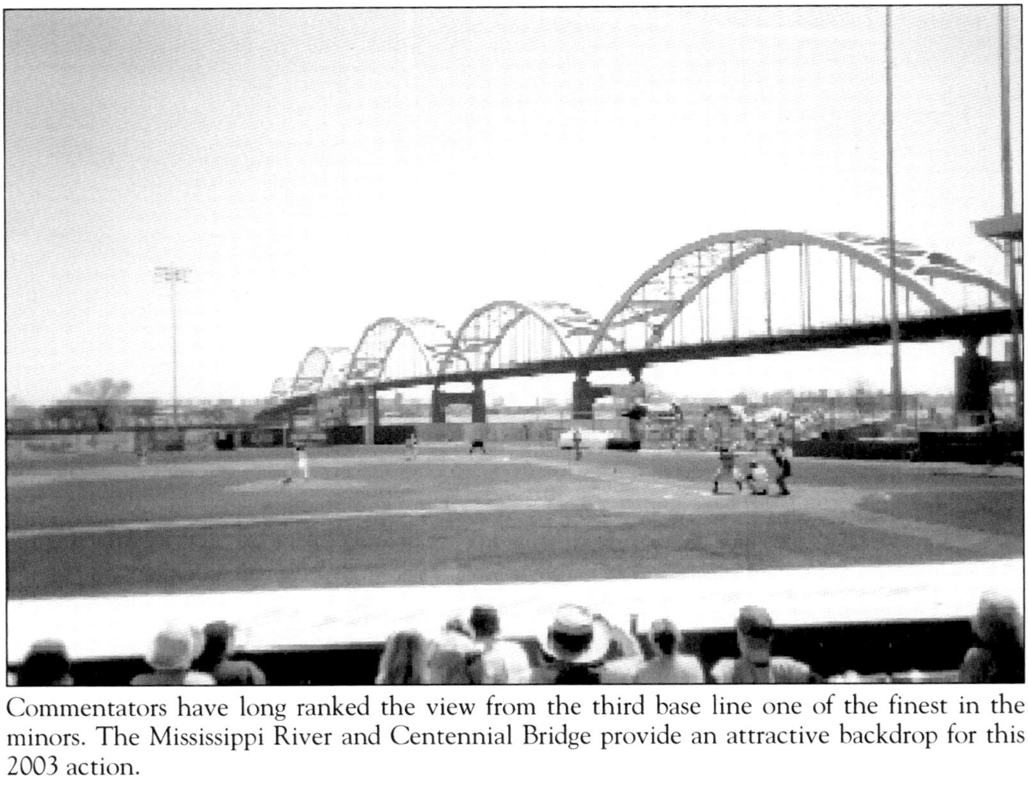

Commentators have long ranked the view from the third base line one of the finest in the minors. The Mississippi River and Centennial Bridge provide an attractive backdrop for this 2003 action.

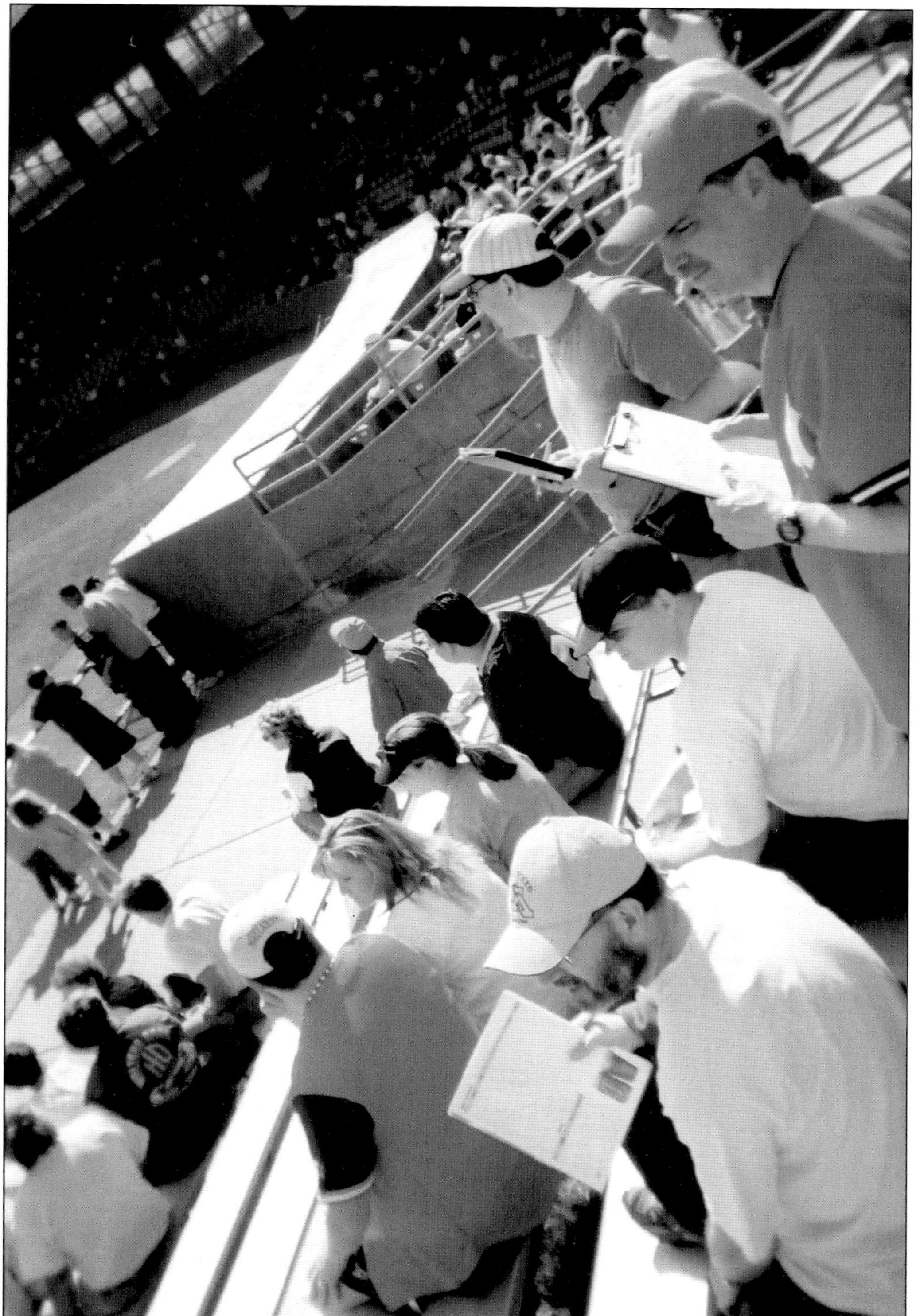

Fans keep score at John O'Donnell in what would be the River Bandit's last summer. The simple aluminum bleachers have been replaced by a full grandstand along the third base line.

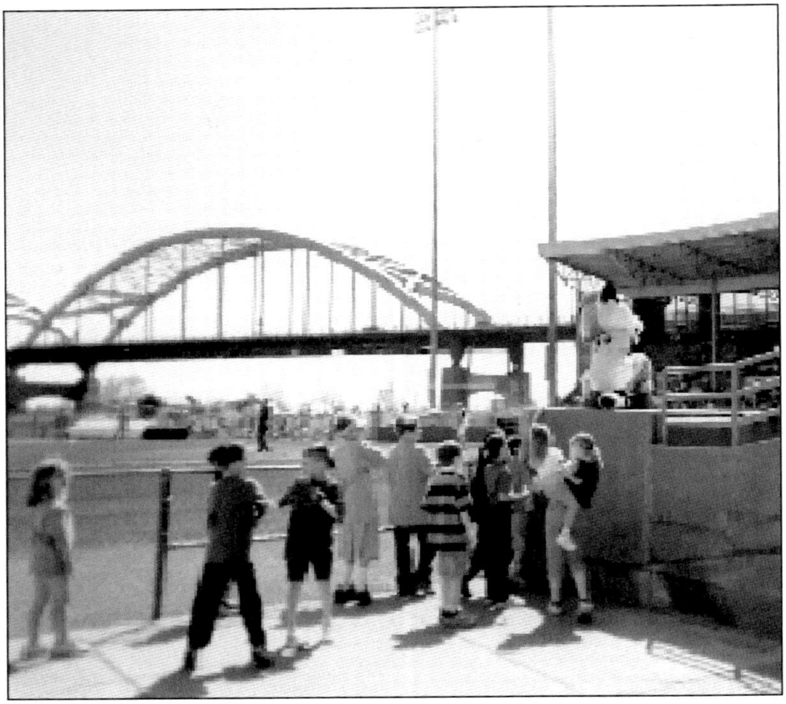

"Rookie," the mascot of the River Bandits, gazes intently from atop the third base dugout during an early season game in 2003. The season would be the club's last as the River Bandits; the ball club unveiled a new name for 2004, "The Swing of the Quad Cities," to accompany their first season in the "new" John O'Donnell.

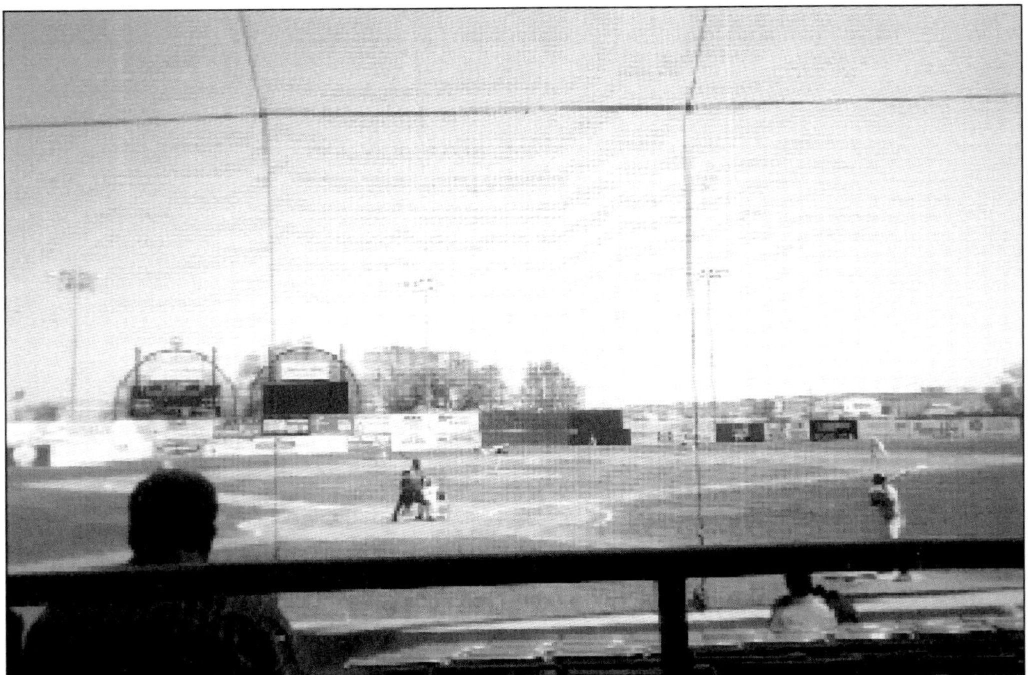

Like most minor league stadiums, John O'Donnell affords fans the opportunity to get close to the action on the field.

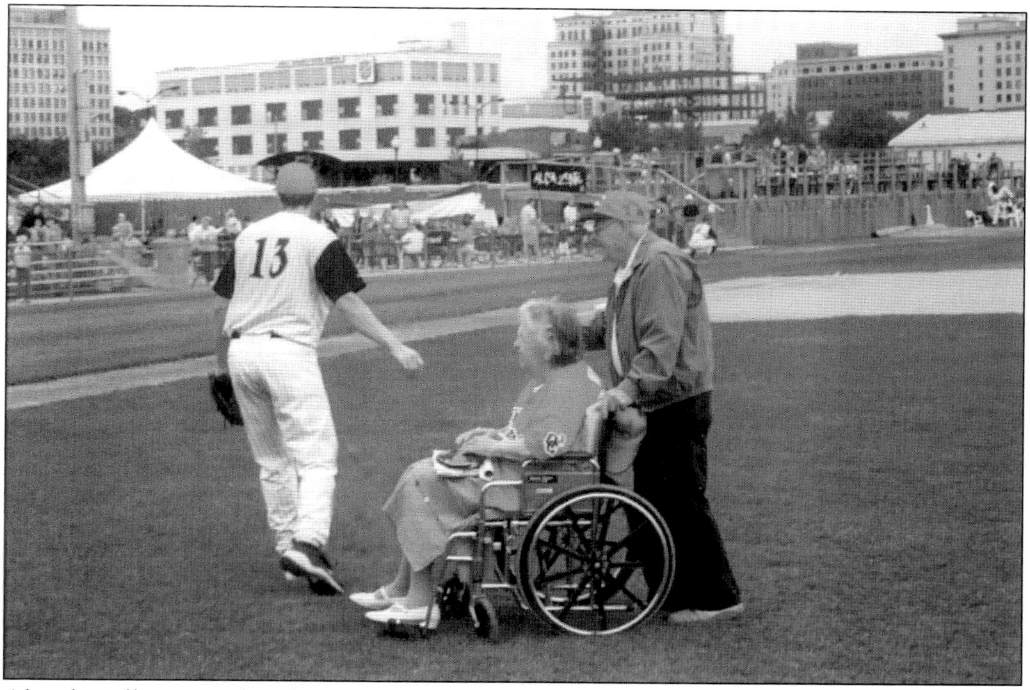

Already well-practiced at throwing out opening pitches, Dorothy Wulf, assisted by her husband Frank, prepares to toss out one of the final pitches at the "old" John O'Donell Stadium—September 1, 2003.

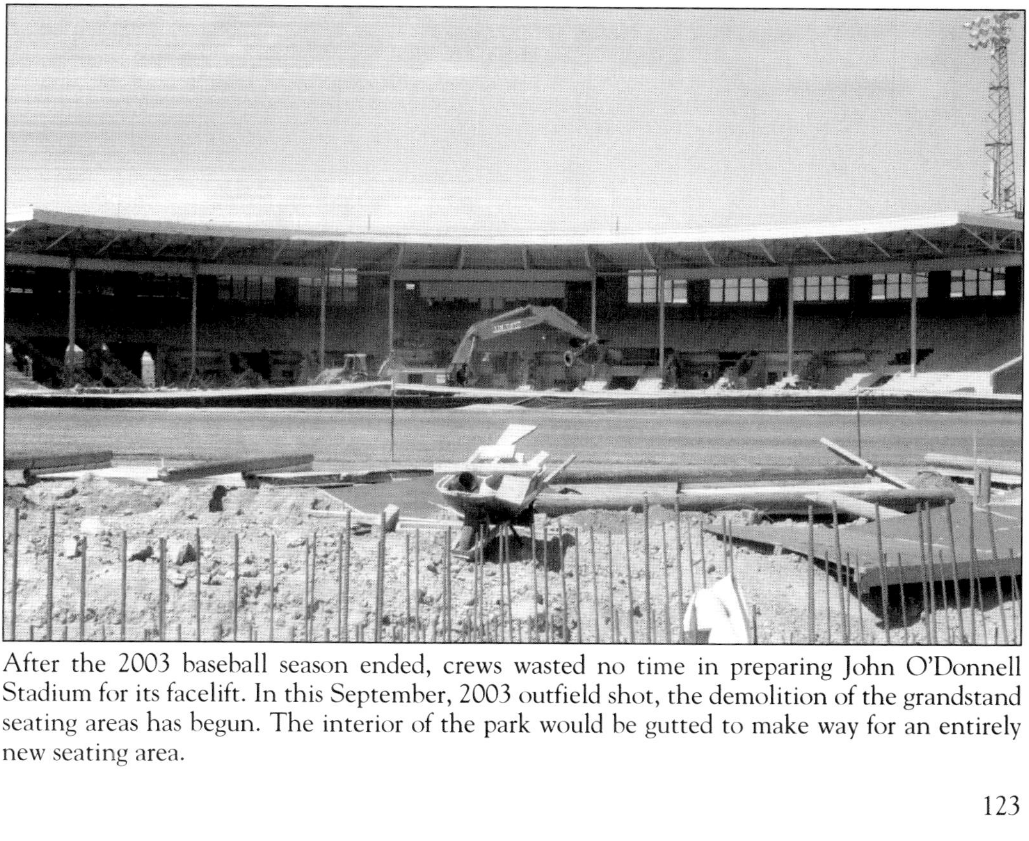

After the 2003 baseball season ended, crews wasted no time in preparing John O'Donnell Stadium for its facelift. In this September, 2003 outfield shot, the demolition of the grandstand seating areas has begun. The interior of the park would be gutted to make way for an entirely new seating area.

APPENDIX A

RECORDS OF DAVENPORT'S MINOR LEAGUE TEAMS DURING THE "MUNY/JOHN O'DONNELL" ERA

Year	Team Name	Parent Club	League	Wins	Losses	Pct.
1931	Blue Sox	Independent	Mississippi Valley Lg.	53	73	.421
1932	Blue Sox	Independent	Mississippi Valley Lg.	78	47	.624
1933	Blue Sox	Independent	Mississippi Valley Lg.	82	32	.719
1934	Blue Sox	Independent	Western League	70	53	.569
1935	Blue Sox	Independent	Western League	70	46	.603
1936	Blue Sox	Independent	Western League	74	52	.587
1937	Blue Sox	Independent	Western League	57	59	.491
1938–1945		No professional baseball in Davenport				
1946	Cubs	Chicago Cubs	Three-I League	76	44	.618
1947	Cubs	Chicago Cubs	Three-I League	55	70	.440
1948	Pirates	Pittsburgh Pirates	Three-I League	41	85	.325
1949	Pirates	Pittsburgh Pirates	Three-I League	67	59	.532
1950	Quads	Independent	Three-I League	49	75	.395
1951	Tigers	Detroit Tigers	Three-I League	56	74	.431
1952	Tigers	Detroit Tigers	Three-I League	54	69	.439
1953–1956		No professional baseball in Davenport				
1957	Dav-Sox	Chicago White Sox	Three-I League	65	65	.500
1958	Dav-Sox	Chicago White Sox	Three-I League	71	58	.550
1960	Braves	Milwaukee Braves	Midwest League	55	65	.458
1961	Braves	Milwaukee Braves	Midwest League	68	56	.548
1962	Angels	Los Angeles Angels	Midwest League	71	54	.568
1963	Angels	Los Angeles Angels	Midwest League	66	57	.537
1964	Angels	Los Angeles Angels	Midwest League	62	56	.525
1965	Angels	California Angels	Midwest League	53	70	.442
1966	Angels	California Angels	Midwest League	63	61	.508
1967	Angels	California Angels	Midwest League	69	51	.579
1968	Angels	California Angels	Midwest League	65	50	.565
1969	Angels	California Angels	Midwest League	64	57	.529
1970	Angels	California Angels	Midwest League	68	53	.562
1971	Angels	California Angels	Midwest League	68	56	.548
1972	Angels	California Angels	Midwest League	69	59	.539
1973	Angels	California Angels	Midwest League	55	66	.455
1974	Angels	California Angels	Midwest League	65	58	.528
1975	Angels	California Angels	Midwest League	78	47	.624
1976	Angels	California Angels	Midwest League	72	59	.550
1977	Angels	California Angels	Midwest League	75	64	.540
1978	Angels	California Angels	Midwest League	67	70	.489
1979	Cubs	Chicago Cubs	Midwest League	77	56	.579
1980	Cubs	Chicago Cubs	Midwest League	74	65	.532
1981	Cubs	Chicago Cubs	Midwest League	77	58	.570
1982	Cubs	Chicago Cubs	Midwest League	79	60	.568
1983	Cubs	Chicago Cubs	Midwest League	68	71	.489

1984	Cubs	Chicago Cubs	Midwest League	50	88	.362
1985	Angels	California Angels	Midwest League	66	74	471
1986	Angels	California Angels	Midwest League	62	78	.443
1987	Angels	California Angels	Midwest League	47	91	.341
1988	Angels	California Angels	Midwest League	60	79	.432
1989	Angels	California Angels	Midwest League	72	63	.533
1990	Angels	California Angels	Midwest League	81	59	.579
1991	Angels	California Angels	Midwest League	74	63	.540
1992	River Bandits	California Angels	Midwest League	91	46	.664
1993	River Bandits	Houston Astros	Midwest League	56	74	.431
1994	River Bandits	Houston Astros	Midwest League	57	81	.413
1995	River Bandits	Houston Astros	Midwest League	76	61	.555
1996	River Bandits	Houston Astros	Midwest League	70	61	.534
1997	River Bandits	Houston Astros	Midwest League	59	75	.440
1998	River Bandits	Houston Astros	Midwest League	77	62	.554
1999	River Bandits	Minnesota Twins	Midwest League	77	62	.554
2000	River Bandits	Minnesota Twins	Midwest League	64	75	.460
2001	River Bandits	Minnesota Twins	Midwest League	80	57	.584
2002	River Bandits	Minnesota Twins	Midwest League	71	65	.522
2003	River Bandits	Minnesota Twins	Midwest League	59	78	.431

Sources: *The Encylopedia of Minor League Baseball, 2nd edition,* by Lloyd Johnson & Miles Wolff (editors), and *The Baseball America Almanac* for 1997–2003. The author would also like to thank fellow SABR member Jerry Jackson for his invaluable assistance in compiling this list.

APPENDIX B
THE QUAD CITY ALL-20TH CENTURY TEAM

During the 2000 season, Quad City fans voted on an All-Century Team, which was announced at the end of that season. Not surprisingly, the team is dominated by recent players, although there are four players who played on pre-1960 teams. Those selected as Davenport's all-time greats included:

First Base: Don Mincher, 1958 Dav-Sox.
Don Mincher put up some terrific offensive numbers for the '58 Sox, batting .330 with 23 home runs, 97 RBI, and 101 runs scored. His 13-year major league career was relatively undistinguished, although he did make the All-Star Team in 1967 and 1969. He ended his career with a pinch hit single in the fourth game of the 1972 World Series that helped boost the Oakland A's to the championship. Mincher later enjoyed a second baseball career as general manager for his hometown Huntsville (Ala.) Stars in the Southern League. In honor of Mincher's service to the Stars, a road near the Huntsville stadium now bears his name.

Second Base: Jerry Remy, 1973 Angels.
Remy was an easy selection as the Midwest League's best second baseman in 1973. His 160 hits lead the league and his .335 batting average is still the best single-season mark by a Quad Cities player since the team joined the Midwest League in 1960. Remy lasted ten years in the majors, playing with the Angels and the Red Sox, and had a lifetime batting average of .275.

Shortstop: Shawon Dunston, 1983 Cubs.
The second player taken in the 1983 draft had a fine professional debut with the Quad City Cubs. The "Shawon O'Meter" registered a batting average of .310 to go with 65 runs scored and 58 stolen bases that season. Although he never developed into a superstar, the cannon-armed Dunston nevertheless was a fixture at shortstop with the Chicago Cubs for 11 seasons, and a popular player with the Wrigley Field fans.

Third Base: Carney Lansford, 1976 Angels
Lansford was a versatile and productive player for Quad Cities, batting .287 with 14 homers, 86 RBI, and 87 runs scored. He also stole 26 bases, splitting his time between third base and the outfield. During a productive 15-year major league career, he was an All-Star only once (in 1988), but the third baseman was an important cog in the Oakland A's machine that won three consecutive American League pennants (1988–1990).

Catcher: Brian Harper, 1978 Angels
Joe Mauer, of the 2001 River Bandits, may well have made this list had he appeared in the Quad Cities before the turn of the century. Harper, however, was no slouch. As an 18-year-old phenom in 1978, Harper batted .293 with 24 homers and a league-high 101 RBI. The following season, Harper was in the majors. After bouncing around several teams, Harper signed as a free agent with the Twins, where he lasted seven seasons and earned a World Series ring as a member of the 1991 champions.

Outfielders: Harvey Kuenn, 1952 Tigers
One year after hitting .340 with the '52 Quad Cities Tigers, Kuenn won the American League Rookie of the Year Award as a member of the Detroit Tigers. He remained a perennial All-Star throughout the 1950s and amassed over 2000 major league hits while maintaining a .303 career batting average. Kuenn also enjoyed success as a manager, leading the 1982 Milwaukee Brewers (aka "Harvey's Wallbangers") to an American League pennant.

Dante Bichette, 1985 Angels
The future Colorado Rockies star had a solid year at Quad Cities in '85 (.265-11-78). He advanced to the majors as a California Angel, but his career really took off when he joined the expansion Colorado Rockies in 1993. Bichette went on to lead the majors in hits twice He was the runner-up for the National League MVP award in 1995, when he slugged .340 with 40 home runs and 128 RBI, leading the league.

Chad Curtis, 1990 Angels
The 1990 Angels won a Midwest League title, thanks in large part to the stellar play of Chad Curtis. He led the league with 151 hits, and hit .307 with 87 runs scored and 64 stolen bases. Curtis moved up to the parent Angels in 1992, but never became more than a journeyman major leaguer. He was a member of the 1999 World Series Champion New York Yankees.

Utility player: Nick Etten, 1933 Blue Sox
As part of Minor League Baseball's 100th Anniversary in 2001, the 1933 Blue Sox were named the 58th greatest team in minor league history. It is only fitting, then, that a member of that club made the All-Century Team. Etten was an outfielder on that club who batted .357 (only good enough for second-best on the club, behind Como Cotelles' .407). Etten also drove in 90 runs, and scored 104. He advanced to the majors in 1938 as a first baseman, and played throughout the WW II years, lasting until 1947. His finest year came in 1945, when as a Yankee he hit .285 with 18 homers and 111 RBI.

Starting Pitchers: Jim Bunning, 1951 Tigers
Bunning was not a great success in Davenport. His record in 1951 was a mere 8-10, although he did post an ERA of 2.88. Bunning's post-Davenport career was phenomenally successful, however. Over a 17-year big league career, primarily with Detroit and Philadelphia, Bunning would win 224 games, including over 100 in each league. He also pitched a no-hitter in each league, including a perfect game on Father's Day, 1964. Bunning was elected to the Baseball Hall of Fame in 1996, becoming the first Davenport player to be inducted (Bid McPhee, who played for Davenport in 1879, became the second when he was inducted into the Hall in 2000). Bunning has also had a hugely successful second career in politics—he currently represents Kentucky in the United States Senate.

Frank Tanana, 1972 Angels
Tanana sparkled for the '72 Quad Cities Angels, going 7-2 with a 2.79 ERA in 129 innings. He would make his major league debut with the California Angels the following season, and stay in the bigs for 21 years, piling up 240 wins as a durable left-handed starter.

Chuck Finley, 1986 Angels;
Like Frank Tanana, this lefty also enjoyed a long and productive major league career. This five-time Major League All-Star won exactly 200 games over 17 seasons. His 161 victories in an Angels uniform makes him the all-time franchise leader. His stay in the Quad Cities was brief, but impressive. He struck out 16 in 12 innings, posting a 1-0 record with no earned runs allowed for the 1986 Q.C. Angels.

Billy Wagner, 1994 River Bandits
Although destined to become an All-Star closer, Billy Wagner pitched as a starter for the River Bandits so he could gain valuable innings of professional experience. His win/loss record was only a so-so 8-9, but the fireballer struck out 204 batters in 153 innings pitched. Wagner would go on to save 225 games for the Houston Astros, pickings up the 1999 Rolaids Relief Man Award along the way. The Philadelphia Phillies acquired Wagner after the 2003 season.

Closer: Saul Rivera, 1999 River Bandits
Rivera was an iron man for the '99 club, making a league-leading 60 appearances. Over the course of 70 innings pitched, he compiled a 4-1 record with 23 saves, an ERA of 1.42, and 102 strikeouts. Rivera did not advance to the major leagues.

Manager: Chuck Tanner, 1963–64 Angles
In something of an upset, Tanner was named to the manager's position over Cletus Dixon, who had led the Davenport Blue Sox to great success in the 1930s. Although Tanner didn't win any titles in his two years at Quad Cities, he did embark on a successful managerial career that took him to the major leagues, most notably with the Chicago White Sox and the Pittsburgh Pirates. His greatest success came with the Pirates, who went 711-685 in Tanner's nine seasons at the helm and won a dramatic seven-game World Series over Baltimore in 1979.